CONTENTS

PROPOSALS

FOR PUBLISHING BY SUBSCRIPTION,

A MAP

OF THE CITIES OF LONDON AND WESTMINSTER,

ON A PRINCIPLE NEVER BEFORE ATTEMPTED.

R. HORWOOD, Land-Surveyor, begs Leave moſt reſpectfully to inform the Public, that he has, for a conſiderable Time paſt, devoted his attention to taking a ſurvey, and engraving a Map of the Cities of LONDON, WESTMINSTER, and their Suburbs, on a Scale ſo extenſive and accurate as to exhibit, not only every Street, Square, Court, Alley, and paſſage therein, but alſo each individual Houſe, the Number by which it is diſtinguiſhed, the Names of all the public Buildings, and other Remarks, ſo as to render it the moſt perfect Plan of the Metropolis, and the beſt Directory, ever publiſhed.

The Public have long been in want of an accurate Map of London; and the various Benefits they will derive from the Execution of this Deſign, are more eaſily conceived than expreſſed. To Gentlemen in every Branch of the Law, as well as thoſe who have the conducting of any Kind of parochial Buſineſs, this Plan cannot fail of being of the utmoſt Uſe; as it will ſhew the Boundary of every Pariſh and Diſtrict with ſo much Exactneſs, that wherever it happens to paſs through a Houſe, which is very frequently the Caſe, it is accurately deſcribed; as the Eight Plates now finiſhed will demonſtrate.—An Object of the utmoſt Importance, as whoever is in Poſſeſſion of this Plan can never be liable to Error, in bringing Ejectments or Actions, in leaſing or conveying Premiſes, &c. &c.

To the Commercial World, the Proprietor has great Confidence this Plan will prove a valuable Acquiſition, particularly to thoſe Gentlemen who reſide in the Country and in Foreign Parts; as it will enable them to point out the Reſidence of every Correſpondent without the leaſt Trouble; and ſhould they have occaſion to viſit the Metropolis of this Kingdom (although never there before) by making a few Memorandums from the Plan, before they leave Home, they will, without the Diſagreeableneſs of Enquiry, be as able to find their neareſt way through London, to their different Connections, as if they had actually reſided in it for the greater Part of their Lives.

The Proprietor flatters himſelf that he need not expatiate any farther on the Advantages ariſing from this Performance; he however begs Permiſſion to mention one Inſtance which may not immediately occur to every Individual; namely, as the Diſtance between any two Houſes will be readily aſcertained by an Application to the Scale which will be annexed to the work, all Impoſitions in Hackney-Coach and Porters' Fares, &c. may be eaſily detected; for Example—if a Coach is taken at No. 200, Piccadilly, and ordered to No. 40, Harley Street, the Diſtance (by the neareſt Coachway) will be found to be 7 Furlongs and 154 Yards, which is conſiderably within a Shilling Fare.—This is an eaſy Experiment, and may be had recourſe to upon all Occaſions.

As this Undertaking will be attended with great Expence, the Proprietor is under the Neceſſity of ſoliciting a Subſcription of Five Guineas for each Plan, to enable him to accompliſh it; one Half to be paid at the Time of ſubſcribing. The whole to be engraved on 32 Plates, containing about 400 Acres each, and delivered in ſheets, which if paſted together, and made to roll and unroll by a Spring, may be pulled down, and any Part brought cloſe to the Eye, or it may be made to fold in a Book, or be paſted in quarters. With each Plan will be given a Book of Reference, containing an alphabetical Arrangement of the Streets, Squares, Courts, &c., ſo contrived that any individual Houſe throughout London may be found upon the Map in an inſtant; to which will be prefixed a Liſt of the Subſcribers.

The Proprietor wiſhes to obſerve, that when he embarked in this Undertaking, he did not intend to take Notice of the back Part of the Houſes, or Gardens, but merely to have confined himſelf to the Manner of the Specimen then publiſhed. He does not preſume to ſay, that in every Part, the Backs of the Houſes, and Gardens, are ſo correct as the Fronts; as of ſome Places it was not in his Power to get a View, nor did he think extreme Accuracy, in that Reſpect, material, but introduced this Addition rather for the Sake of Ornament than Uſe.

Thoſe Noblemen or Gentlemen who chooſe to have the back Parts, and the whole of their own Premiſes or Property accurately inſerted, or in any way diſtinguiſhed, may, at a very trifling additional Expenſe, by Application to the Proprietor. Gentlemen in the Law, who have occaſion for Plans of different Premiſes they have to Leaſe or Convey, may be likewiſe ſupplied at a very ſmall Expenſe. Merchants and Tradeſmen who ſubſcribe to this Work, may have their Names, and the Branch of Buſineſs they follow, engraved oppoſite their Reſidences, which will make their Situations known in the faſhionable World; and in hopes of rendering the Performance as acceptable and complete as poſſible, the Proprietor will be happy to make any other Addition to the Plans ſubſcribed for, that may be required.

As many Gentlemen have expreſſed a Wiſh to patronize this Work by a different Mode of Subſcription, the Proprietor, deſirous of offering the moſt agreeable Method to the Public, propoſes to ſuch as do not approve of the foregoing Terms, to ſubſcribe 7s. 6d. for the firſt, and 5s. for every ſubſequent Plate, except the laſt, which will be 2s. 6d.—Each plate to be paid for when delivered.

This Plan includes the Borough of Southwark, St. George's Fields, Lambeth, Newington, Kennington, Walworth, Rotherhithe, Limehouſe, Stepney, Hoxton, Pentonville, Somer's Town, Knightſbridge, Part of Iſlington and Chelſea; ſhewing the River Thames from Cheyne Walk, Chelſea, to Deptford, with a Plan and Names of all the different Chains and Moorings; forming a Square of Six Miles from Eaſt to Weſt, and Three Miles and Three Furlongs from North to South.

N. B. No Money to be paid by Subſcribers till Eight Plates of the Work are delivered, and upon a Receipt from the Proprietor.

Their MAJESTIES, and their Royal Highneſſes the PRINCE of WALES, DUKES of YORK, CLARENCE, and GLOUCESTER, and many of the Firſt Nobility of this Kingdom, have been pleaſed to expreſs their higheſt Approbation of the Deſign, and have honoured the Subſcription with their Names; and the Proprietor humbly hopes the Public will give it ſuch Encouragement and Support as an Undertaking ſo uſeful, and on a Principle ſo entirely new, may appear to merit.

HACKNEY, Dec. 1, 1795.

A LIST OF SUBSCRIBERS to this WORK, to December 1, 1795.

HIS MAJESTY
HER MAJESTY
H. R. H. the Prince of Wales
H. R. H. the Duke of York
H. R. H. the Duke of Clarence
H. R. H. Prince Erneſt
H. R. H. the Duke of Glouceſter
Aſhburnham, Earl of
Aylesford, Earl of
Admiralty, Lords Commiſſioners
Adair, Serjeant
Arden, John, eſq., *Arden Hall*
Angerſtein, J. Julius eſq. *Pall-Mall*
Atkinſon, Jaſper, eſq. Banker
Allen, Mr. Brewer, *Wapping*
Adams, —, eſq. *Bond-ſtreet*
Apothecary's Hall
Archers, *Henrietta-ſtreet*
Alkin, Mr. *Francis-ſtreet*
Aſtley, Mr. *Weſtminſter bridge*
Armſtrong, Mr. *Conduit-ſtreet*
Aſkew, —, eſq. *Doctors-commons*
Agricultural Society
Alliſon, Mr. William, *Long Lane*
Aubert, Alexander, *Highbury Houſe*
Arnold and White, *Marybone*
Atkinſon, Mr. Thomas
Allen, Mr. *St. John's, Southwark*
Agar, Mr. *Artillery Place.*
Allop, Mr. *Marybone*
Atkinſon, Mr. *Bermondſey*
Arris, Mr.
Atkinſon and Clarence
Bedford, the Duke of, 2 ſets
Bridgwater, the Duke of
Buccleugh, the Duke of
Bath, the Marquis of
Blandford, the Marquis of
Buckingham, the Marquis of
Beverly, Earl of
Bagot, Lord
Boringdon, Lord
Bayham, Lord
Breadalbane, Lord
Banks, Sir Joſeph, *Soho Square*
Broughton, Sir Thomas, *Broughton*
Blake, Sir Francis
Buckley, Mr. and Son, *Strand*
Bonomi, —, eſq. *Titchfield-ſtreet*
Bickley and Lardner, *Berners-ſtreet*
Bowers, Meſſrs. *Bond-ſtreet*
Beauchamp, Mr. *Holborn*
Barratty, Mr. *Gracechurch-ſtreet*
Boverie, Hon. Edward
Blades, Mr. *Ludgate-ſtreet*
Buxton, Mr. *Coleman-ſtreet*
Bramah, Mr. *Piccadilly*
Burton, Mr. *Newcaſtle-ſtreet*
Braſsbridge, Mr. *Fleet-ſtreet*
Broderip, Mr. *Haymarket*
Bank, the Gov. and Co. of England
Biſhton, John, Eſq. *Kelſal*
Bill, Mr. *Farley*
Bell, Mr. *Stone*
Blackwell, Mr. *Cobridge*
Burgeſs, J. Bland, eſq. *Treaſury*
Baker, William, eſq. *Hill-ſtreet*
Barber, Robert, eſq. *Charter-Houſe*
Barlow, Mr. Builder, *Baker-ſt.*
Bland, —, eſq.
Buſh, Mr.
Buchnan, J. eſq. City Comp. 2 ſets
Berners, —, eſq. *Berners-ſtreet*
Boyd, Walter, eſq. *Albemarle Street*
Bodenham, C. eſq. *Rotherwas*
Bolton, —, eſq. *Soho, Birmingham*
Baker, —, eſq. *Portman Square*
Burton, Mr. *Chatham Square*
Booth, Mr. *Guilford-ſtreet*
Burdett, Francis, eſq.
Boucherett, A. eſq. *Wyndham*
Baldwin, Joſeph, eſq. *Serjeants Inn*
Barclay, Robert, eſq. Banker
Birbeck, R. eſq. *Fox-ordinary-court*
Bolton, Rev. Mr.
Bullock, Meſſ. and Co. Brewers
Battier, Meſſ. and Co. *Devonſhire Sq.*
Bate, Mr. at the Hotel, *Adelphi*
Budd, Doctor
Barrett, Bryan, eſq. *Stockwell*
Beach, Mich. Hicks, eſq. *M. P.*
Burrow, Edward, eſq. *Bromley*
Beaufoy, Meſſrs. *Cuper's-bridge*
Boyd, Benfield, and Co.
Barlow, Mr. Joſeph, *Newington*
Bull, Mr. William, *Covent Garden*
Baumgartner and Hoofſtetter, *George ſtreet, Minories*
Browninge and Nottige, Meſſieurs, *Bermondſey*
Bourne and Evans, *Fleet-ſtreet*
Bowver and Coates, *Bermondſey*
Bradley, Mr. Richard
Bendelack, Mr.
Brandon, Mr. D. *Tabernacle Walk*
Brazen-noſe College, *Oxford*
Bourne, Mr.
Brodie, Mr. Alexander, *Cary-ſtreet*
Browning, Mr. *Bank-ſide*
Betts, Mr. Samuel, jun. *Lambeth*
Bird, Mr. Joſeph, *Radcliffe*
Bowles, Mr. G. *Wanſtead Grove, Eſſex*
Bound and Clarkſon, *Ray-ſtreet*
Bond, Edward, eſq. *Golden Lane*
Barton, Mr. *Bermondſey*
Benezick and Co. *Beaufort-buildings*
Balenger, Mr. *Old Fiſh-ſtreet*
Biggerſtaff, J. Eſq. *Iſlington*
Bracken, Rev. Mr.
Baynes, Wood, and Co. *Black-friars*
Blackley, Mr. Charles
Carliſle, Earl of
Cheſterfield, Earl of
Carliſle, Lord Biſhop of
Clinton, Lord
Craven, Lord
Cornewall, Sir George
Curtis, Alderman
Creſwell, —, eſq. *Bedford Row*
Corporation of London, 2 ſets
Croſier, Mr. *Leiceſter Fields*
Commiſſioners of Sewers for *Clerken.*
Cuncannon, Lucias, eſq. *Grafton ſt.*
Clark, John, eſq. *Hatton Garden*
Commiſſioners of the Trinity Houſe
Crellin, Mr. *Henrietta-ſtreet*
Caſwell, J. eſq. *Davies-ſtreet*
Coutts, Thomas, eſq. *Strand*
Collett, Richard, eſq. *Chancery Lane*
Codrington, Chriſtopher, eſq.
Cockerell, —, eſq. *Saville Row*
Cheſter, Edward, eſq. *Curzon-ſtreet*
Charter-Houſe, Governors of the
Coyney, William, eſq.
Commiſſioners of Sewers, *Weſtminſter*
Ditto of Sick and Hurt Seamen
Cantwell, —, eſq. *Gr. Pulteney-ſt.*
Collyer, J. eſq.
Chaſe, Francis, eſq. *Mincing Lane*
Crofts, Meſſ. and Co. Bankers
Creſſwell, —, eſq. *Doctors Commons*
Crop, R. eſq. *Brook-ſtreet*
Curling and Nelſon, *Dockhead*
Chounet, Mr. *Bermondſey*
Crutchfield, J. and W. *Holborn Bridge*
Collins, J. eſq. *Berners-ſtreet*
Coles, Mr. William, *Buſh Lane*
Curwen, J. C. eſq. *M. P. Workington Hall, Cumberland*
Champion, Mr. William, *City Road*
Cary, Mr. P. *Goſwell-ſtreet*
Crankſhaw, Mr. J. *Hertford-ſtreet, Fitzroy-ſquare*
Cawne, Robert, Eſq. *Mercers Hall*
Clark, John, Eſq. *Hatton Garden*
Crawfurd, —, Eſq. *Soho Square*
Calvert, Felix, and Co. Brewers
Cole, —, Eſq. *Albion Place*
Cummings, G. Eſq.
Campbell, Mr. *Marybone-ſtreet*
Crowder, W. H. Eſq. *Finſbury Sq.*
Croſbie, General, *Seymour-ſtreet*
Coades, Mr. *Lambeth*
Cruickſhank, Dr. *Leiceſter-ſquare*
Cope, Mr. Thomas, *Rood Lane*
Collins and Co. *Weſtminſter-bridge*
Claridge, Mr. John, *Craven-ſtreet*
Coxhead and Stevens
Combrane, Mr. Gideon, *Golden Lane*
Clowes, Newbery, and Co. Brewers
Coles, Child, & Sons, *Lower T.-ſt.*
Clark, Mr.
Cox, Mr. William, *Strand*
Curtis and Son, *Wapping*
Coſlet, Mr. *Whitechapel*
Crawſhay, Son and Co. *George Yard, Thames-ſtreet*
Coverdale and Norris, *Blackwall*
Charrington, Mr. *Mile End*
Curtis, and Clark *Wapping*
Donegall, the Marquis of
Downſhire, the Marquis of
Dorcheſter, Earl of
Darnley, Earl of
Dacre, Lord
Duncannon, Earl of
Dartmouth, Earl of
Douglas, Earl of
Dundas, Sir Thomas
Dundas, the Right Hon. Henry
Dimſdale, Baron, and Co. Bankers
Drew, —, Eſq. *Exeter*
Dibdin, Mr. *Strand*
Dickie, William, Eſq. *Caroline-ſtreet*
Denniſon, Joſeph, Eſq.
Daykin, Mr. *Duke Street*
Denner, Mr. *Furnival's Inn Coffee Ho.*
Dixon, Mr. *St. Mary's Hill*
Downer, Mr. *Fleet-ſtreet*
Drury, Mr. *Strand*
Dorant, Mr. Dorant's Hotel, 2 ſets
Devall, Mr. Statuary, *L. Portland St.*
Deering, Henry, Eſq.
Dance, George, Eſq. *Gower-ſtreet*
Drummond, Robert, Eſq. Banker
Dutens, Rev. Mr.
Dupre, Rev. Dr. *Berkhampſtead*
Dimſdale, Meſſ. and Co. *Broad-ſtreet*
Down, Thornton, and Free, Bankers
Dubois, Meſſ. and Co.
Dorſet, Johnſon, and Co. Bankers
De Valenger, Dr. *Pentonville*
Dickenſon, Mr. *St. John-ſtreet*
Dudley, Ryder, Eſq. Pay Office
Dunkin, Mr. Chriſt. *Horſleydown*
Dudman, Mr. J. *Grove-ſtreet, Deptford*
Dunbar, Mr. W. *Tottenham-court Road*
Daniel, T. and Co. *Mincing Lane*
Daviſon, Mr. *Shadwell*
Dell, Mr. *Broad Wall, Lambeth*
Doune, Mr. William, *Eaſt Smithfield*
Dirs, Mr. C. *Well-cloſe ſquare*
De Veime, Mr. Gerard
Dowding, Rd. and Co. *Wapping wall*
Egremont, Earl of
Euſton, Earl of
Elliott, Hon. Edward James
Eades, Mr. *Ruſſell-ſtreet*
Egerton, William, Eſq.
Edwards, John, Eſq. *Bridge-ſtreet*
Ewer, Francis, Eſq.
Equitable Aſſurance Office
Exciſe Office
Elliot and Co. Brewers
Edmonds', St. the King's Pariſh
Eccard, Mr. *Chelſea*
Eggers, Henry, Eſq. *Whitechapel*
Fauconberg, Earl of
Fitzwilliam, Earl of
Fife, Earl of

Proposals for Horwood's Plan of London dated December 1st 1795 (reproduced by permission of the Guildhall Library). The list of 838 subscribers continues onto the reverse side.

The A to Z of Regency London

Introduction by
Paul Laxton

Index compiled by
Joseph Wisdom

LONDON TOPOGRAPHICAL SOCIETY
Publication No. 131
1985

ISBN 0 902087 19 3

Published for the London Topographical Society by Harry Margary, Lympne Castle, Kent, in association with Guildhall Library, London.

London Topographical Society
3 Meadway Gate
London NW11 7LA

Printed in Great Britain by Headley Brothers Ltd The Invicta Press Ashford Kent and London

RICHARD HORWOOD'S MAP AND THE FACE OF LONDON, 1799–1819

I will introduce you to a magnificant plan of London, which will enable us to see the bearings and quality of each district, and, perhaps, more easily to discover the parts where improvements are most wanted.

[G. G. Stonestreet], *Domestic Union, or London as it should be!!* (1800)[1]

THE FAMILIAR POCKET *A to Z* is a cheap and handy means of finding one's way around the city: its rudimentary street plans soon become dog-eared with constant use and eventually have to be discarded in favour of a slightly more up-to-date but equally ephemeral replacement. This historical *A to Z* has a different purpose; it too affords a means of finding the main streets and back lanes of London (no less than 6,500 of them) but the map upon which the index grid is superimposed is far more than a mere street plan. Richard Horwood's plan, here adapted and reproduced in its third edition of 1813 at approximately half the original scale, is one of the most richly detailed maps of London ever produced, and one of the largest cartographic ventures in Britain before the age of the Ordnance Survey map. For those interested in the history of London it is not just a means of finding places that have long since been removed; it is a portrait of the capital during the Regency. The topographical context for the social, economic and political history of London is described in an economical and accessible way, as only detailed maps can. This introduction provides a brief guide to the history of the map, its qualities and significance, and presents the little we know about its maker. It also draws attention to some of the ways in which the map reflects the striking topographical changes that were taking place in London in the years covered by the four editions.[2]

As fine a work as Horwood's huge map might, at least to those already knowledgeable in the topography of London, seem to speak for itself; to describe so eloquent a description any further might appear to gild the lily. But no map can fail to be better understood in the light of its history, or better appreciated after critical evaluation. The specialist in London's topography will soon discover—if he has not already done so—that his knowledge provides as much a commentary on London maps as the maps upon his knowledge. The spurious authority with which finely engraved maps are generally endowed, and their effectiveness in communicating much topographical detail so economically, tend to obscure their very obvious limitations as historical evidence. Most maps are, of course, out of date from the moment they are printed, often before, but in the days before aerial photography maps were also of necessity patchworks of surveys taken at different times. Horwood's map of London was surveyed over several years and revised three times after its author's death. As evidence for the topographer, therefore, it is as ambivalent as it is eloquent.

On a principle never before attempted

During the 1780s the London map trade was as busy as ever. Almost every year Bowles, Kitchin, Sayer, Faden, Cary, and other lesser arm-chair geographers and print shop proprietors, published between them several new maps in a variety of styles for an ever growing popular market.[3] But most of them were at scales of less than six inches to a mile and were, inevitably, derivative. They served their customers well enough, but the task of meeting the more exacting demands of public officials and landowners, and of advancing the practice of cartography, fell to those impecunious but heroic surveyors who, every half-century or so, made the large-scale plans for the hacks of the map trade to plagiarize and adapt at will. Richard Horwood, like John Rocque fifty years before, was such a surveyor.

By 1790 Rocque's plan of London was well out of date, not just because it was over forty years old, but because it fell far short of the specification needed for a large-scale survey of the city by the end of the eighteenth century.[4] Horwood planned something far more ambitious; as he put it in the heading of his prospectuses, his plan was to be 'on a principle never before attempted'. It was, in fact, to be the first map of London to attempt to show each individual property since Ogilby and Morgan's map of 1676, and in its numbering of premises it was to be unmatched until the 1930s.[5] The sheer size of the task that Horwood completed raises many intriguing questions about the way the survey was undertaken—questions to which we have very few answers.

The little we know about the making of Horwood's map comes from his own advertisements, brief documentary records of his attempt to gain financial support, and the map itself. Of Horwood himself we know even less, far less than we do of Rocque and many other map-makers of the period. He published only one other map, a six-sheet plan of Liverpool similar in style to the London one. He may have worked as a surveyor from time to time for the Phoenix Fire Office, but he is first recorded in 1790 when he began to canvass subscriptions for his London map.[6] In October of that year he published a map of an area of about 22 acres around Leicester Square and Haymarket 'as a specimen of a Plan of LONDON'.[7]

In March of the following year he sought the support of the Royal Society for the Encouragement of Arts, Commerce and Manufactures, but without success.[8] He must, however, have obtained enough subscriptions to encourage him to make a start, for we next learn of his progress from the publication of the first of the 32 sheets: sheet B2 (12 in this reproduction), covering the most fashionable parts of the West End, bears the date June 22nd 1792. The adjoining sheet to the north, B1 (2), has the date October 25th 1793. In January and February 1794 three further sheets appeared: A1–3 (1, 11 and 21). At about this time (for it is undated) the earliest of the two prospectuses for the map was published from an address in Arundel Street: in describing the virtues of the map to encourage further subscriptions, it draws the attention of the public to 'the five Plates now finished'—which probably means that they were published and not merely drawn for the engraver.[9] The next sheet to be published is dated 10 April, 1794 and it seems likely that subscribers received in March the four sheets published at the beginning of that year in a batch, with a printed circular from Horwood apologizing for the slow progress of the map, which had originally been promised for 1792. The letter, rashly, promises that 'a great part [of the map] will be finished by the end of the summer' and, to keep impatient subscribers sweet, expresses the hope that 'the improvement made in shewing the boundaries of parishes, &c. will in some degree compensate for the delay'. Ever desperate for more subscribers, Horwood undertook to replace any sheets that got damaged through being shown by subscribers to their friends 'to encourage the undertaking'.[10]

Two further sheets, B3 and B4 (22 and 32), appeared in January 1795, thereby completing the western quarter of the whole map. Encouraged by this milestone, Horwood wrote to the Royal Society of Arts again asking for their support and sending them copies of the completed eight sheets. The minutes of the Committee for Polite Arts, who considered such matters for the Royal Society of Arts, give the first tantalizingly brief glimpse of the survey itself:

> Mr Horwood attending was called in and being asked
>
> Q How long is it since he began the Plan, and in what time he thought it would be completed.
>
> A It was begun in the year 1791 and thinks it will be completed in 1796; It would have been completed sooner had he not been obliged to survey it himself.[11]

Again he was unsuccessful; the Committee considered that the map was 'executed in a very accurate manner, and on a scale that promises to be of considerable Utility' but that it could not be considered for a prize until it was completed.[12] But no further sheets were to appear until 1799.

Meanwhile, Horwood made a further attempt to raise support and to propitiate those who had paid him five guineas five years earlier. From his address in Mare Street, Hackney, he issued a second prospectus dated December 1st 1795 and listing the names of 838 subscribers. This prospectus is reproduced as the frontispiece to this volume.[13] On the assumption that each of the names, including the King and Queen who are listed separately, represented a subscription of five guineas, Horwood should by that date have received £4,562.5s.0d, at least twice the sum needed to survey and publish a large-scale county-map. For a project of this magnitude, however, it seems that this was insufficient, for in January 1798 Horwood wrote to the Phoenix Fire Office in Lombard Street, who had already subscribed for five copies, 'proposing to Dedicate a Map of London . . . to the Office in consideration of the Directors granting him a Loan of £500 to enable him to proceed and finish the work'. The loan was approved 'on the Securities that he proposes', a reference to a letter from Horwood offering (presumably) some or all of the eight plates that were already printed. The name of the Phoenix duly appeared on the map, an early example of sponsorship by the insurance industry, and the loan was redeemed in June 1799, the directors resolving to return 'the Plates relating to the large Map of London, deposited in the Office by Mr. Horwood.' In the following month the Phoenix board agreed that 'a sum not exceeding £20 be expended in advertising Horwood's Plan of London and its Environs'.[14]

Horwood's proposals, like those of many map-makers of the time, are a characteristic blend of vague promises and pardonable exaggeration of the kind found in most publishers' blurbs. But they do allow us to estimate the gap between what Horwood intended to do and what he actually achieved. For example, there was to have been a set of eight plates engraved with 'Perspective Views of Hampstead, Highgate, Primrose-Hill, Islington, &c. &c.' to form a kaleidoscopic panorama of the northern fringes of London and the nearby countryside.[15] Two of these were engraved on separate copper plates and appear as the top part of sheets A1 and B1 (1 and 2) in some copies of the first edition.[16] The plates are not mentioned in the proposals of 1795 and it seems that the other six views were never engraved. More significant for the quality of the cartography itself are several other features of the proposals. Particular stress is laid upon the delineation of parish boundaries: 'To Gentlemen in every Branch of the Law, as well as those who have the conducting of any kind of parochial Business, this Plan cannot fail of being of the utmost Use; as it will shew the Boundary of every Parish and District with so much Exactness, that wherever it happens to pass through a House, which is very frequently the Case, it is accurately described . . . An Object of the utmost Importance, as whoever is in Possession of this Plan can never be liable to Error, in bringing Ejectments or Actions, in leasing or conveying Premises, &c. &c.'[17] The picture of scrupulous grey lawyers checking with Horwood's plan before evicting some hapless tenant is touching, but Horwood overestimated his cartographic abilities as well as human nature; he did not attempt the awesome task of plotting the parish boundaries within the City of London, and even outside the City, despite a brave attempt to show many of the small extra-parochial liberties, his boundaries were left incomplete.

On the first edition of the map, beneath the 'EXPLANATION' on sheet G4 (37), Horwood added to the plate, after several copies had been pulled from it and distributed to subscribers, the following note: 'The Proprietor thinks it his Duty to state to the Public, that he never pledged himself to shew the interior or extent of the back parts of Premises or in any way to distinguish property unless specially required, nor in an undertaking of such Magnitude and difficulty wou'd it have been possible in any length of time—But if any Gentleman wishes to have his Property or Premises more particularly shewn. The Proprietor will make any addition required at the least posible expence [*sic*]'. The sixth paragraph of the Proposals, in both versions, repeats this disclaimer in a slightly different and more defensive form, adding that 'in some Places it was not in his Power to get a View' and that, in any case, showing the backs of buildings was 'rather for the Sake of Ornament than Use'. Such excuses, and particularly the offer to show the premises of individual subscribers in greater detail, would have cut little ice with George Dance the Younger, Surveyor to the City of London, whose opinion on the map was later to be sought by the Royal Society of Arts. He would immediately have recognized this obvious defect in the map. The fact that Horwood's disclaimers appear in the Proposals and on the map suggests that the criticism had already been made to him.

Completion: the First Edition

Whatever its defects, and they are many, the final appearance in 1799 of the full 32 sheets was a remarkable achievement, the result of nine years dogged work by what we must assume was no more than Horwood himself and a small, and doubtless changing team of assistants.[18] It was the largest map ever printed in Britain and, if we discount the maps of the Ordnance Survey, has probably never been exceeded in size.[19] The amount of engraving required far exceeded that of the large-scale county surveys, even allowing for the extensive use of punches for numbers and some smaller lettering. The cost of the plates and the engraving would almost certainly have exceeded £700. Although it is unlikely that all of the 1,142 copies listed as subscribed for in the list of subscribers supplied with the map were actually delivered, it seems more than likely that over 1,000 copies were printed.[20] So much paper was required that Horwood seems to have had it specially made: nearly all copies in which the 2½-inch margin above and below each sheet has not been cropped have his watermark, 'HORWOODS PLAN' along one edge and 'OF LONDON' along the other.[21] Because the process of printing from copper plates allowed map-makers to make alterations with ease during printing, most large-scale maps and plans were issued in different editions (often referred to as 'states' since they were pulled from the plate in its *n*th state) and all but three of the 32 sheets of the first edition of Horwood's map have been found in at least two states. Copies were assembled from stock for mounting or binding, or for issue as sets of mint sheets, so that in theory the number of possible unique copies of the first edition far exceeds the total number printed.[22] Most of the variants are minor, and it would not be appropriate to describe them in detail here.

In December 1800 Horwood once again approached the Royal Society of Arts for their favour but in the following May the Committee on Polite Arts decided that the report they had received from George Dance was not sufficiently enthusiastic for Horwood to be granted a bounty. Horwood advertised the map in August 1799 from 'his apartments at No. 11 Haymarket'.[23]

Although Horwood, like most map-makers of the period, looked to the aristocracy and gentry for most of his subscriptions, with a map of this kind he clearly had in mind a clientele with a more practical need for maps. The subscription lists are a rich source of speculation about the map and its users. Of the 1,116 names on the final list issued with the map 123 were members of the Royal Family, Peers or Knights; 152 were commercial firms or professional partnerships; and about 750 were private individuals, including eleven Members of Parliament. Among the remainder were: 13 parish vestries, mostly outside the City itself; 27 central or local government departments or their officials, including the police offices; 8 or 9 insurance companies; 7 water companies; and a miscellaneous collection of institutions ranging from Brazenose College Oxford to the Office for Sick and Hurt Seamen. Not all those listed can have received their copies; some, like John Hunter F.R.S., died before Horwood managed to finish the map.[24] Prominent among both firms and individuals were bankers, lawyers and industrial concerns with large premises, many of whom are named on the map, especially brewers (Meux, Barclay and Whitbread included) and sugar bakers. The Royal Society of Arts was not alone in recognizing the map's 'considerable Utility'.

Yet none of this brought financial success to Horwood. He wrote to the R.S.A. in July 1801 still determined to gain one of their prizes and (more important, for the best prize he could have hoped for would not cover more than a fraction of his costs) their 'approbation'.[25] Meanwhile, in July or August 1800, he had approached the Mayor and Corporation of Liverpool seeking their patronage for a survey of their town, second in size only to London among English towns. He received immediate support, the promise of assistance from the Corporation's surveyors, and a subscription for ten copies from the Treasurer.[26] He began the survey, which followed the specification of the London map, in May 1801, and published its six sheets in July 1803: it carries the names of no fewer than 760 subscribers.[27] After his struggles in London this was plain sailing. Moreover, in April 1803 the R.S.A., whose secretary Charles Taylor he had badgered yet again, resumed consideration of the London map and finally on 4 May granted him a bounty of 50 guineas.[28] But it did little more than give Horwood the satisfaction of finally making his point. He wrote before learning of his success explaining that illness prevented him from attending a meeting of the Committee of Polite Arts, and again a few days later asking that his prize be sent via an intermediary; 'I am extremely unwell and the weather is much against an invalid . . . I have been so ill having taken a fresh Cold . . . now you will perceive I am scarcely able to write'.[29] His handwriting reveals no such malady, but whether he had a cold or not he was certainly ill. On 2 October 1803 he died, aged 45, and was buried in the ancient Toxteth chapel about a mile outside Liverpool.[30] In one of his letters to Charles Taylor, which otherwise reveals a disillusioned, careworn and ill man, he forcefully defends his work:

> You once mentioned to me something had been said about an Error or Omission somewhere by the River—To which I can only say to you *I know of no such Error or Omission either by the River Side or elsewhere* was I at the Office I coūd point out to you many proofs of accuracy—& I doubt not many parts have been so altered & added to *since* that the accuracy of the Work has frequently been impeached with injustice—It is an Undertaking which cost me 9 years of the most valuable part of my Life——I took every Angle meas^{d} almost every line & after that Plotted the whole work and compared it—The Engraving considering the immense Mass of Work—I flatter myself is well done.[31]

Today, when copies of the map are hawked around the antique map trade at sums exceeding Horwood's total printing costs, and when the hacks and spivs of the eighteenth-century map trade get far more attention than they deserve, it would take a harsh critic to gainsay the justice of Richard Horwood's own epitaph on his work. It is honest and rings true; quite a rare thing in the history of cartography.

William Faden's editions

By some means or other the 32 plates passed to William Faden, the country's leading seller and publisher of large-scale maps. Faden had acquired the plates of most of the large-scale county maps of the late eighteenth century and reissued most of them under his own imprint. He also commissioned new surveys of five counties and published the first maps of the Ordnance Survey in 1801.[32] Although he is not listed as a subscriber Faden would certainly have been following the progress of Horwood's project and in the circumscribed world of the London map business, concentrated around the Strand, the two men could hardly fail to become acquainted; in fact Faden's shop in Charing Cross was one of the places where subscriptions were taken, and it seems likely that copies were supplied there after Horwood's departure for Liverpool.[33] Faden was nothing if not a good businessman and may have acquired the plates very cheaply, for he must have realised that there was little money to be made from reissuing them, and even less in revising them. Yet he did revise them, substantially in some respects, and republished them in 1807, 1813 and 1819. The 1819 edition was listed in his catalogue of 1822 at double Horwood's subscription price of five guineas.[34] The 1813 edition, then, reproduced in this *A to Z*, contains a considerable contribution from Faden; but it is still essentially the work of Richard Horwood, whose name Faden (as was his practice when reissuing other men's plates) retained, prominently re-engraved on the new title plate. For all the expense of revision, the number of copies printed by Faden must have been very small: the first edition appears regularly at auction sales and has survived in quite large numbers, but the Faden editions are extremely rare. Perhaps Faden had some private obligation to Horwood or, perhaps more likely, simply wished to gain the esteem from being the publisher of the best map of the largest city in the world. Faden took trouble to incorporate major revisions in the county maps he reissued (adding new turnpikes and canals for example)[35] but at this scale the rapid growth of streets and buildings demanded something more systematic. Although he could not possibly have accounted for every new development, Faden was not content simply to add major public buildings and extensive new residential development. One rather obvious revision was not undertaken in any of Faden's editions; Horwood's parish boundaries were neither completed nor corrected.[36]

Some of the significant changes to the metropolitan townscape which are reflected in these editions, and in the 1813 edition in particular, will be discussed shortly but to take the history of the plates further we can briefly summarize the major revisions Faden made. Most of them were already incorporated in the 1807 edition. Eight new plates were added, extending the coverage to the River Lea;[37] the title was removed from the plate H1 (8) and a new elaborate one beautifully engraved on one of the new plates; minor changes are to be found on all of the original 32 plates and most plates were substantially revised. In particular Faden's engravers added house numbers in many streets, back lanes and courts. Business premises, such as warehouses, lying behind street frontages were delineated with greater precision and the vague, incomplete shading that Horwood left was tidied up extensively. Architectural details were added to many churches and other public buildings which Horwood had depicted with stark regularity; porticos, bays and steps can be seen added to many prominent buildings. Faden also labelled hitherto unnamed buildings, open spaces and gardens. Altogether, on most sheets the differences found between the first edition and this reproduction were effected on the 1807 edition.[38]

In 1813, presumably anxious to incorporate major public works that were changing the face of London, Faden issued this third edition. The major change was the engraving of two new plates for sheets A1 and B1 (1 and 2). The imminent creation of Regent's Park necessitated such wholesale revision that rather than re-engrave the existing plates (two large and two smaller copper plates for each of the two sheets) Faden started afresh. Apart from major public works, which will be discussed later, additions and revisions for the 1819 edition were relatively minor. They are widely spread across the map and often involved unspectacular building developments, but only detailed local studies would reveal whether the revision was the result of systematic field work or merely the assimilation of randomly acquired information.

In addition to the main plates Faden issued an index map in 1814.[39] It proved to be a popular general map of London and was revised and reissued no less than twenty times by Faden and by the man who took over his business in 1823, James Wyld. Whether or not Wyld kept the 40 plates of the large map intact his son, James Wyld junr, certainly revised two of them for printing.[40] In 1842 he published a map of the City of London using plates D2 and E2 (14 and 15) and copying parts of the adjacent sheets to complete his map. In the case of plate D2 (14) not only was the information on the map considerably updated but Wyld had the map so comprehensively restyled with mechanical tinting, the bold mechanical lettering then becoming fashionable, and other stylistic devices, that one wonders why he did not start afresh.[41] Whatever the reasons for this belated revival of Horwood's plates, it repeated the familiar tendancy for the copper plates of maps to be reprinted until the the very last saleable copy had been pulled from them. In this case it must reflect the high investment represented by such dense and intricate engraving compared with other aspects of map production. On the other hand, many of the streets and buildings of eighteenth-century London must have survived just as Horwood plotted them about 45 years earlier: the major street works and new office buildings that altered the face of London were essentially a Victorian phenomenon, and the few early-nineteenth-century schemes were easily plotted on existing map plates. The longevity of the townscapes may justify the longevity of the copper plates.[42]

The contents of the map and the changing face of London

As an historical document Horwood's map informs and interests in a variety of ways. The sheer detail, for all that it is idiosyncratic, provides an endless source of information for the topographer and impresses the student of cartography. Individual rooms of the Chelsea Hospital (sheet 31) are numbered and described, on the first edition the Earl of Leicester's house was similarly treated (sheet 11), and on the 1819 edition Faden provided a similar guide to the buildings around Horse Guards Parade. Readers will find other examples of such detail, more appropriate to the Ordnance Survey's town plans of later years at scales of five and ten feet to one mile. Faden even managed to draw in the outlines of the buildings inside the Tower of London (doubtless from his connections with the Ordnance Survey whose operation was based there) whereas Horwood, with a hint of irritation had noted on the first edition 'The Internal Parts not distinguished being refused permission to take the Survey'.

But beyond all these details, which it would be neither possible nor appropriate to describe or comment upon here, the map is a unique *general* guide to the growth of London between 1799 and 1819. The appearance of four editions in that span of twenty years makes it possible to trace significant developments in the geography of the capital.

Since Rocque's survey in the 1740s London had grown at a modest rate; its population had increased more slowly than the country as a whole and a comparison of the maps of Rocque and Horwood reveals similarly restrained expansion onto new building land. Generally speaking new building had been for the middle and lower-middle classes—the West End, Knightsbridge, Sloane Square and its environs, and the laying out of Kennington, Walworth and St George's Fields south of the river. There were smaller, more concentrated developments for artisans, clerks and others of lesser means—the Christchurch district of Southwark, Shoreditch and parts of St Luke's Old Street, and portions of Whitechapel, Bethnal Green and St George's in the East—but the poor presumably colonized the attics and back yards of commercial districts and residential areas deserted by those who could afford to move to more desirable locations. Much of the new building in the second half of the eighteenth century occupied tenter grounds made redundant as the London cloth trade declined in the face of northern competition and other forms of metropolitan enterprise. But in the years covered by the editions of Horwood's plan London's growth accelerated sharply. On the basis of the census of 1801 we can estimate that Horwood had surveyed an area containing approximately 110,000 inhabited houses containing about 730,000 inhabitants; by the time of the last edition in 1819 the area covered by the original 32 sheets contained about 150,000 houses and a population of approximately 1 million.[43] Not only do these figures reinforce the immensity of the task of producing the map and revising it, they also add emphasis to some fundamental changes in the face of London which can be very clearly detected by comparing the editions of Horwood's plan.

That late eighteenth-century London was socially and politically turbulent is common knowledge, but it has not deflected some from a tendency to equate Georgian London with the Golden Age of the Adam brothers, and Regency London with John Nash and the society whose tastes he fulfilled. But of course the grubby rough parts of London did not suddenly appear with Charles Dickens, and the division, however rough and ready, between the East and West Ends had sharpened through the seventeenth and eighteenth centuries and was evident enough in the early nineteenth.[44] For Sir John Summerson the lack of surviving buildings from the years of the French Wars reflects a lack of government spending on building and a shortage of Baltic timber, and marks a period of distinct inactivity in the London building industry for over twenty years.[45] But this conclusion needs qualifying, for while it is true that in many (though not all) of the fashionable districts in which architectural taste might be expected to find expression building was carried on at a modest scale, the scene was quite different elsewhere. The industrial end of the city was expanding, with inevitable effects upon the building industry, especially after 1800. The giant breweries, for example, broke new records in output and profit, and the Port of London and its associated riverside districts were transformed by massive and unprecedented dock and warehouse construction.[46] Consequently mean streets of small houses spread over the East End and in districts south of the Thames. Horwood and Faden allow us to see all this with particular clarity.

At the time of the publication of the first edition London had only eighteen acres of enclosed dock; the old Greenland Dock (opened in 1699) and John Perry's Brunswick Dock of 1790 near the mouth of the Lea. By the time of the 1813 edition the area of enclosed dock had increased tenfold to almost 180 acres including basins. London Dock, Wapping Basin, the Grand Surrey Docks, the East India Docks, West India Docks and the City Canal across the Isle of Dogs had all been completed in time to appear on the 1807 edition of Horwood's plan.[47] Faden moved in the sort of circles that would have enabled him to obtain plans of the docks without having to survey them; indeed, many such plans were published. His detailed portrayal even extends to the Royal Dockyard in Deptford. A significant addition to the plates in 1807 were the soundings in the Thames. Again, Faden had simply plundered an official source, *The Second Report for the Select Committee upon the Improvement of the Port of London,* though in doing so he confused the soundings taken by Trinity House in 1750 with those 'reduced to the lowest tide that happen'd between the 10th. May and 8th. June, 1794' which were distinguished in the original report in italic numerals.[48] A mariner eccentric enough to rely upon this map would at the very least be confused.

The building of London Dock and its associated warehouses probably displaced about 5,000 persons from their homes. Moreover, dock construction on this scale required a huge labour force. All this, together with other commercial development in the East End, must have pushed up demand for cheap accessible houses. The effects can be seen dramatically by comparing the four editions of plate G2 (17): Commercial Road was constructed in 1800 and in each successive edition of the map short terraced streets filled the adjacent fields—about 1500 houses were added to that plate by 1813, chiefly in the parish of St George in the East.[49] Upstream from all this fever of dock building the three existing bridges across the Thames were proving inadequate, or at least inadequate enough to encourage the speculative building of three more in quick succession. Regent's Bridge was begun in May 1811; it languished for want of funds, was restarted again in 1813, and was completed as Vauxhall Bridge, with nine iron arches, in 1816. The foundation stone of Strand Bridge was laid on 11 October 1811 and the magnificent structure of Cornish and Aberdeen granite was opened in the presence of the Regent and the Duke of Wellington on 18 June, 1817; it was by then, of course, called Waterloo Bridge. Southwark Bridge, with the widest iron span in the world, was built between September 1814 and April 1818, like Waterloo Bridge to the designs of John Rennie, senior.[50] All three bridges were added to the plates for the 1819 edition of Horwood, but Faden, up to date as ever, also showed Vauxhall and Strand Bridges in outline on the 1813 edition; though the approach roads did not appear until the 1819 edition. (See Appendix to this introduction.)

To complete the picture of major public works taking place in the years around 1813 and 1819 we turn to the schemes of John Nash.[51] Their impact was made all the more obvious by the modest scale of other changes in the West End. The great artery of Regent Street and Waterloo Place, connecting Regent's Park and its fashionable residential district with the centres of Court and Government around St James's Park and Whitehall, had been proposed at the turn of the century but did not appear on paper in its final form until 1813, too late for the third edition of Horwood. But it was Faden who published a plan of the scheme in 1814.[52] By 1819 he was able to depict the incomplete scheme on plate B2 (12) of the big map with the quadrant and the famous colonnade in place. (See Appendix.) The plans for Regent's Park, however, were public knowledge a little earlier and caused Faden to effect substantial alterations to Horwood's plates.

In re-engraving of sheets A1 and B1 (1 and 2) Faden once again took advantage of his ready access to sources. The Regent's Park depicted here on the 1813 edition is quite different in many respects from the Park that actually took shape; but it is identical to that shown in Faden's own *PLAN of the Improvements now Executing in the REGENT'S PARK, Designed by John Nash Esqr.* which bears the same date as the revised Horwood, 4th June 1813.[53] At that time little of Nash's scheme had been achieved; the Regent's Canal was being dug in early 1813 on a more southerly course, through what Faden shows as Cumberland Square, one of the many blocks of proposed houses that never assumed the form imagined here.[54] Of Regent's Circus only the southern half was built to form Park Crescent. The lake when flooded did not assume the shape shown here, nor was it crossed by a carriageway running westwards from the circus in the middle of the park. But the most important point to note is that with few exceptions the residences in and around the park were not erected until between 1820 and 1827.[55] By plundering the plans of the Commissioners of Woods, Forests and Land Revenues Faden was, characteristically, ahead of himself.

Other developments in the West End and other residential districts of the well-to-do and middling classes were unremarkable. Chelsea, Marylebone and St Pancras can be seen filling up block by block; the tentative building lines of the Bedford Estate between Russell Square and Euston await attention; Belgravia was not to be shown in project outline until the 1819 edition; gardens and the Chelsea Water Works were to occupy Pimlico for some years yet, though south Westminster was about to expand into the proposed streets around Vincent Square and Regent (now Regency) Street in the shadow of that 'long forgotten humanitarian Bastille', the new Millbank Penitentiary, just begun in 1813 and completed in 1816.[56]

Horwood in perspective: evaluation and conclusion

The value of a map and thus, very often, the reputation of its author, depend more upon the requirements of its users than upon any objective criteria. Moreover, the requirements of historians and those of contemporaries may diverge sharply. For the topographer Horwood is a constant source of reference, a common base against which to see the myriad changes to the streets and buildings of London. For the historian of London as a whole, the four editions provide a sequence of documents which through careful analysis, particularly beside directories and other systematic sources, may reveal solid evidence of building and land use changes in these crucial years of London's physical development. Moreover, such an analysis may suggest lines of investigation for the student of the changing geography and structure of the capital which are of wider significance than the details of topographical change. In this sense the detailed maps provide the assembled evidence for synthesis.

There has not been the space here to comment on more than a few of the major developments manifested in the Horwood editions. William Faden seems to have kept the plates up to date with considerable care, but there is room for far more detailed comparison with other sources—particularly contemporary plans, views, directories and topographies—to *evaluate* the map at every level. Parochial plans are the most readily available source of comparison, though to be fair to Horwood the parochial surveyors faced a far easier task. Tompson's plan of St Pancras, surveyed from about 1796 and published in May 1804 at about half the scale of Horwood, provides the most direct comparison of all.[57] Similarly Thomas Hornor's plan of Clerkenwell was published in the same year as this third edition, at the same scale as Horwood.[58] These, and several slightly later parochial surveys, often giving house numbers, provide the first line of attack and many plans in manuscript, several of them reproduced in the volumes of the *Survey of London*, facilitate even sharper tests.[59] Not unexpectedly, many of the details in these local plans, especially the interior parts of blocks and the backs of buildings, were generalized or omitted altogether by Horwood, though it cannot be assumed that Horwood was always the less reliable, and making due allowance for the conventions of map production at this scale there is very little in Horwood's plates that would actually mislead. House by house he seems to be reliable. The total number of names of streets, courts, yards, and all manner of public buildings is, as the index to this volume shows (though it includes all of Faden's additions) very substantial. Certainly there are minor names which appear in parish surveys and not on these plates, but it is difficult to accept the claim of John Lockie, Inspector of Buildings to the Phoenix Fire Office that he was about to produce a map of London 4 foot by 2 foot whose 'Copiousness . . . far exceeds that of any other Plan of London now extant, containing upwards of Two Thousand Places, the Names of which are not to be found in the *large Map of Thirty-Two Sheets, by* HORWOOD'. Lockie's *Topography*, however, contains a little over 8,000 entries in its gazetteer, rather more than the number of names on Horwood's first edition. Horwood had originally proposed to publish a 'Book of Reference' or index to his map, perhaps not unlike the index to this *A to Z*.[60] All he provided in the event was a two-page sheet with 1,691 streets, etc., with street numbers. The temptation to suspect Lockie of professional jealousy here is irresistible in view of the connection through the Phoenix.[61]

There is no doubt that the imperfections in Horwood's map were remarked upon by contemporary surveyors. The rather cool reception by the City Surveyor, George Dance, has already been mentioned, though Dance, whose own published plans are certainly superior, probably recognized that for such a modest cost in money and manpower Horwood's achievement was remarkable. With the benefit of hindsight and after half a century of progress in scientific surveying, Henry Austin, Charles Dickens's brother-in-law, was less sympathetic. Acting as consulting engineer for Chadwick and the Metropolitan Commission of Sewers, his job was to back the call for a scientifically sound large-scale plan of London by the Ordnance Survey and to destroy the manifestly wrong-headed but influential arguments of James Wyld that existing parochial surveys would suffice.[62] In 1848 Austin stated firmly:

> From the time of Horwood to the present there can be no doubt that more money has been wasted in repeated Surveys of large portions of the Metropolis than would have produced a perfect detailed plan of the whole area over and over again, under general arrangements. Horwood's map, concocted some half century ago, probably in the same faulty manner to which it is now desired by some to resort, was known to be trigonometrically wrong, and has consequently never been trusted.[63]

Although Austin was right in his acerbic comment that 'second-class towns in the north [are] surveyed with all the completeness of minute detail . . . every door-step, every lamp-post . . . while London is denied the simplest skeletal plan', and that for the engineer all the previous plans were practically useless, his failure to state his evidence against Horwood may betray the propagandist: he was, after all, no more disinterested than James Wyld, aptly named spokesman for the private map-maker. For the historian a map's geodetic or trigonometrical accuracy may not be the prime criterion of its value. In some ways the hopelessly unscientific judgement of the author of our epigraph is just as appropriate:

> The plan of London lately completed by Mr Richard Horwood, is particularly valuable at this time, whilst so many improvements are in agitation; affording more ample means than any other of discovering the situation and bearings of every street and road. It would be an appropriate ornament to public halls, colleges, and libraries, and must prove a very acceptable present to persons in remote situations in Great Britain, and in places abroad.[64]

NOTES

1. p. 12. This pamphlet is attributed to George Griffin Stonestreet, first chief executive of the Phoenix Fire Office, now Phoenix Assurance. It is an idiosyncratic polemic advocating town planning measures for London. Stonestreet expresses his admiration for Horwood's plan and was probably the link between Horwood and the Phoenix which is discussed later in the text.
2. A fuller study of the publication history of Horwood's map, particularly of the first edition, is being prepared by the author for the *London Topographical Record*. Carto-bibliographical details are not given in full in this Introduction. The words map and plan are used interchangeably even though the latter is conventionally applied to scales exceeding six inches to one mile.
3. For a descriptive catalogue see James Howgego, *Printed Maps of London circa 1553–1850* (2nd edn, Folkestone, 1978).
4. John Rocque's *A Plan of the Cities of London and Westminster, and Borough of Southwark;* (1747) was surveyed between 1739 and 1746. It is described by Ralph Hyde in *The A to Z of Georgian London* (Lympne Castle, Kent, 1981). Although it is remarkably comprehensive in showing yards and courts, it does not otherwise distinguish the details of the interior of blocks or individual buildings.
5. The Ordnance Survey did not publish large-scale plans (1:2500 and 1:1250) with numbered premises until after the Second World War but the London County Council added them to a special series of 1 : 1056 plans in the 1930s.
6. Howgego, *op. cit.* p. 22 says that he 'was almost certainly working for the Phoenix Assurance Company on *ad hoc* surveying jobs', and the popular in-house histories of that company issued in 1960 and 1982 give Horwood a prominent place to the extent of having fanciful pictures of him at work surveying the streets of London, supervising assistants pushing odometers. (See note 1.) But there is no evidence to support these speculations.
7. *A small SKETCH as a specimen of a Plan of LONDON . . . Published . . . Octr. 22d. 1790.* British Library 3495 (113). Another copy in Cambridge University Library is accompanied by a similar plan of the Cavendish Square area: *Rough Sketch of a few Streets as a specimen of the manner in which the Plan is to be finished.* Atlas.1.79.3. This is cruder in execution and perhaps therefore earlier, but it is undated. From its title it seems to have accompanied a proposal or similar document.
8. R[oyal] S[ociety of] A[rts] Minutes Comm. (Pol. Arts) 16 March 1791. The Committee on Polite Arts resolved that he should complete the map before approaching them again for consideration for a prize or bounty.
9. Bodleian Library, Gough Gen. Top. 364, fol. 636.
10. British Library, 3495 (113). This copy is signed and dated in manuscript 'R. Horwood 9 March, 1794'.
11. RSA Minutes Comm. (Pol. Arts) 20 February 1795.
12. *Idem.* The role of the RSA in encouraging map-making is fully documented by J. B. Harley, 'The Society of Arts and the Surveys of English Counties 1759–1809' *Jnl of the Royal Society of Arts* 112 (1963–64) 43–46, 119–124, 269–275 and 538–543.
13. Guildhall Library, Broadside 6.100.
14. Phoenix Assurance Company, Minutes of the Board of Directors: Volume 7, 24 and 31 January 1798; Volume 8, 26 June and 17 July 1799.
15. Bodleian Library, Gough Gen. Top. 364, fol. 636.
16. The viewplates are quite rare and only found in combination with early states of plates A1 and B1 of the first edition. They will be discussed further in the *London Topographical Record*.
17. This passage is identical in both sets of proposals. See notes 9 and 13.
18. The imprints on all the sheets of the first edition except the eight at the western end have the date 24 May 1799.
19. The area inside the border at just over 94 square feet is larger than the largest of the county maps, Andrews, Dury and Herbert's map of Kent (1769).

20. To speculate upon Horwood's costs is to raise some puzzling issues. 32 copper plates 20.7 ins. by 22.6 ins, engraving, about 35,000 sheets of specially made paper, printing from the plates, printing the list of subscribers and short street index, and publicity must have cost between £1500 and £2000: the engraving could have inflated this sum considerably. If the manpower engaged in the surveying was as modest as Horwood claimed, then allowing for the fact that little travelling was required compared to a county survey, £2000 would be a reasonable guess. Even if the subscription list is wishful thinking and represents no more than, say, 800 subscribers, the income from that would be £4,200. That leaves a substantial margin unaccounted for.
21. The library accounts of Brazenose College, Oxford, record the payment of half subscriptions in 1795 and 1803: from the evidence of watermarks, the copy received was not printed until 1802 at the earliest and bound in 1803.
22. The maximum number of variants found on any one plate of the first edition is 6 and the total number of possible combinations of variant sheets exceeds 69 (British) billions!
23. *The Morning Herald* 2, 9 and 24 August 1799. The advertisement is headed 'In a few days will be published'.
24. Judging from its printed catalogue of 1802 the Liverpool Athenaeum never received the copy for which it supposedly subscribed. John Hunter died on October 16th 1793 yet is named in both subscription lists.
25. R.S.A. ms Transactions 1802–03, section 17, contains six letters received from Horwood between 20 May 1800 and 26 May 1803. The letter dated 20 May 1800 printed in the R.S.A. *Transactions* for 1803, p. 321, and quoted in Howgego, *op. cit.* p. 22, is an edited conflation of two letters (20 May 1800 and 21 April 1803) and is therefore misleading.
26. Sir James A. Picton, *City of Liverpool Municipal Archives and Records 1700–1835* (Liverpool, 1886) vol. 2, p. 275.
27. *PLAN of the Town and Township of LIVERPOOL Shewing every House By R. HORWOOD 1803.* Proposals stating that the survey 'will be begun next month' and dated 4 April 1801 appeared in *Billinge's Liverpool Advertiser* 13 and 27 April 1801. Over 800 copies were subscribed for.
28. R.S.A. Minutes Comm. (Pol. Arts) 30 April 1803 and *Transactions* 1803, p. 311.
29. Letter 19 May 1803. See note 25.
30. *Gore's General Advertiser* 6 October 1803. Liverpool Central Libraries, microfilm copy of the registers of the Ancient Chapel of Toxteth. His gravestone records 'Rd. Horwood who with great Ingenuity & Indefatigable Industry designed & executed the celebrated Plans of London & Liverpool'.
31. Letter 21 April 1803. See note 25.
32. Elizabeth M. Rodger, *The Large Scale County Maps of the British Isles 1596–1850. A Union List* (2nd edn, Oxford, 1972). On Faden and the early Ordnance Survey see J. Brian Harley and Yolande O'Donoghue's Introduction to *The Old Series Ordnance Survey Maps of England and Wales. Vol. 1* (1975) pp. xxxi–xxxii; and W. A. Seymour (ed.), *A History of the Ordnance Survey* (Folkestone, 1980) pp. 68 and 73–74.
33. *The Morning Herald* 2 August 1799.
34. *Catalogue of the Geographical Works, Maps, Plans etc. published by W. Faden, 5 Charing Cross, Geographer to His Majesty* (1822. Reprinted 1963) p. 9.
35. See for example J. Brian Harley and Paul Laxton (eds), *A Survey of the County Palatine of Chester, P. P. Burdett 1777* (Historic Society of Lancashire and Cheshire, Occasional Series vol. 1, Liverpool, 1974) pp. 9–12, 35.
36. See key map. The boundaries of Limehouse, Bethnal Green and Rotherhithe remain incomplete.
37. The additional sheets are numbered: I1 (9), K1 (10), I2 (19), K2 (20), I3 (29), K3 (30), I4 (39) and K4 (40).
38. Sheet C2 (13) illustrates Faden's revisions. 1,438 house numbers were added to the plate between the first and third editions, nearly all of them by the second edition; the area between Soho and Lincoln's Inn Field was comprehensively revised in this way with many mews and yards depicted in greater detail; steps and porticos were added to St Paul's Covent Garden and St Martin in the Fields; and many other changes were effected by the 1807 edition.
39. Howgego, *op. cit.*, no. 272. It was issued in at least 20 editions but the earliest listed with a date is 1818. There are two copies of the 1814 edition in the library of the Royal Institute of Chartered Surveyors bound with two of their copies of Horwood.
40. *Dictionary of National Biography xxi*, pp. 1148–49. Ida Darlington has suggested that Wyld's vigorous opposition in 1848 to the Ordnance Survey in London was partly motivated by the threat it posed to his scheme to republish Horwood's plates (though there is no direct evidence for such a scheme): Ida Darlington, 'Edwin Chadwick and the First Large-Scale Ordnance Survey of London', *Trans. London and Middlesex Archaeol. Soc.* 22 (1968–70) pp. 58–63; Ralph Hyde, 'The *Act to Regulate Parochial Assessments* 1836 and its Contribution to the Mapping of London', *Guildhall Studies in London History* 2 (1976) pp. 54–68. If the Horwood plates survived they may have passed with Wyld's extensive business to the firm of G. W. Bacon in 1894. (Information from Ralph Hyde.)
41. Howgego, *op. cit.*, no. 374, says that *WYLD'S PLAN OF THE CITY OF LONDON* is 'based upon Horwood', but there is a no doubt that the old plates were used with some additional engraving and a decorative border *pasted* around them. The undated copy noted by Howgego is simply one in which the date has been erased by hand after printing.
42. King William St and Victoria St (now Farringdon Rd) were initiated in the early 1830s and schemes of a smaller kind, such as the widening of the Strand around St Clement Danes in 1810 [described and illustrated with a map in *Londina Illustrata*, vol. 1, plate 10 (published by Robert Wilkinson, 1819)] were undertaken long before 1830, but otherwise the old street plan and most pre-1800 buildings remained until well into the Victorian period. For a general comment see H. J. Dyos's introduction to *Collins' Illustrated Atlas of London* (Leicester, 1973) pp. 18–19.
43. The census figures are conveniently retabulated in J. Marshall, *Mortality of the Metropolis* (London, 1832).
44. M. Dorothy George, *London Life in the Eighteenth Century* (London, 1925). Chapter 2 is an excellent account of the housing of the lower classes and a necessary complement to Sir John Summerson's studies.
45. Sir John Summerson, *Georgian London* (Harmondsworth, 1962) p. 154. The sharp downturn in the building industry was reversed after 1799 and the recovery complete by about 1807 if national trends are a guide: A. K. Cairncross and B. Weber, 'Fluctuations in Building in Great Britain, 1785–1849', *Economic History Review* 9 (1956) pp. 283–97.
46. Peter Mathias, *The Brewing Industry in England, 1700–1830* (Cambridge, 1959) pp. 21–7, 133 and 551–2. James Bird, *The Major Seaports of the United Kingdom* (London, 1963) pp. 328–50. John Pudney, *London's Docks* (London, 1975).
47. A. W. Skempton, 'Engineering in the Port of London, 1789–1808' *Trans. Newcomen Soc.* 50 (1978–79) pp. 87–108 and 'Engineering in the Port of London, 1808–1834' *Trans. Newcomen Soc.* 53 (1981–83) pp. 73–96.
48. *Plan of the RIVER THAMES, from the TOWER to BLACKWALL, taken by the Corporation of the TRINITY HOUSE, in the Year 1750.* This plate was adapted for the First and Second Reports from the Select Committee

upon the Improvement of the Port of London of 1796 and 1799: *Reports from Committees of the House of Commons. Reprinted by Order of the House* Volume 14 (1803) plates 13 and 22.

49. Despite the demolition of almost 1,000 houses in the parish to accommodate London Dock (and making due allowance for possible inaccuracy in the census figures) the number of inhabited houses in St George in the East rose from 4029 to 4423 between 1801 and 1811. The number of inhabited houses enumerated in Mile End Old Town was 1627 in 1801, 2598 in 1811 and 4284 in 1821. J. Marshall, *op. cit.*
50. The bridges are described and illustrated in [Samuel] *Leigh's New Pictures of London* (3rd edn, London, 1819) pp. 267–75. See also Summerson, *Georgian London* pp. 238–41. The name Waterloo Bridge was confirmed by its third Act of Parliament in 1816.
51. Sir John Summerson, *The Life and Work of John Nash Architect* (London, 1980) provides a full account of his schemes for Regent Street and Regent's Park and reproduces many of the plans.
52. *PLAN OF A Street Proposed FROM CHARING CROSS TO PORTLAND PLACE DESIGNED BY I. NASH ESQR . . . Published . . . By W. FADEN . . . MAY 11TH. 1814.* Plate 25 in Summerson, *John Nash.* See also Hermione Hobhouse, *A History of Regent Street* (London, 1975).
53. Reproduced in Herbert Spencer, *An Illustrated History of the Regent's Canal* (London, 1961) p. 41. The date on Horwood is conventional; only the year was updated in the imprint.
54. *Idem,* p. 40. See also Ann Saunders, *Regent's Park: A Study of the Development of the Area from 1086 to the Present Day* (London, 1969).
55. Summerson, *Georgian London,* pp. 320–21 for a listing with dates.
56. *Idem,* p. 210
57. *A MAP of the PARISH of SAINT PANCRAS . . . by J. TOMPSON No. 29 Grafton Street, Fitzroy Square. May 30th 1804.*
58. *PLAN OF THE PARISH OF CLERKENWELL LONDON FROM A SURVEY & DRAWING BY T. HORNOR* [1813]. Described in Ralph Hyde, 'Thomas Hornor: Pictorial Land Surveyor', *Imago Mundi* 29 (1977) pp. 23–34.
59. *Plan OF the Parish of SAINT MARY LE BONE . . . Constructed pursuant to an Order of the Vestry, 1st July 1820. By PETER POTTER* was published in 1821, 1823 and *c.*1832 (facsimile of 3rd edn, with an introduction by Richard Bowden, published by Westminster City Libraries, 1979). The volumes of the *Survey of London* often allow plans of the most minute detail for appropriate dates to be compared with Horwood.
60. See frontispiece of this volume.
61. John Lockie, *Lockie's Topography of London; Giving a Concise Local Description of and Accurate Direction to every Square, Street, Lane, Court, Dock, Wharf, Inn, Public-Office, &c. in the Metropolis and its Environs* (London, 1810. Later editions in 1813 and 1816).
62. Darlington, *op. cit.*
63. *Metropolitan Commission of Sewers. Proceedings with Respect to the Ordnance Survey. A Report of Mr Austin . . . read at the Meeting of the General Purposes Committee, March 28, 1848.* p. 2.
64. [G. G. Stonestreet], *Domestic Union, or London as it should be!!* (London, 1800) p. 12.

ACKNOWLEDGEMENTS

Thanks are due to several librarians who have assisted me by making available many copies of Horwood's map and associated documents, in particular: Margaret Swarbrick (Westminster Public Library), John Phillips (Greater London Record Office) and Roger Fairclough (Cambridge University Library). Ray Tye of the Phoenix Assurance Company gave much enthusiastic help. Above all Ralph Hyde at the Guildhall Library has been a constant source of advice, erudition and hospitality and my debt to him is enormous.

APPENDIX

The copy of Horwood's map reproduced in this volume is held by the Department of Prints and Maps in the Guildhall Library. It has some amendments added in manuscript which cannot be distinguished from the original engraved lines in a reproduction of this kind. They are located on the Key Map as described below.

[A] The outlines of the proposed Regent Street from Portland Place to Pall Mall, including Lower Regent Street and Waterloo Place. (Sheet 12, upper centre to bottom right corner; sheet 13, bottom left corner; sheet 22, top right corner; sheet 23, top left corner.)

[B] The outlines of the proposed new Waterloo Bridge with its approach roads, from the Strand to what was to become St George's Circus, Southwark; including Wellington Street and Waterloo Road. In the 1813 edition of Horwood's map the outlined bridge was named 'STRAND BRIDGE',* but in this copy the word 'STRAND' has been erased and replaced in manuscript by 'WATERLOO'. Only the approach roads are in manuscript; the outline of the bridge and the waterside works are engraved. (Sheet 13, bottom right corner; sheet 23, top right corner; sheet 24, top left corner to lower centre.)

[C] The outlines of the proposed new Vauxhall Bridge with its approach roads, from Chelsea Road (now Buckingham Palace Road) to Kennington Lane, Vauxhall; including Vauxhall Bridge Road. In the earliest state of plate C4 (33) it was named 'Projected VAUXHALL BRIDGE'* but the word 'Projected' is not in this copy. The broken lines denoting the bridge itself are engraved on the original map. (Sheet 22, bottom centre; sheet 32, top centre to right centre; sheet 33, left centre.)

These manuscript amendments must have been added within a year or so of the publication of the map in 1813. The dates of the schemes concerned are described in this Introduction.

* Copy of the 1813 edition in this Greater London Record Office.

PUBLISHER'S NOTE

The value of this *A to Z* to serious students is enormously enhanced by the Introduction very kindly prepared by Paul Laxton, Lecturer in the Geography Department of Liverpool University. The publishers wish to record their appreciation of the very great amount of research that its preparation has entailed. The publishers also wish to record their thanks to Joseph Wisdom for undertaking the truly monumental task of compiling the Index.

READERS' NOTES

KEY

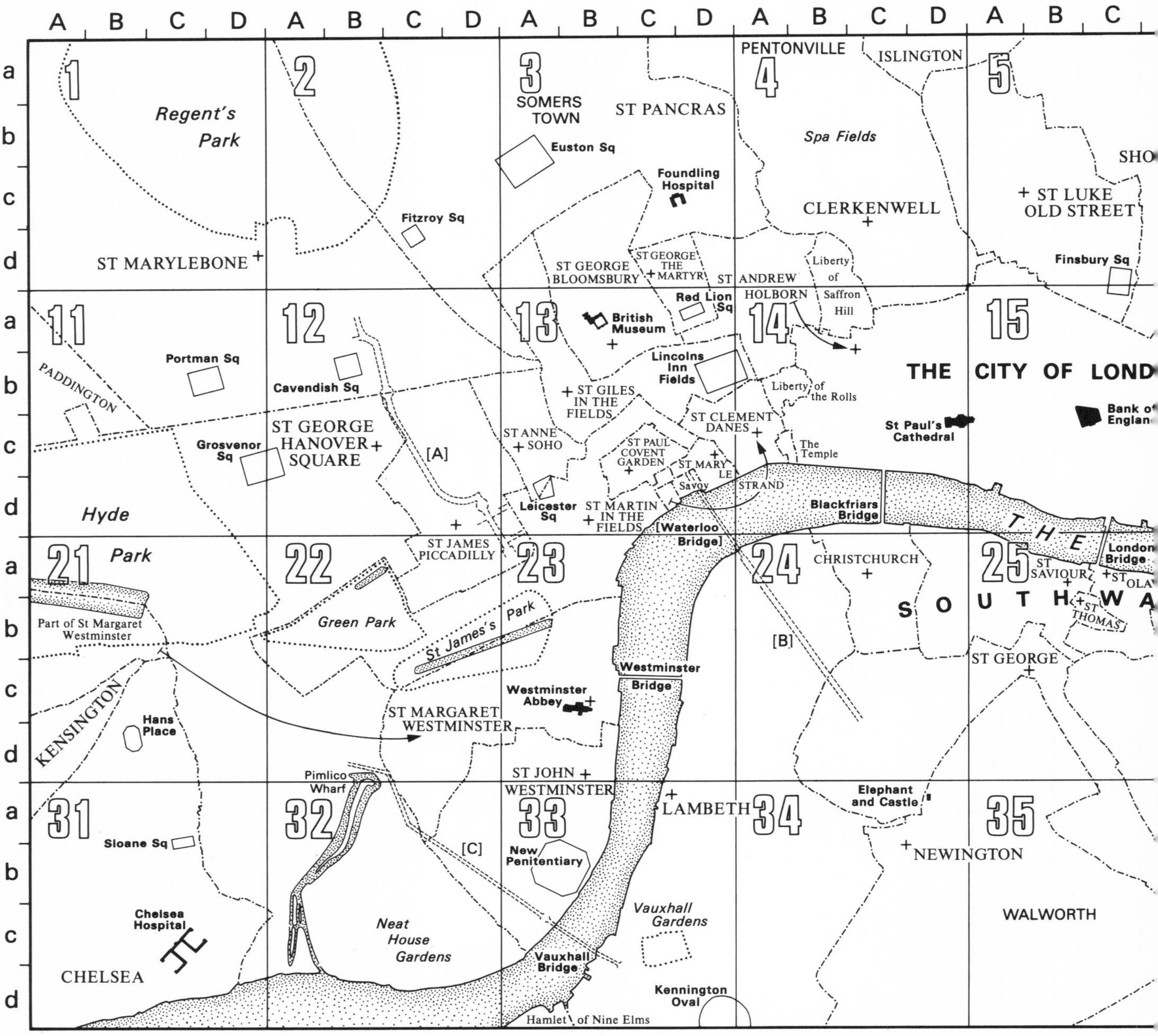

A B C D A B C D A B C D A B C D A B C

a b c d a b c d a b c d a b c d

1 Regent's Park
ST MARYLEBONE
2
Fitzroy Sq
3 SOMERS TOWN
ST PANCRAS
Euston Sq
Foundling Hospital
4 PENTONVILLE
ISLINGTON
Spa Fields
CLERKENWELL
5 SHO
ST LUKE OLD STREET
Finsbury Sq
ST GEORGE BLOOMSBURY
ST GEORGE THE MARTYR
ST ANDREW HOLBORN
Liberty of Saffron Hill
Red Lion Sq
11 PADDINGTON
Portman Sq
12 Cavendish Sq
ST GEORGE HANOVER SQUARE
Grosvenor Sq
[A]
13 British Museum
ST GILES IN THE FIELDS
Lincolns Inn Fields
14 Liberty of the Rolls
15 THE CITY OF LOND
Bank of England
St Paul's Cathedral
ST ANNE SOHO
ST PAUL COVENT GARDEN
ST CLEMENT DANES
ST MARY LE STRAND
Savoy
The Temple
Hyde Park
Leicester Sq
ST MARTIN IN THE FIELDS
[Waterloo Bridge]
Blackfriars Bridge
THE
London Bridge
21
22 ST JAMES PICCADILLY
23
24 CHRISTCHURCH
25 ST SAVIOUR
ST OLAVE
ST THOMAS
SOUTHWA
Part of St Margaret Westminster
Green Park
St James's Park
[B]
ST GEORGE
KENSINGTON
Hans Place
ST MARGARET WESTMINSTER
Westminster Bridge
Westminster Abbey
Pimlico Wharf
ST JOHN WESTMINSTER
LAMBETH
Elephant and Castle
31 Sloane Sq
32
33 [C]
New Penitentiary
34
35 NEWINGTON
Chelsea Hospital
CHELSEA
Neat House Gardens
Vauxhall Gardens
Vauxhall Bridge
Kennington Oval
Hamlet of Nine Elms
WALWORTH

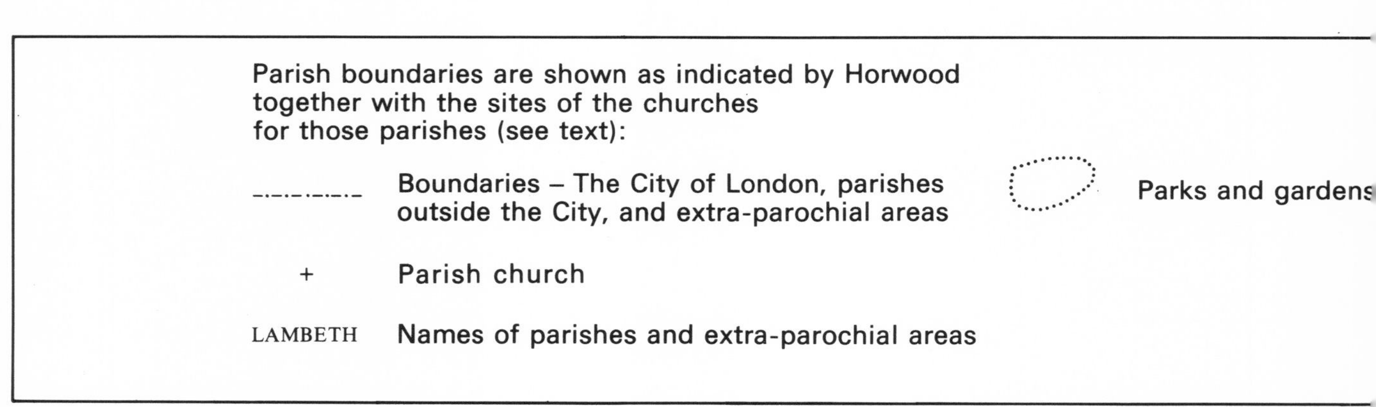

KEY

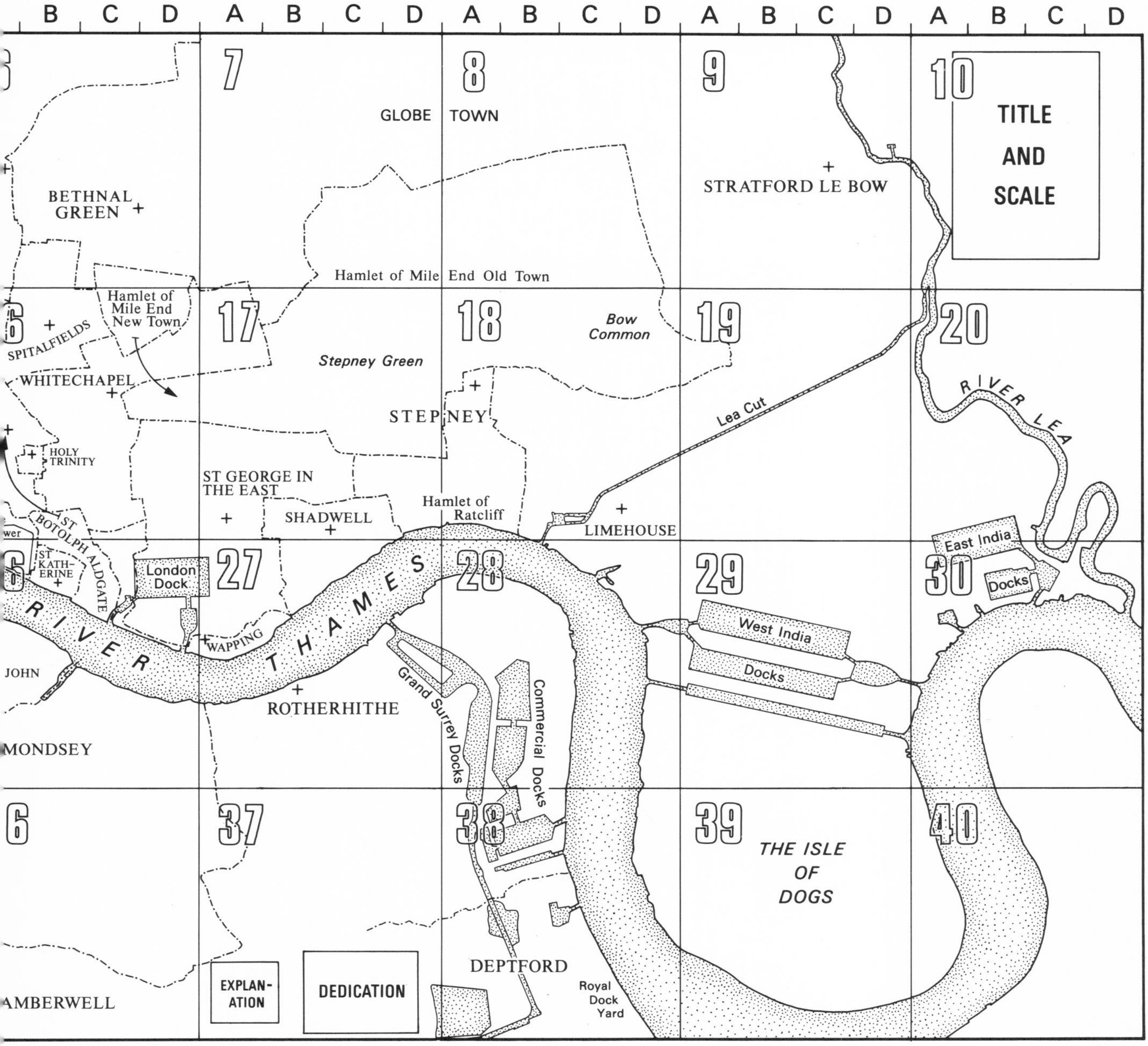

B C D A B C D A B C D A B C D A B C D

7 8 9 10

GLOBE TOWN

TITLE AND SCALE

BETHNAL GREEN

STRATFORD LE BOW

Hamlet of Mile End Old Town

Hamlet of Mile End New Town

17 18 19 20

SPITALFIELDS

Bow Common

Stepney Green

WHITECHAPEL

STEPNEY

Lea Cut

RIVER LEA

HOLY TRINITY

ST GEORGE IN THE EAST

Hamlet of Ratcliff

SHADWELL

LIMEHOUSE

ST BOTOLPH ALDGATE

ST KATHERINE

London Dock

27 28 29 30

East India Docks

RIVER THAMES

WAPPING

West India Docks

JOHN

ROTHERHITHE

Grand Surrey Docks

Commercial Docks

MONDSEY

6 37 38 39 40

THE ISLE OF DOGS

DEPTFORD

Royal Dock Yard

EXPLANATION

DEDICATION

AMBERWELL

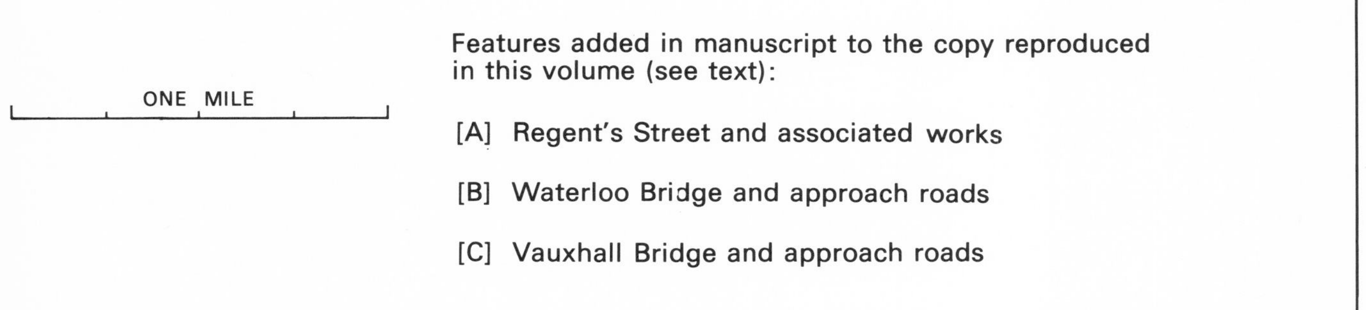

Features added in manuscript to the copy reproduced in this volume (see text):

[A] Regent's Street and associated works

[B] Waterloo Bridge and approach roads

[C] Vauxhall Bridge and approach roads

1
A
B
C
D
a
b
Strathern Place
THE REGENT'S CANAL
Kent Terrace
Teviot Street
Cumberland Terrace
Cumberland Square
Armagh Street
Inverness Street
Sussex Place
ROAD
PRINCE of WALES CIRCUS
Princess Charlotte's Circus
Princess Charlott's Circus

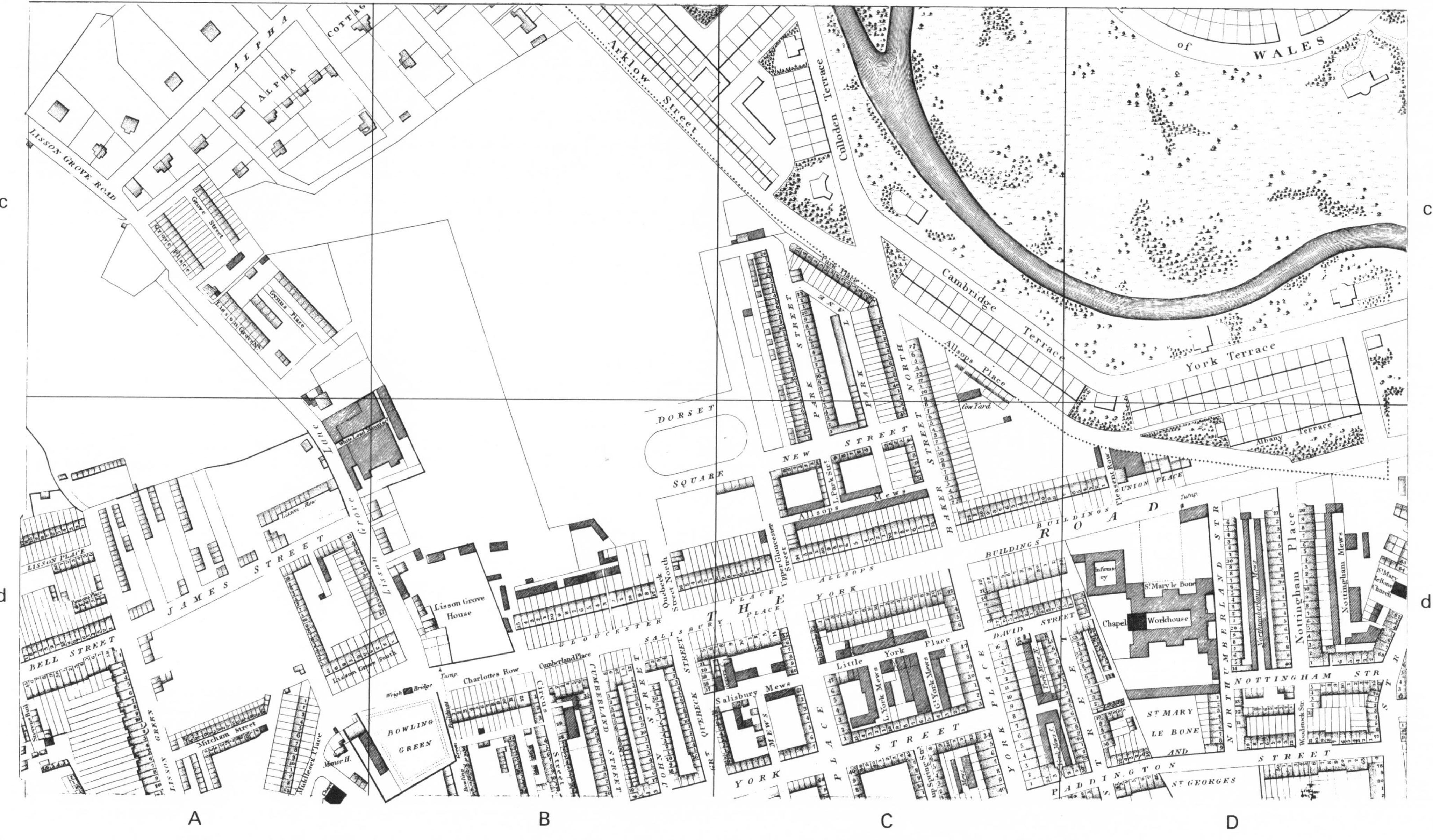
c
d
A
B
C
D
1
of WALES
York Terrace
Albany Terrace
Cambridge Terrace
Culloden Terrace
Arklow Street
Allsops Place
Cow Yard
Nottingham Mews
Nottingham Place
Northumberland Mews
NORTHUMBERLAND STR
NOTTINGHAM STR
Woodstock Str.
St. Mary le Bone Church
St. Mary le Bone Workhouse
Chapel
Infirmary
ST MARY LE BONE AND PADDINGTON
ST GEORGES
UNION PLACE
Pleasant Row
BUILDINGS
THE ROAD
DAVID STREET
YORK PLACE
BAKER STREET
NORTH STREET
PARK STREET
NEW STREET
L. Park Str.
Allsops Mews
ALLSOPS PLACE
YORK PLACE
Little York Place
L. York Mews
Gt. York Mews
Upper Gloucester Street
Salisbury Mews
SALISBURY PLACE
DORSET SQUARE
Quebeck Street North
GT. QUEBECK STREET
JOHN STREET
GLOUCESTER PLACE
CUMBERLAND STREET
Cumberland Place
Circus Street
Charlottes Row
Lisson Grove House
BOWLING GREEN
Manor H.
Middlesex Place
Lisson Grove Lane
Lisson Row
Lisson Grove South
JAMES STREET
Gyms Place
Grove Street
Grove Place
LISSON GROVE ROAD
ALPHA
COTTAG
Mitcham Street
LISSON GREEN
BELL STREET
LISSON PLACE

2

a b

D C B A

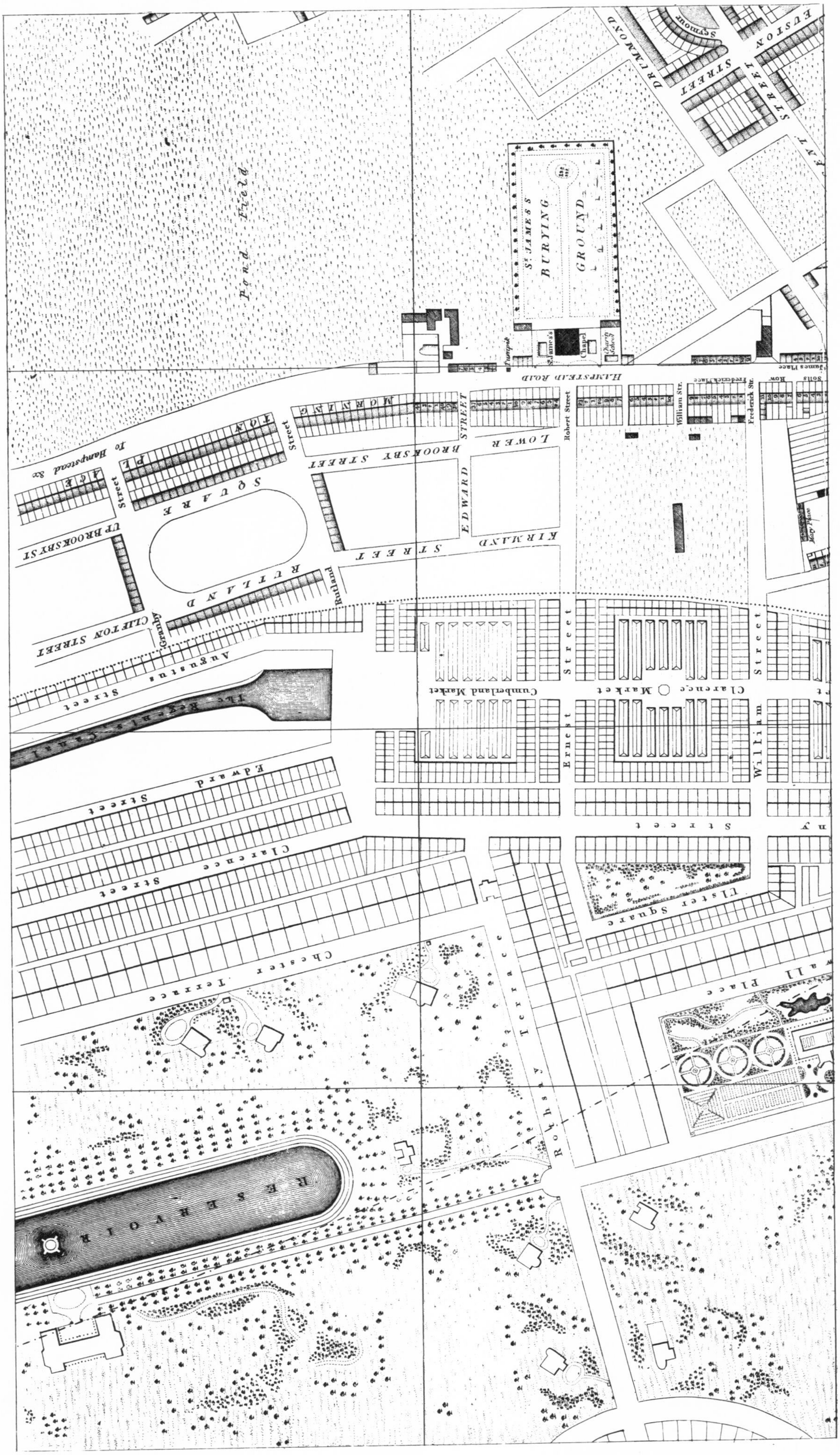
Pond Field
To Hampstead &c
ST JAMES'S BURYING GROUND
St James's Chapel
Charity School
Turnpike
HAMPSTEAD ROAD
DRUMMOND STREET
EUSTON STREET
Seymour
James Place
Solls Row
Frederick Place
Frederick Str.
William Str.
Robert Street
Mary Place
UP BROOKSBY ST
BROOKSBY STREET
LOWER BROOKSBY STREET
EDWARD STREET
KIRMAND STREET
MORNINGTON PL
SQUARE
RUTLAND
Rutland Street
CLIFTON STREET
Granby
Augustus Street
The Regent's Canal
Edward Street
Clarence Street
Cumberland Market
Clarence Market
Ernest Street
William Street
Ulster Square
Chester Terrace
Rothsay Terrace
Place
RESERVOIR

a b

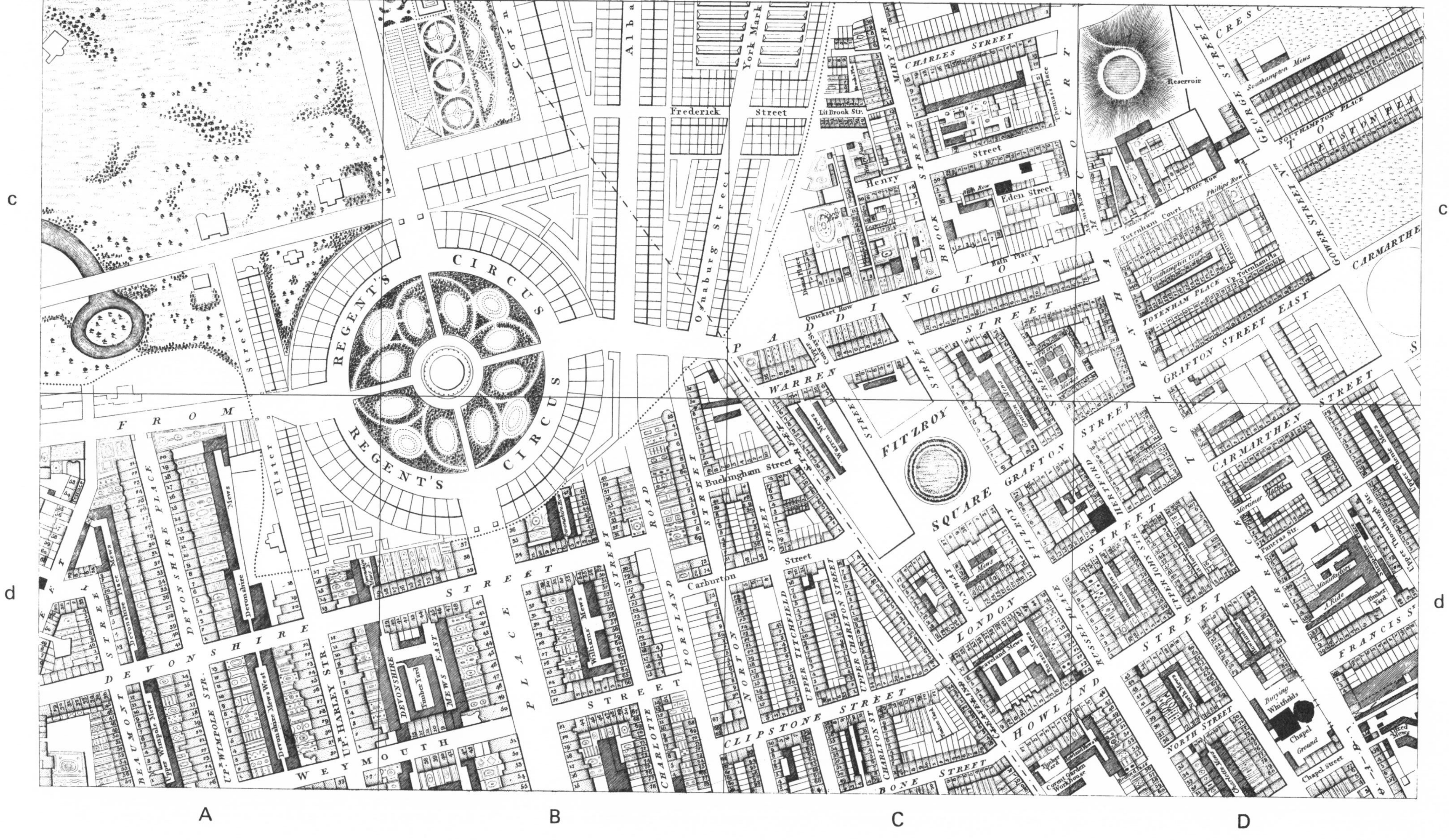
c
d
A
B
C
D
2
REGENT'S CIRCUS
FITZROY SQUARE
PORTLAND ROAD
DEVONSHIRE STREET
DEVONSHIRE PLACE
UPPER CHARLTON STREET
NORTON STREET
CLIPSTONE STREET
LONDON STREET
CONWAY STREET
GRAFTON STREET
HOWLAND STREET
UPPER JOHN'S STR.
Osnaburg Street
Frederick Street
Buckingham Street
Carburton Street
WARREN STREET
Warren Mews
Devonshire Mews West
UP. HARLEY STR.
UP. WIMPOLE STR.
BEAUMONT STREET
WEYMOUTH STREET
CHARLOTTE STREET
Ulster Street
Reservoir
MARY STR.
CHARLES STREET
BROOK STREET
Henry Street
Eden Street
GEORGE STREET
GOWER STREET N.
CARMARTHEN STREET
EAST MEWS
Timber Yard
Williams Mews

3

a b

D C B A

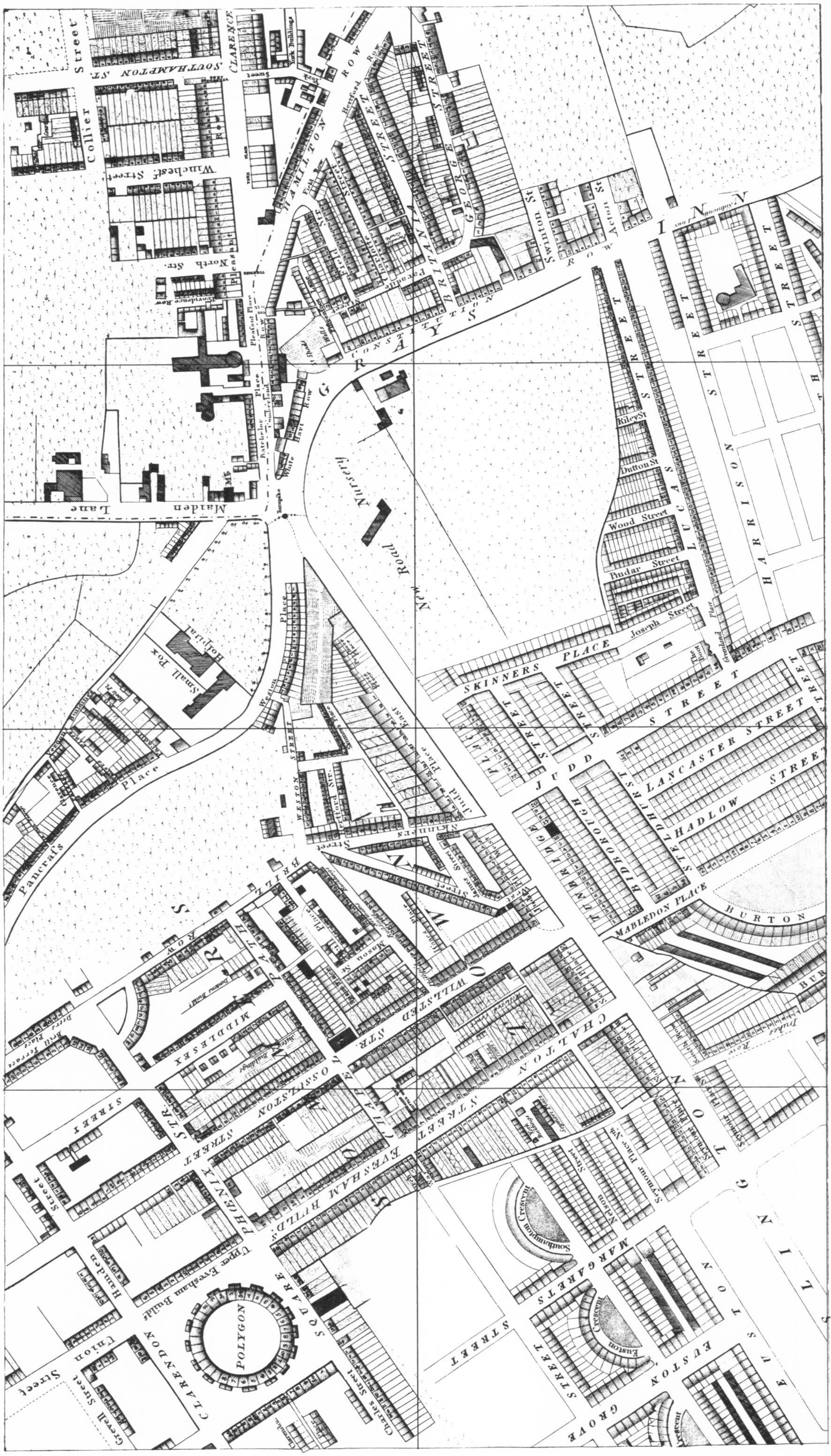
Southampton St.
Clarence
Collier Street
Winchester Street
North Str.
Hamilton Row
Britannia Street
George Street
Constitution Row
Swinton St
Acton St
Gray's Inn
Maiden Lane
Turnpike
Nursery
New Road
Small Pox Hospital
Pancras Place
Weston Place
Weston Street
Skinners Place
Joseph Street
Pindar Street
Wood Street
Dutton St
Riley St
Lucas Street
Harrison Street
Judd Street
Tunbridge Street
Bidborough Street
Lancaster Street
Hadlow Street
Mabledon Place
Burton
Brill Row
Middlesex
Somers Town
Wilsted Str.
Ossulston Street
Chalton Street
Phoenix Street
Evesham Build.
Upper Evesham Builds
Polygon
Clarendon Square
Union Street
Southampton Crescent
Euston Crescent
Margarets Street
Grove Street
Euston Square
Seymour Place
Nelson Street

a b

TAVISTOCK SQUARE
CRESCENT
LEIGH
SIDMOUTH
Tavistock Chapel
COMPTON STREET
HUNTER STREET
The Pavilion
St. George Bloomsbury Burying Ground.
St. George the Martyr Burying Ground.
MECKLENBURGH SQUARE
Welch Charity School
LANE
Garden
Foundling Hospital
Boys Side
Girls Side
TAVISTOCK PLACE
MARCHMONT STREET
KENTON STREET
HENRIETTA STREET
Henrietta Mews
BRUNSWICK SQUARE
Little Coram Street
Tavistock Mews
GREAT CORAM STREET
EVERETT STREET
WILMOT STREET
Brunswick Mews
Woburn Mews
Bernard Mews
Woburn Place
BERNARD STREET
Greville St.
Guilford Mews
Lansdown Place
Caroline Place
Doughty Street
GUILFORD STREET
Guilford Place
Mews
Long Yard
New Millman St.
Millman St.
Upper Gower Mews
Upper Gower Str.
Street
UPR. BEDFORD PLACE
Upper Bedford Mews
THE COLONNADE
UPPER GUILFORD STREET
Saint Pancras Parish
Saint George the Martyr
Lansdown Mews
NEW ORMOND ST.
CHAPEL STR
Francis
GOWER STREET
THORNHAUGH STREET
CHENIES STREET
RUSSELL SQUARE
ROW
SOUTHAMPTON
QUEEN SQUARE
St. George the Martyr
GREAT ORMOND STREET
ORMOND MEWS
LAMB'S CONDUIT STREET
GREAT JAMES STREET
Robert
KEPPEL STREET
Lt. Keppel Street
PLACE
BED
EAST STREET

c c
d d

A B C D

3

A
B
C
D
a
b

Collier Street
CUMMING STR.
Pentonville Chapel
RODNEY STR.
HENRY STR.
Ann Str.
Hermes Street
PENTON ST.
WHITE STR.
Dobneys Place
WINCHESTER PLACE
BARRON STR.
LION STREET
HIGH - STR.
PENTONVILLE
KINGS ROW
QUEENS ROW
PENTON PLACE
Weston Street
Upper Pond
Cow Yard
CITY ROAD
Duncan Place
York Place
Owens Row
Owens Place
Alfred Place
Sidney Street
Quakers Workhouse
Nelson Terrace
Howards Green
SADLERS WELLS FIELD
New River Company
HANGING FIELD
New River Company
SADLERS WELLS
NEW RIVER HEAD
New Reservoir
SPA TEA GARDENS
RAWSTORNE STREET
WYNYATT STREET
Goswell Terrace
CHARLES STREET
SPENCER STREET
SMITH STREET
NORTHAMPTON
UP. ASHBY STREET
NORTHAMPTON SQUARE
Spencers Row
St. Bartholomew and Bedlam Hospitals Lands
St. Bartholomew's Hospital Land
ISLINGTON
Turnpike
Ditch
Mill Yard
Merlins Place
WATERHOUSE FIELD
New River Company
NORTHAMPTON FIELD
RIVER FLEET
Bagnigge Place
London Light Horse Target Ground
Tile Kiln Company
Tile
Kilns
Brook

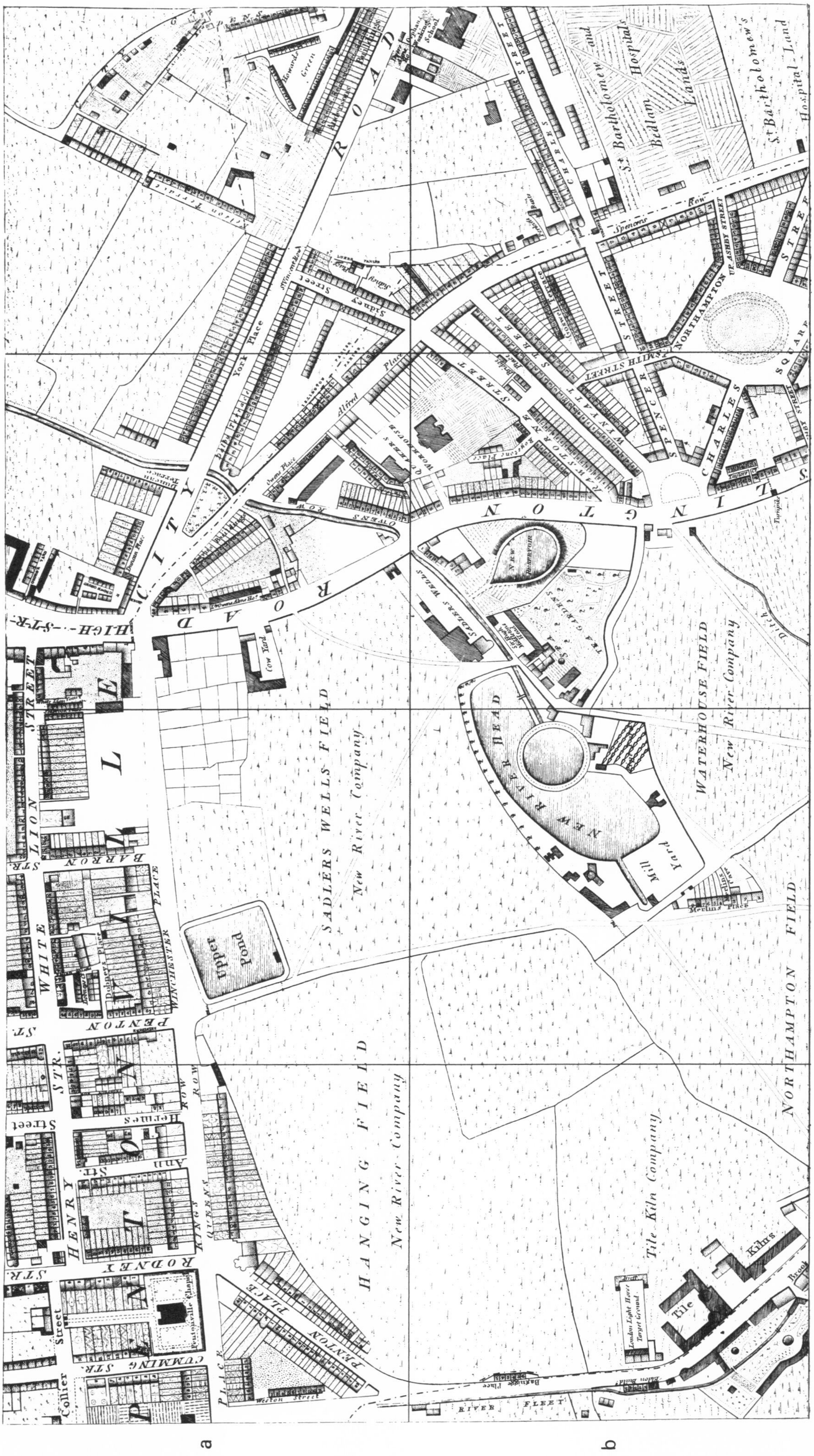

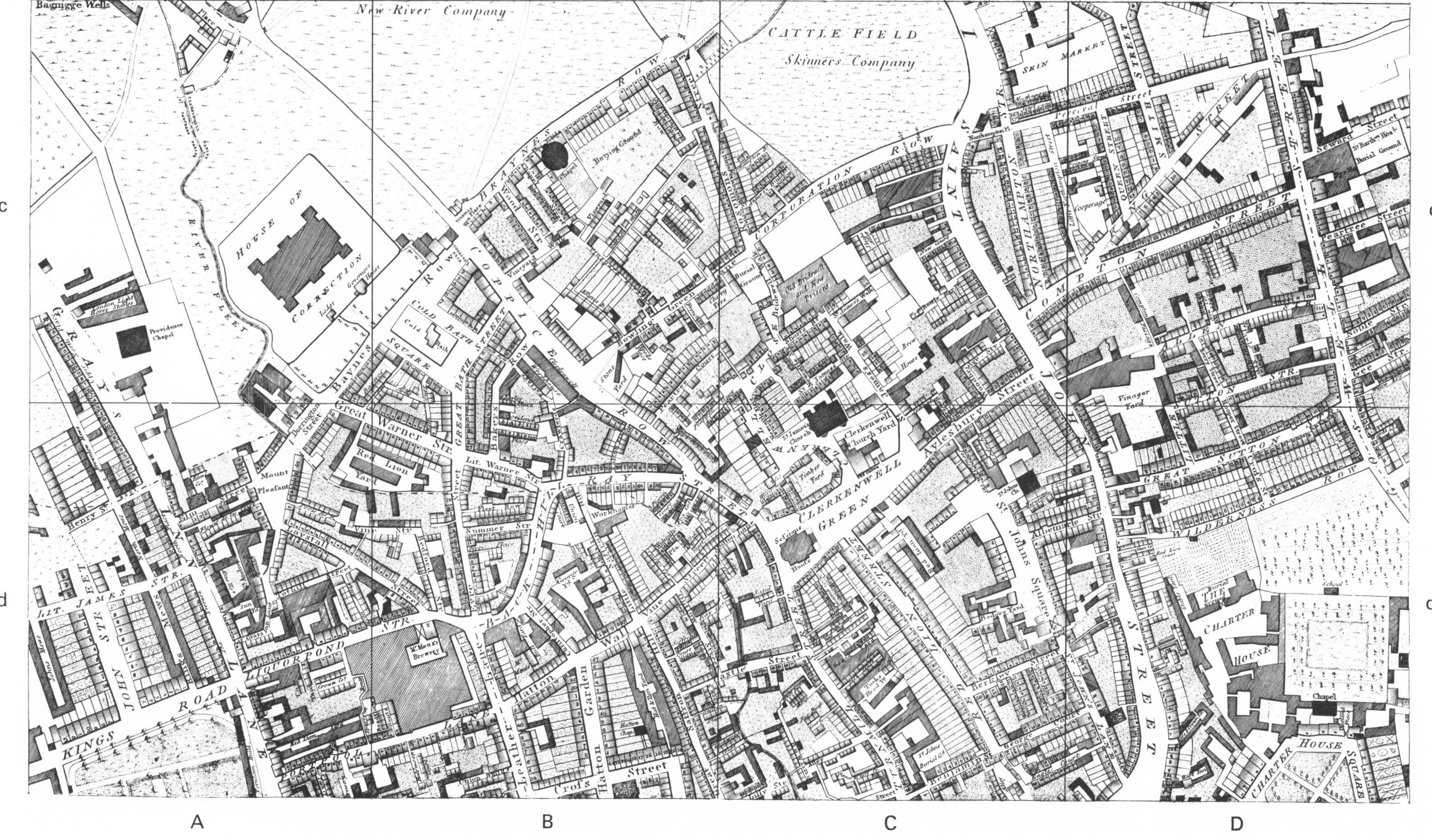

Bagnigge Wells
New River Company
CATTLE FIELD
Skinners Company
SKIN MARKET
HOUSE OF CORRECTION
RIVER FLEET
Providence Chapel
COLD BATH SQUARE
Burying Ground
CORPORATION ROW
COPPICE ROW
BRAYNES ROW
NORTHAMPTON
COMPTON STREET
SAINT JOHN STREET
Clerkenwell Church Yard
CLERKENWELL GREEN
Aylesbury Street
St. Johns Square
GREAT SUTTON
WILDERNESS ROW
THE CHARTER HOUSE
Chapel
CHARTER HOUSE SQUARE
Great Warner Str.
Lit. Warner Str.
Red Lion Yard
Mount Pleasant
Baynes
LIQUORPOND STR.
Mr. Meux's Brewery
KINGS ROAD
JOHN STR
LIT. JAMES STREET
GRAYS
Hatton Garden
Leather Lane
Crofs Street
Seward Street
Peartree Street
Vinagar Yard
Sessions House
A
B
C
D
c
d

4

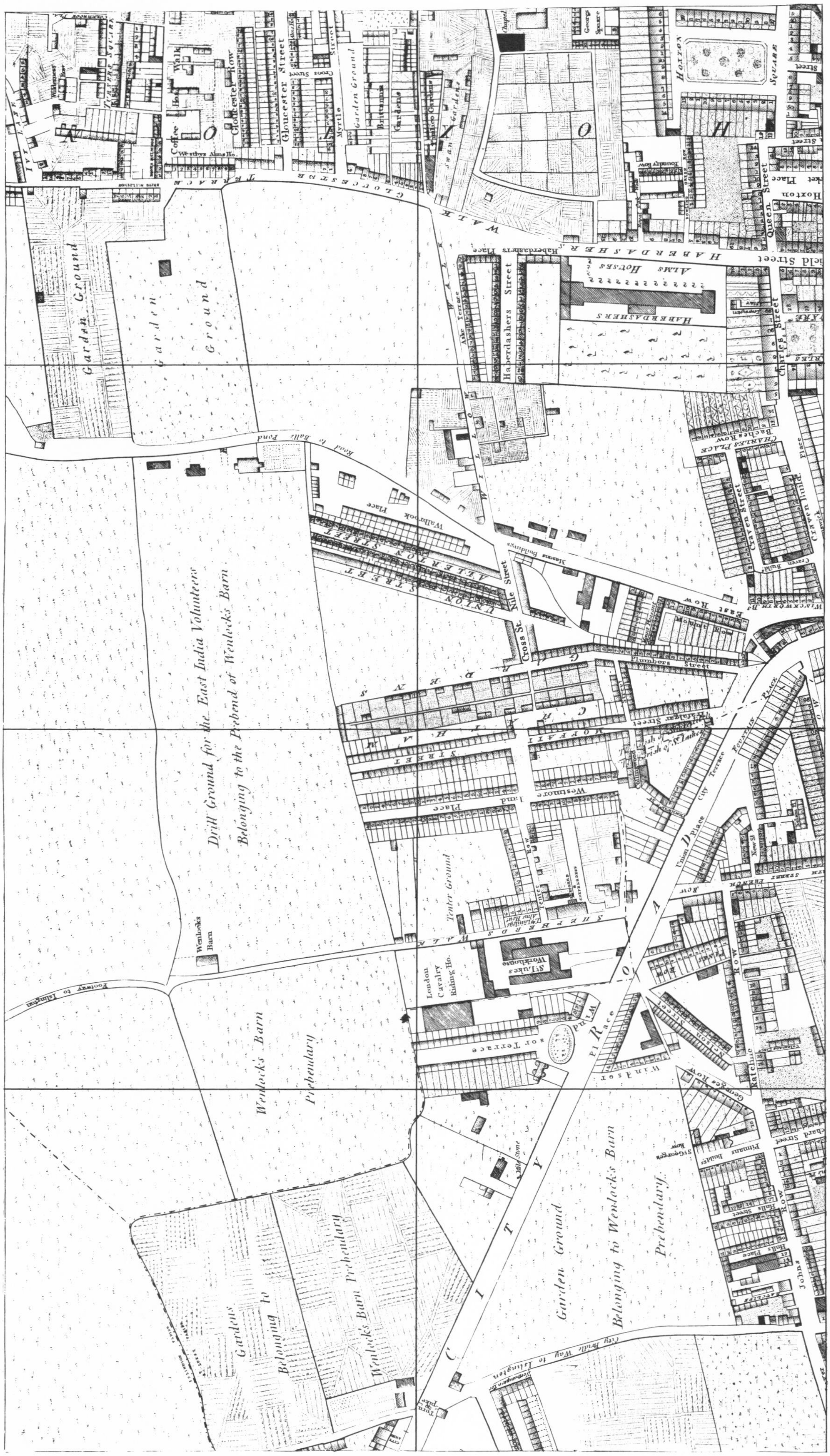

5

A B C D

a b

Garden Ground

Garden Ground

Drill Ground for the East India Volunteers Belonging to the Prebend of Wenlock's Barn

Wenlocks Barn

Wenlock's Barn Prebendary

Gardens Belonging to Wenlock's Barn Prebendary

Garden Ground Belonging to Wenlock's Barn Prebendary

Footway to Islington

City Bridle Way to Islington

Turn pike

Mile Stone

CITY ROAD

Race

Windsor Terrace

London Cavalry Riding Ho.

St. Lukes Workhouse

Tenter Ground

Tenter Row

Shepherds Walk

Westmoreland Place

Moffatt Street

Charles Street

Cross St.

Nile Street

Union Street

Allerton Street

Walbrook Place

Road to Balls Pond

Willow Walk

Aske Terrace

Haberdashers Street

Haberdashers Place

Haberdashers Alms Houses

Gloucester Terrace

Gloucester Row

Gloucester Street

Cross Street

Myrtle Street

Coffee Ho. Walk

Britannia Gardens

Swan Gardens

Chapel

George Square

Hoxton Square

HOXTON

Ivy Lane

Wilderness Row

Turners Square

Queen Street

Hoxton Place

East Row

Craven Street

Craven Build.

Charles Place

Baches Row

Union Place

City Terrace

Fountain Place

New St.

Ratcliffe Row

Nelson Street

Georges Row

St. Georges Row

Pitmans Builds.

Hills Street

Hills Place

Johns Row

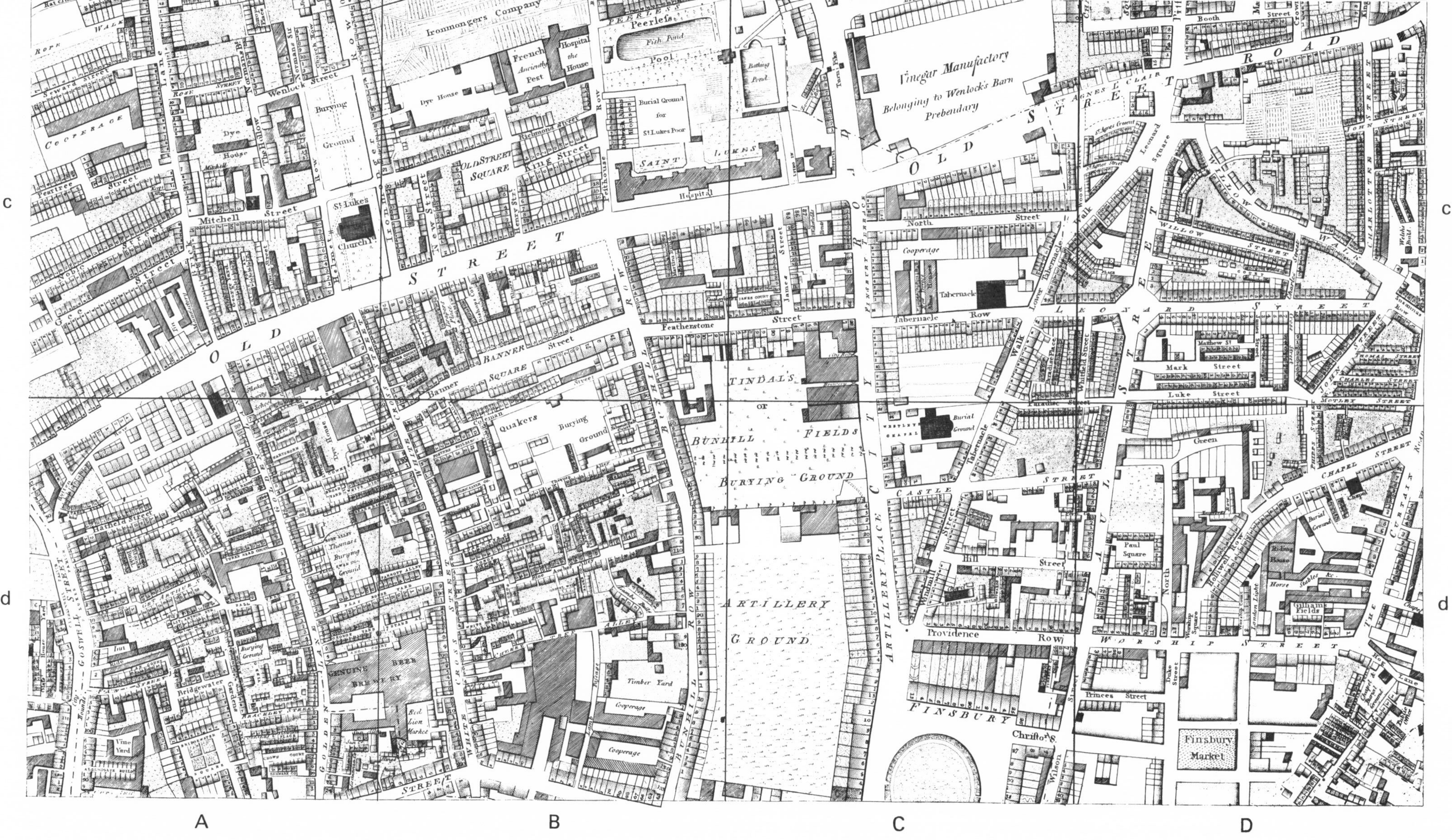
c
d
A
B
C
D
5
Vinegar Manufactory Belonging to Wenlock's Barn Prebendary
OLD STREET
ROAD
Ironmongers Company
French Hospital
Peerless Pool
Fish Pond
Bathing Pond
Burial Ground for St. Lukes Poor
SAINT LUKES Hospital
St. Lukes Church
Burying Ground
OLD STREET SQUARE
King Street
Richmond Street
BANNER SQUARE
Banner Street
Featherstone Street
TINDAL'S or BUNHILL FIELDS BURYING GROUND
Quakers Burying Ground
ARTILLERY GROUND
ARTILLERY PLACE
BUNHILL ROW
Tabernacle Row
Tabernacle
Cooperage
Timber Yard
Providence Row
FINSBURY
Princes Street
Finsbury Market
WORSHIP STREET
Paul Square
LEONARD STREET
Mark Street
Luke Street
Green
GOLDEN LANE
WHITE CROSS STREET
GENUINE BEER BREWERY
Red Lion Market
Vine Yard
Bridgewater Gardens
GOSWELL STREET
Mitchell Street
Dye House
Wenlock Street
CHARLOTTE STREET
WILLOW WALK
CHAPEL STREET

6

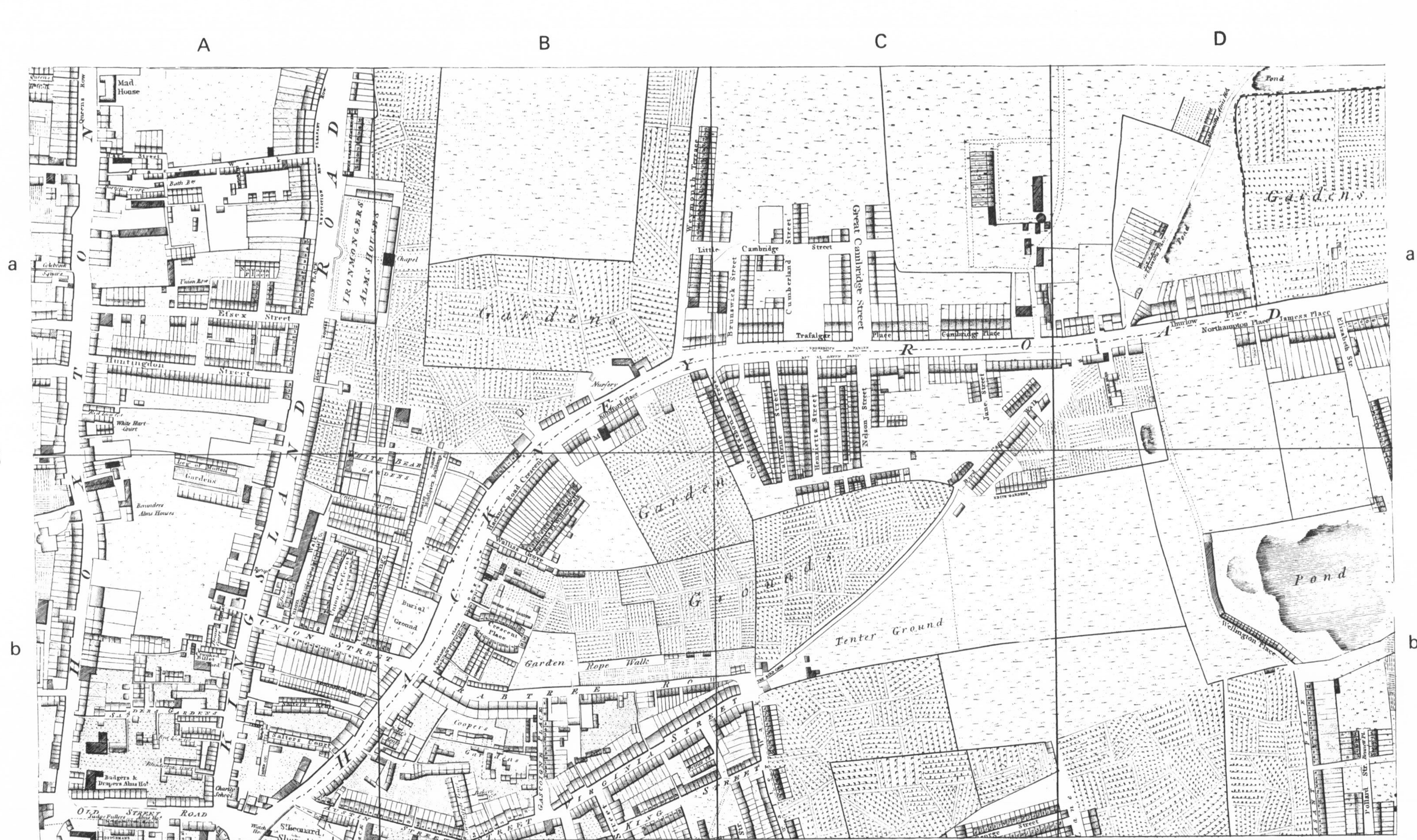

A
B
C
D
a
b
Mad House
Bath Pl
Union Row
Essex Street
Huntingdon Street
White Hart Court
Gardens
Boundary Alms Houses
Ironmongers Alms Houses
Chapel
Nursery
Little Cambridge Street
Brunswick Street
Cumberland Street
Great Cambridge Street
Trafalgar Place
Cambridge Place
Northampton Place
James Place
Elizabeth Str
Nelson Street
Henrietta Street
Jane Street
Pond
Gardens
Garden Grounds
Tenter Ground
Garden Rope Walk
Burial Ground
Union Street
Crabtree Row
Coopers Gardens
Virginia Street
Salters Court
Badgers & Drapers Alms Ho.
Charity School
Old Street Road
St. Leonard
Wellington Place
Pollard Str

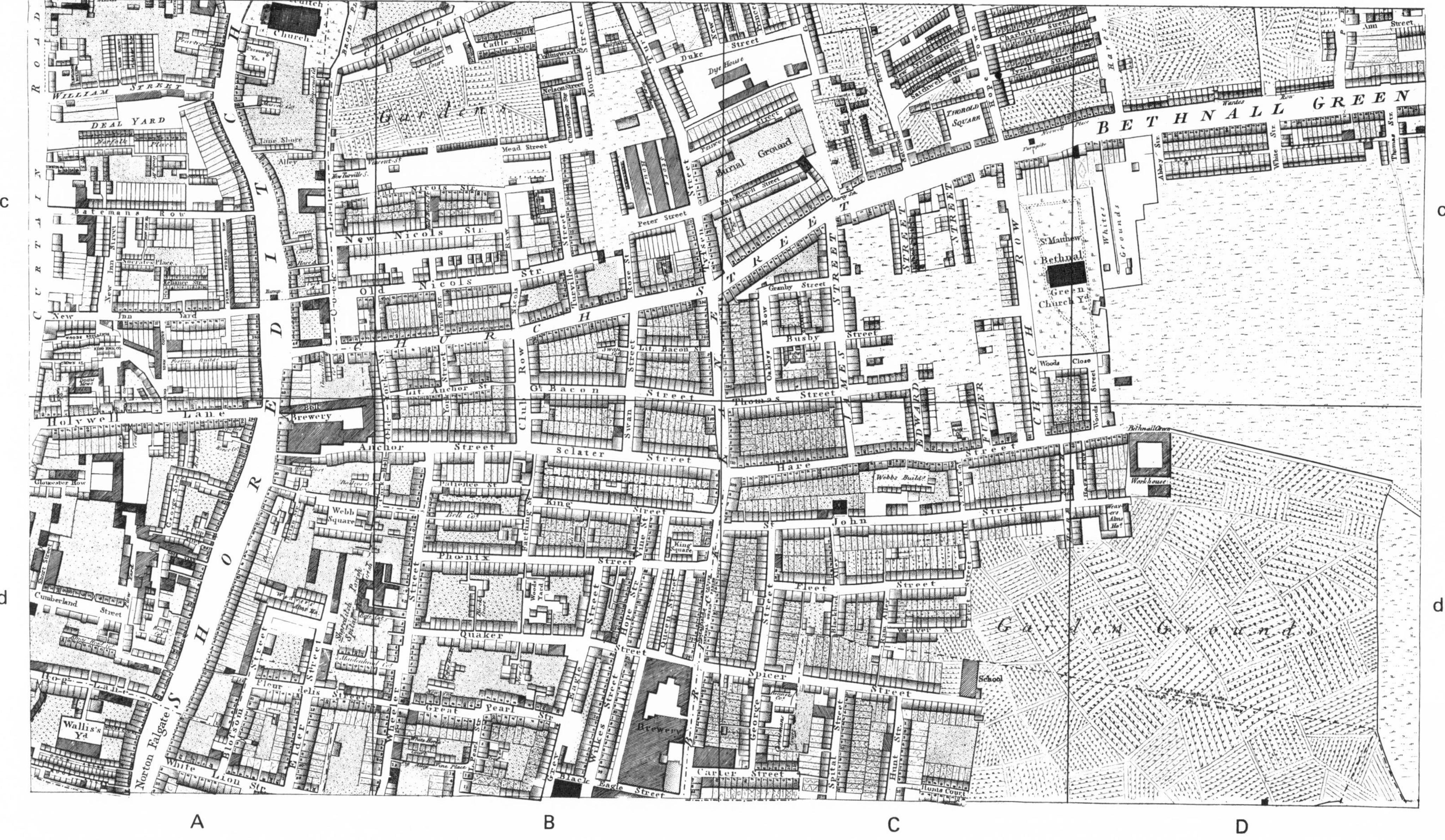

c
d
A
B
C
D
6
BETHNALL GREEN
SHOREDITCH
CHURCH STREET
CHURCH ROW
St. Matthew Bethnal Green Church Yd.
Whites Grounds
Hares
Abbey Str.
White Str.
Thomas Str.
Ann Street
Charlotte Street
Thorold Square
Hope Town
Burial Ground
Dye House
Duke Street
Peter Street
Mead Street
Mount Street
Nelson Street
Christopher Str.
Castle St.
Gardens
Church
Parsonage Yd.
Alley
WILLIAM STREET
DEAL YARD
Batemans Row
New Inn Street
New Inn Yard
Holywell Lane
CURTAIN ROAD
Old Nicols Str.
New Nicols Str.
Nicols Row
Turville Str.
Rose St.
Granby Street
Oakleys Row
Busby Street
JAMES STREET
EDWARD STREET
FULLER STREET
Woods Close
Woods Street
Thomas Street
Gt. Bacon Street
Lit. Bacon St.
Club Row
Swan Street
Lit. Anchor St.
Anchor Street
Sclater Street
Hare Street
Webbs Build.
Brewery
Workhouse
King Street
John Street
Phoenix Street
Quaker Street
Fleet Street
Spicer Street
Weaver St.
Garden Grounds
School
George Street
Carter Street
Spital Street
Hunt Str.
Hunts Court
Brewery
Eagle Street
Wilkes Street
Great Pearl Str.
Fleur de lis Street
Elder Street
Blosom Street
White Lion Str.
Norton Falgate
Wallis's Yd.
Cumberland Street
Short Street
Glocester Row
Webb Square
King Square
Bell Ct.
Patience St.
Hope Str.
Queen Street

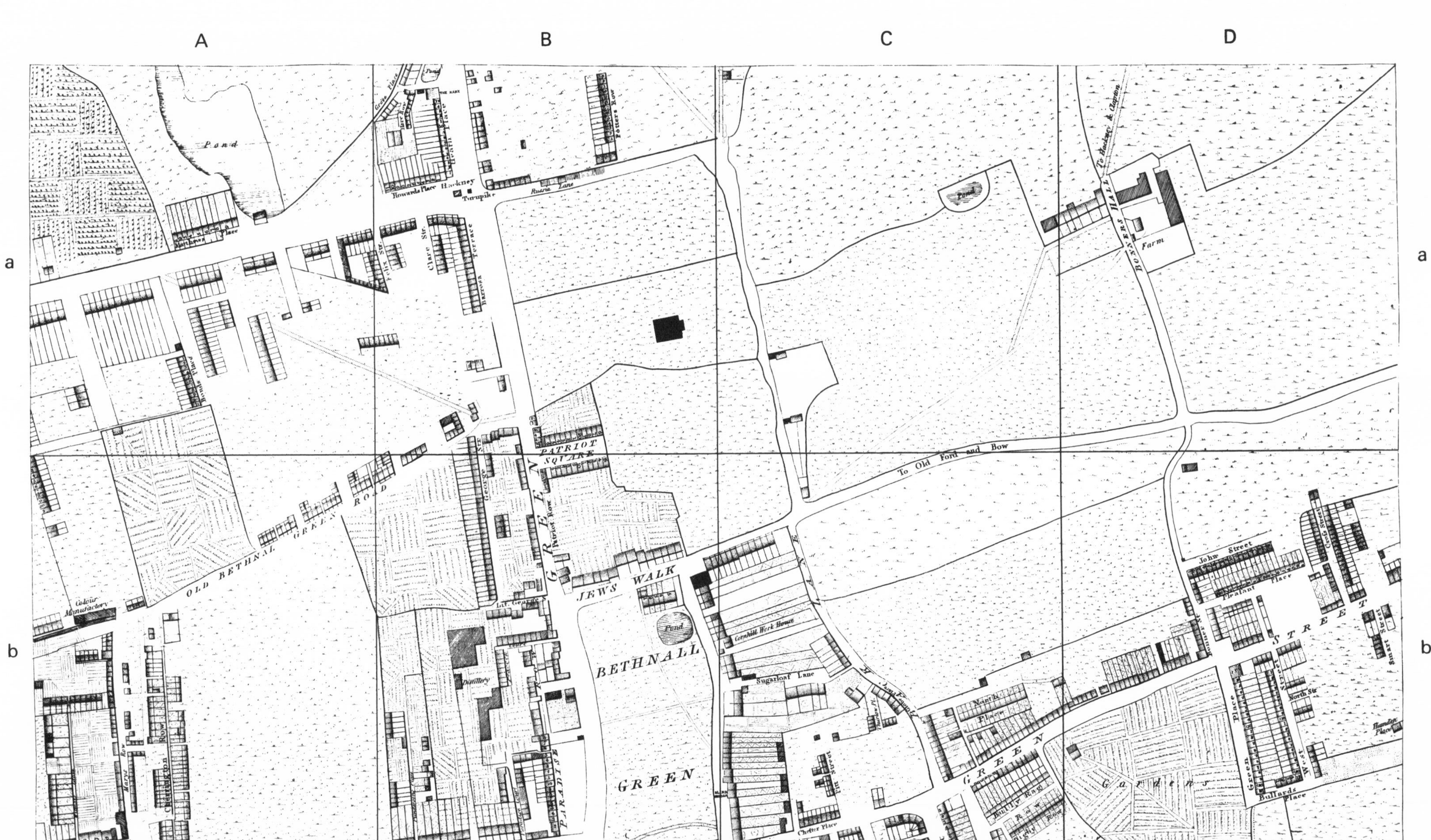
7
A
B
C
D
a
b
Pond
Potters Row
Howards Place
Hackney
Turnpike
Barossa Terrace
Clare St.
Felix Str.
Bonds Place
Bonners Hall
To Hackney & Clapton
Farm
Pond
To Old Ford and Bow
Patriot Square
Patriot Row
George Str.
Jews Walk
Bethnall
Green
Pond
Distillery
Paradise
Old Bethnal Green Road
Colour Manufactory
Marys Row
Cherrington Row
Cornhill Work House
Sugarloaf Lane
Chester Place
North Place
John Street
Pleasant Place
Green Street
Smart Street
North St.
Green Place
West Street
Bullards Place
Gardens
Bullys Row

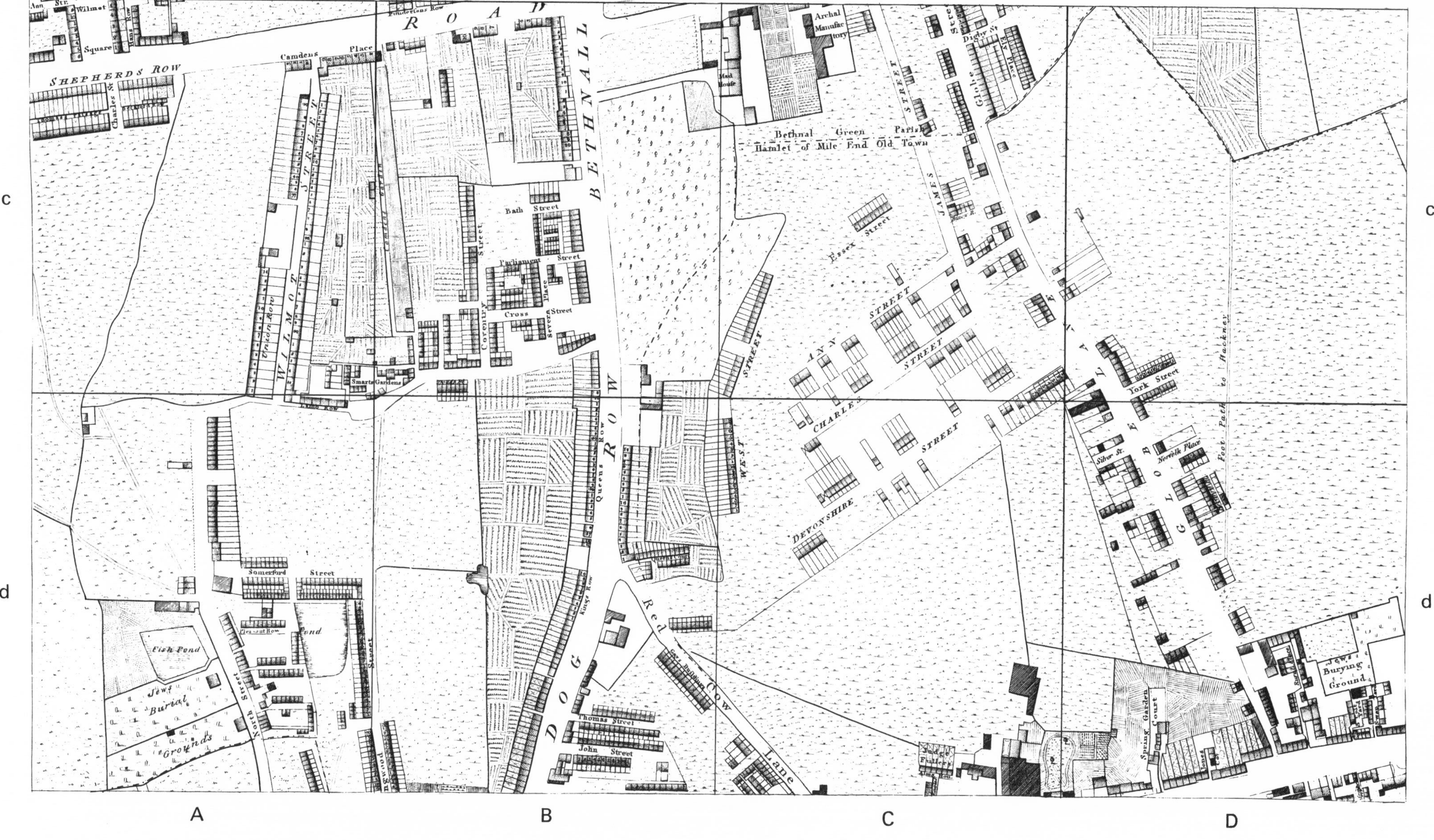
Ann Str.
Wilmot
Square
SHEPHERDS ROW
Charles St.
Camdens Place
ROAD
BETHNALL
WILMOT STREET
Union Row
Bath Street
Parliament Street
Cross Street
Severn Street
Place
Coventry Street
Smarts Gardens
Mad House
Archd Manufactory
Bethnal Green Parish
Hamlet of Mile End Old Town
JAMES STREET
Globe
Digby St.
Ely Place
Essex Street
ANN STREET
CHARLES STREET
DEVONSHIRE STREET
WEST STREET
GLOBE LANE
York Street
Silver St.
Norfolk Place
Foot Path to Hackney
Queens Row
ROW
Kings Row
DOG
Red Cow Lane
Thomas Street
John Street
Somerford Street
Pond
Fish Pond
Pleasant Row
North Street
Jews Burial Grounds
Spring Garden Court
Jews Burying Ground
A
B
C
D
c
d
7

8
A
B
C
D
a
b
TO OLD FORD
King's Arms Row
To Hackney and Clapton
From Bethnal Green to Old Ford Bow &c
G R O V E
To Old Ford & Bow
Norton Street
Twig Folly
East Street

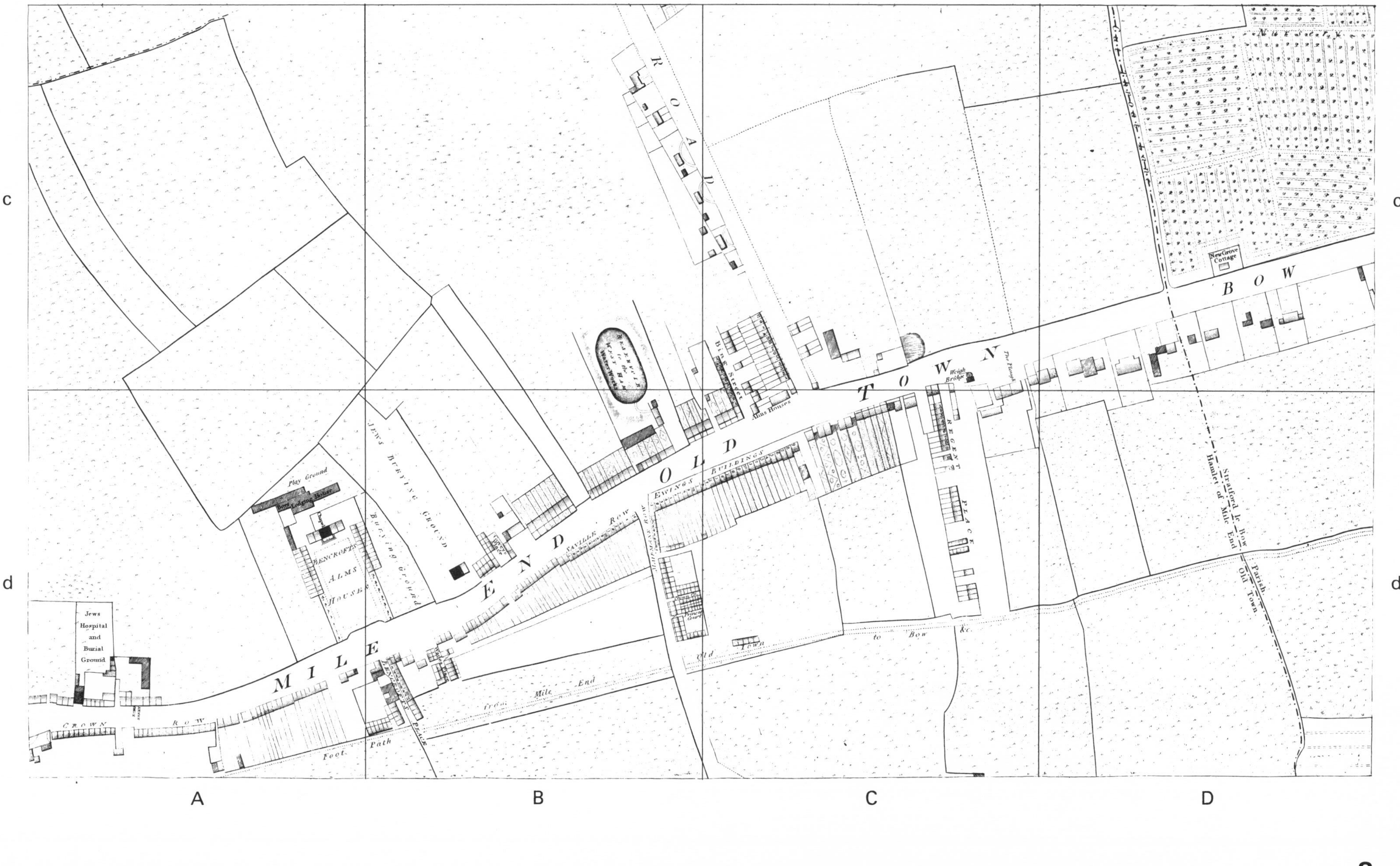
c
d
A
B
C
D
8
MILE END OLD TOWN
BOW
ROAD
New Grove Cottage
Stratford le Bow Parish
Hamlet of Mile End Old Town
The Plough
Weigh Bridge
REGENT PLACE
Bing Street
Alms Houses
EWINGS BUILDINGS
SAVILLE ROW
Reservoir to the West Ham Water Works
JEWS BURYING GROUND
Burying Ground
Play Ground
Chapel
BENCROFTS ALMS HOUSES
Old Town to Bow &c.
from Mile End
Foot Path
CROWN ROW
Jews Hospital and Burial Ground

9

A
B
C
D
a
b
Reservoir
Clay Hall Gardens
Pond
Pond
East London Water Works
Towing Path
Barebinder Lane
Hermitage
Five Bells Bridge
Windmill
Dock
Bow Bridge
GARDEN
FAIR
Union Row
Charles Street

Farm Yard
B
O
Church
Alms Houses
DRAPERS
ALMS HOUSES
Brew House
Halley Place
Bakers Alley
Stewards Buildings
ORCHARD
ORCHARD
GARDEN
NURSERY
NURSERY
Foot Path to Bow and Bromley
2 M. 1 Stone
Pound
New Prospect Place
Dull Shed Building
Dyers Row
St. Leonards Church Bromley
Dye House
c
c
d
d
A
B
C
D
9

A B C D

a a

A Plan of the CITIES of
LONDON & WESTMINSTER,
with the
Borough of Southwark
including their adjacent
SUBURBS,
In which every Dwelling House is described & numbered;
Surveyed and first published by

b b

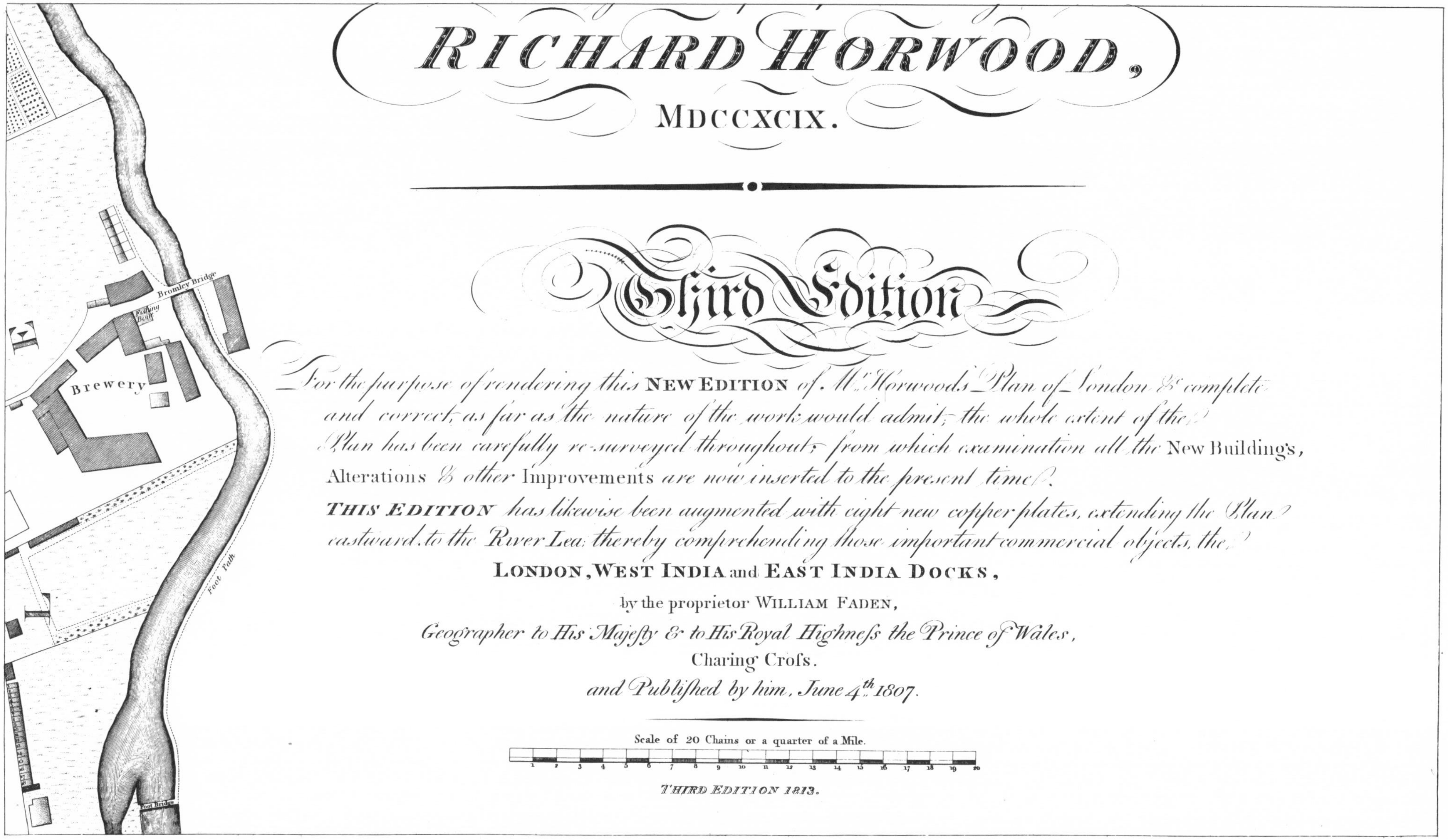

RICHARD HORWOOD,

MDCCXCIX.

Third Edition

For the purpose of rendering this **NEW EDITION** of Mr. Horwood's Plan of London &c. complete and correct, as far as the nature of the work would admit; the whole extent of the Plan has been carefully re-surveyed throughout; from which examination all the New Buildings, Alterations & other Improvements are now inserted to the present time.

THIS EDITION has likewise been augmented with eight new copper plates, extending the Plan eastward, to the River Lea: thereby comprehending those important commercial objects, the

LONDON, WEST INDIA and EAST INDIA DOCKS,

by the proprietor WILLIAM FADEN,

Geographer to His Majesty & to His Royal Highness the Prince of Wales,

Charing Cross.

and Published by him, June 4th 1807.

Scale of 20 Chains or a quarter of a Mile.

1 2 3 4 5 6 7 8 9 10 11 12 13 14 15 16 17 18 19 20

THIRD EDITION 1813.

Bromley Bridge

Fishing Boat

Brewery

Foot Path

Foot Bridge

c c d d

A B C D

11

A B C D

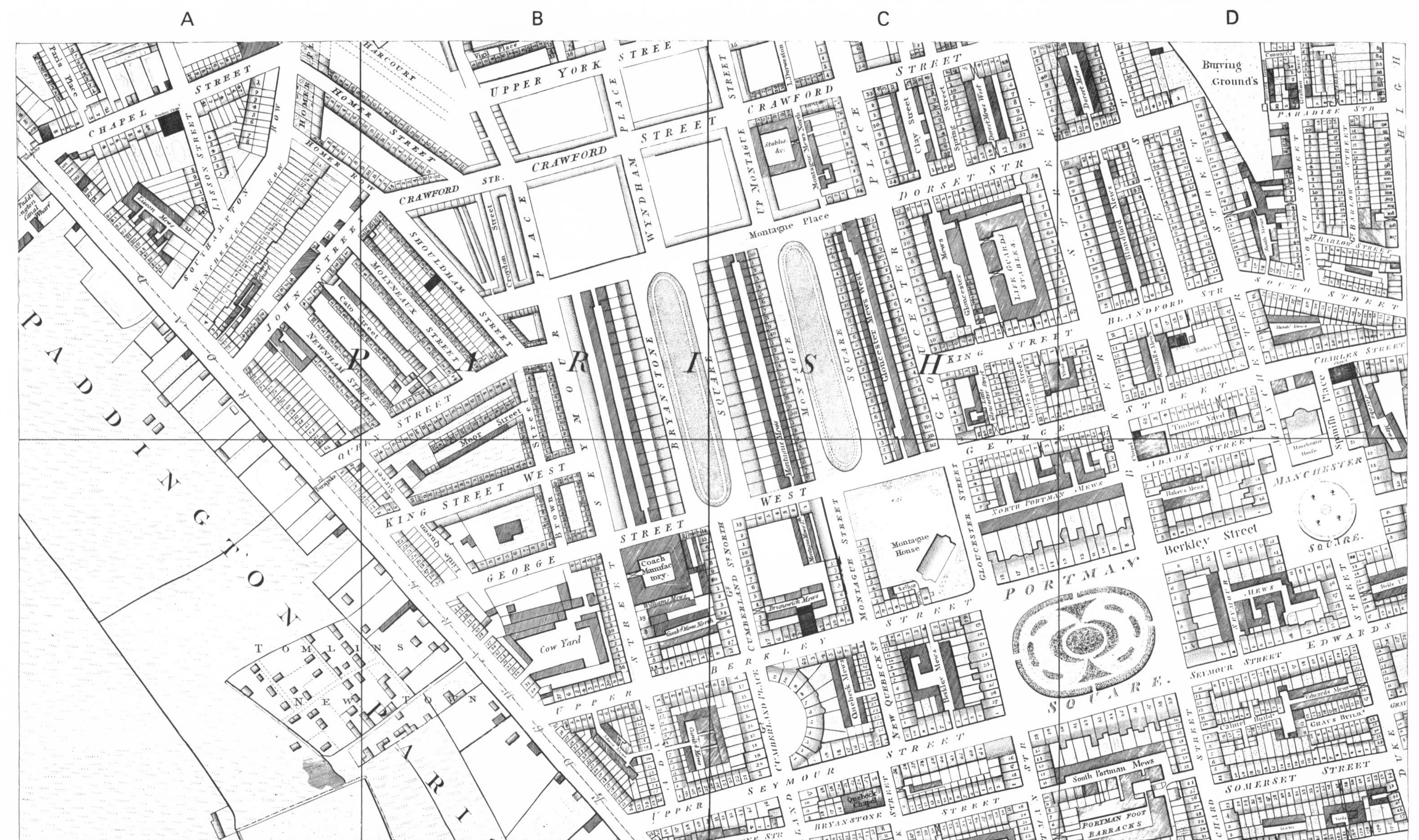

PADDINGTON
PARISH
PORTMAN SQUARE
MONTAGUE SQUARE
BRYANSTONE SQUARE
MANCHESTER SQUARE
Berkley Street
Burying Ground's
Montague House
Manchester House
LIFE GUARDS STABLES
PORTMAN FOOT BARRACKS
Quebeck Chapel
Cow Yard
Coach Manufactory
TOMLINS NEW TOWN
Paddington Canal Wharf
UPPER YORK STREET
CRAWFORD STREET
WYNDHAM PLACE
UP MONTAGUE PLACE
Montague Place
DORSET STREET
GLOUCESTER PLACE
BLANDFORD STREET
KING STREET
GEORGE STREET
WEST STREET
KING STREET WEST
SEYMOUR PLACE
SEYMOUR STREET
UPPER SEYMOUR STREET
NEW QUEBECK STREET
CUMBERLAND PLACE
UPPER BERKLEY STREET
ADAMS STREET
EDWARDS STREET
SOMERSET STREET
DUKE STREET
SOUTH STREET
NORTH STREET
PARADISE STR
BARLOW STREET
CHARLES STREET
SHOULDHAM STREET
MOLYNEAUX STREET
NEWNHAM STREET
JOHN STREET
HOMER STREET
HOMER ROW
HARCOURT
CHAPEL STREET
LISSON STREET
SOUTHAMPTON ROW
WINCHESTER ROW
Paris Place
Clay Street
Spring Street
Croydon Street
Cato Street
Brown Street
Moor Street
Queen Street
Blandford Mews
Dorset Mews
Dorset Mews West
Gloucester Mews
Gloucester Mews West
Montague Mews
Montague Mews North
Brunswick Mews
Berkley Mews
Quebeck Mews
South Portman Mews
North Portman Mews
Bakers Mews
Lisson Mews
Timber Yard
Spanish Place
Stables &c.

a b

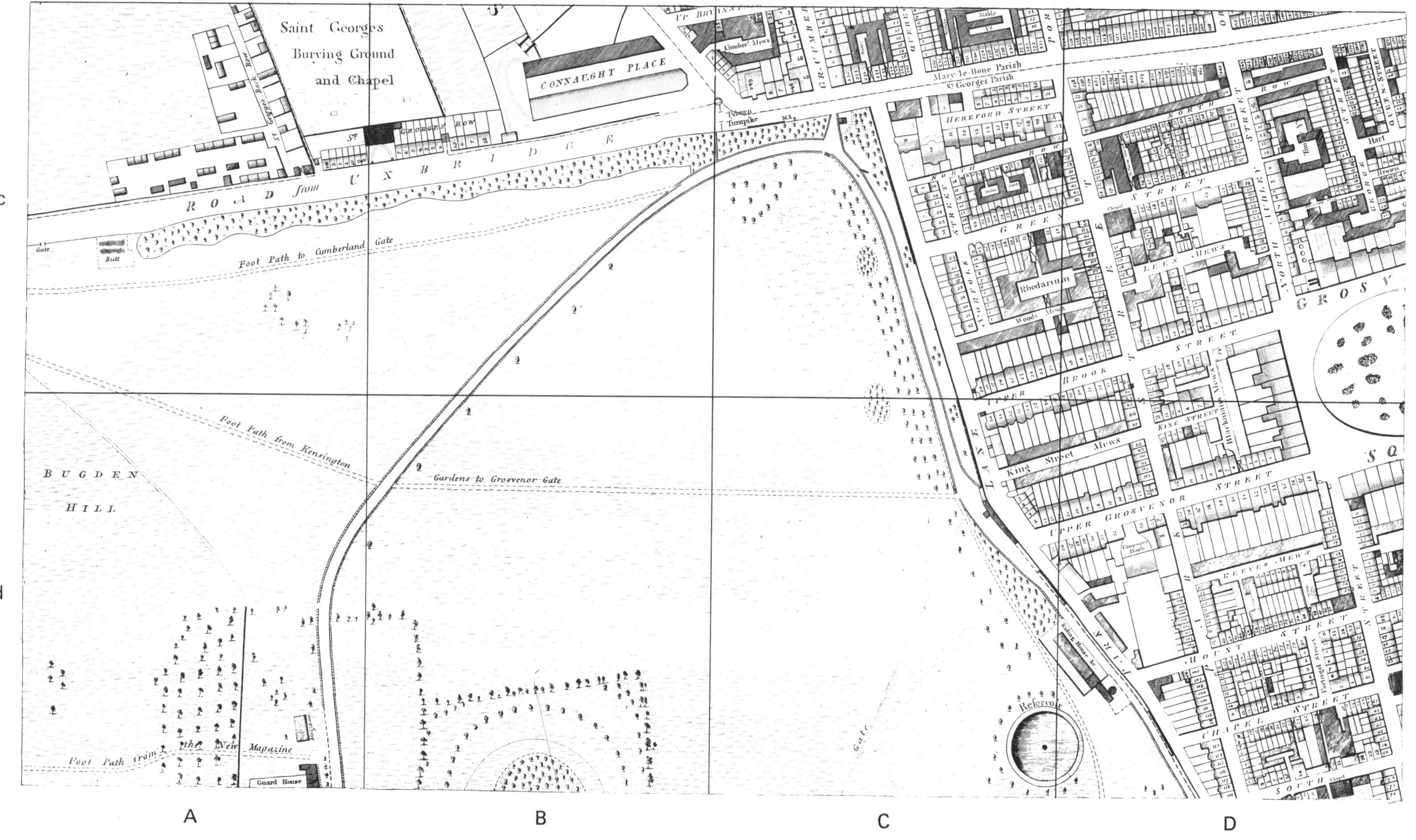
c
d
A
B
C
D
11
Saint Georges
Burying Ground
and Chapel
CONNAUGHT PLACE
St. Georges Back Row
St. GEORGES ROW
ROAD from UXBRIDGE
Foot Path to Cumberland Gate
Foot Path from Kensington
Gardens to Grosvenor Gate
BUGDEN HILL
Foot Path from the New Magazine
Guard House
Tyburn Turnpike
Mary-le-Bone Parish
St. Georges Parish
HEREFORD STREET
NORFOLK STREET
Rhedarium
Woods Mews
UPPER BROOK STREET
King Street Mews
UPPER GROSVENOR STREET
NORTH AUDLEY STREET
LEES MEWS
REEVES MEWS
MOUNT STREET
CHAPEL STREET
PARK LANE
Reservoir
Riding House
GROSV
SQ

12

A
B
C
D
a
a
b
b
WEYMOUTH
Chesterfield Street
GREAT MARY LE BONE STREET
NEW CAVENDISH STREET
PORTLAND PLACE
UPPER MARY LE BONE STREET
QUEEN ANN STREET EAST
TOTTENHAM STREET
CHARLOTTE STREET
GOODGE STREET
Middlesex Hospital
Little Titchfield Street
Repository
MORTIMER STREET
CAVENDISH SQUARE
OXFORD MARKET
WIGMORE STREET
HENRIETTA STREET
HOLLES STREET
CHANDOS STREET
Queen Anns Mews
Mill Hill Mews
Phoenix Yard
St. Mary le bone Parish
St. James's Parish
Timber Yard
THAYRE STREET
BENTINCK STR
STRATFORD PLACE
PRINCES STR
Harewood Place

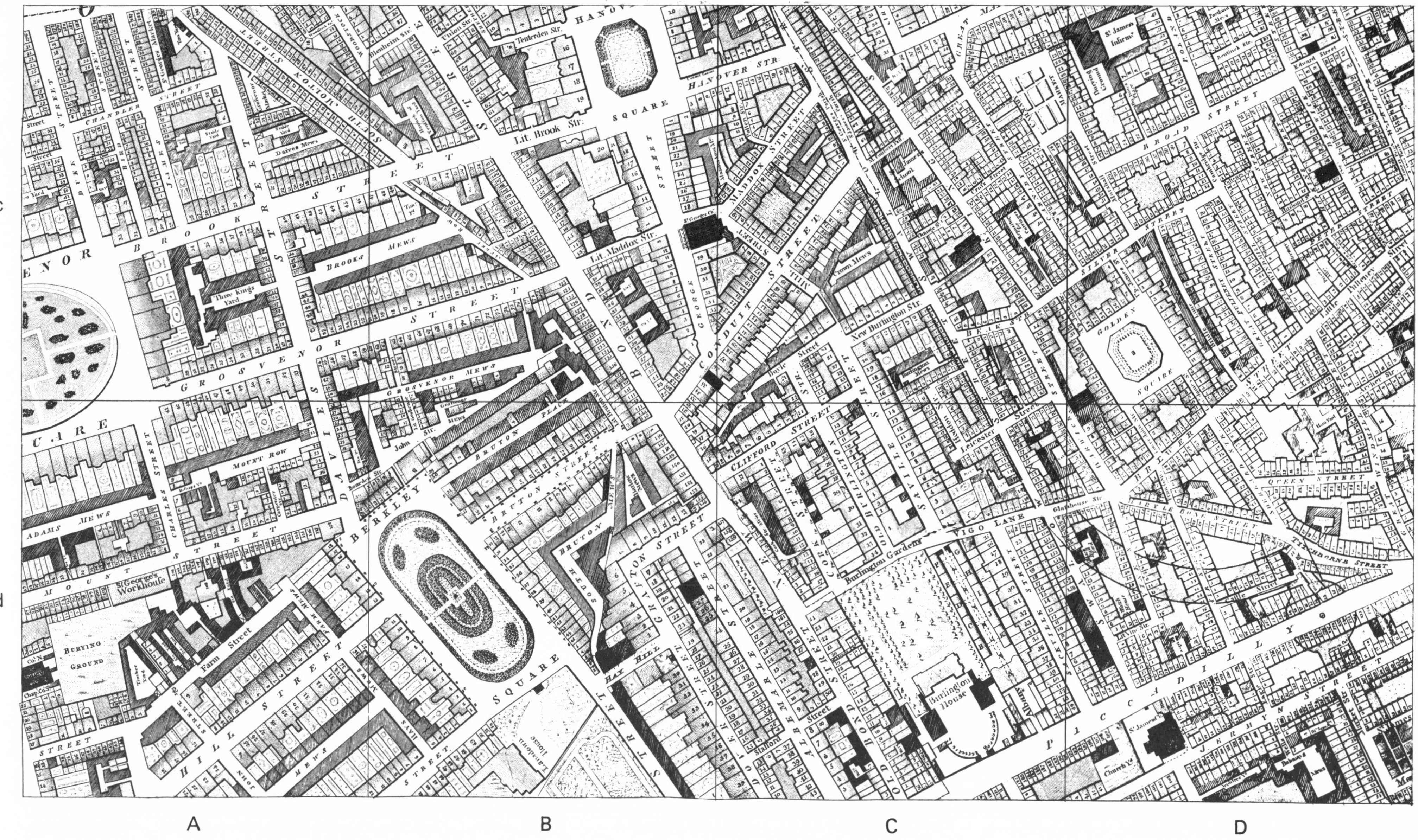

c
c
d
d
A
B
C
D
Lit. Brook Str.
Tenterden Str.
Lit. Maddox Str.
New Burlington Str.
Three Kings Yard
Brooks Mews
Grosvenor Mews
Mount Row
Bruton Street
Clifford Street
Vigo Lane
Burlington Gardens
Burlington House
Albany
St. George's Workhouse
Burying Ground
Farm Street
Hill Street
Hay Hill
Square
Golden Square
St. James's Infirmary
Piccadilly
Jermyn Street
Queen Street

12

13

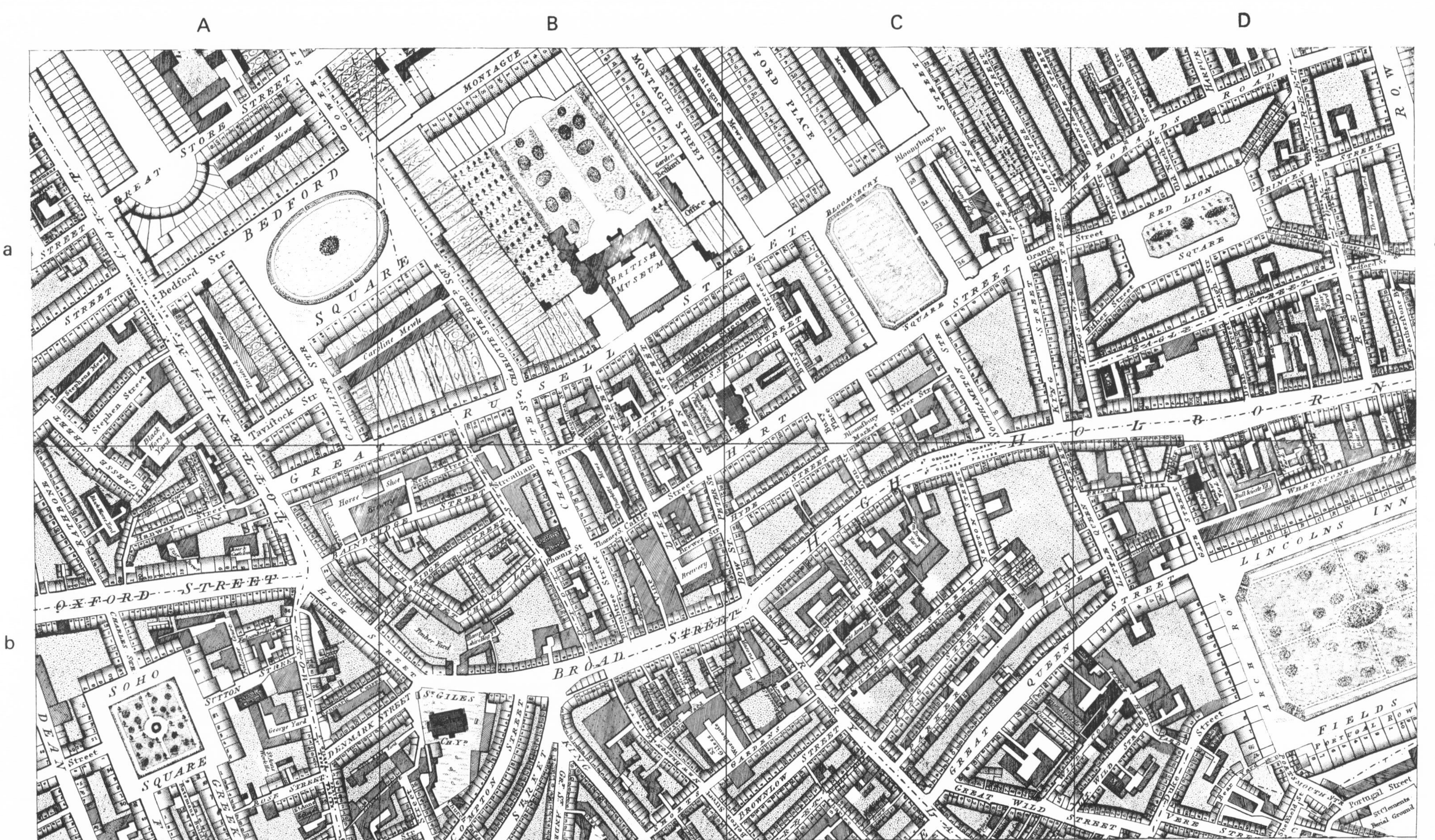

A
B
C
D
a
b
MONTAGUE STREET
MONTAGUE
FORD PLACE
BRITISH MUSEUM
BLOOMSBURY SQUARE
BEDFORD SQUARE
GREAT STORE STREET
RED LION SQUARE
LINCOLNS INN FIELDS
BROAD STREET
HIGH STREET
OXFORD STREET
SOHO SQUARE
GREAT RUSSELL STREET
HIGH HOLBORN
ST GILES
GREAT QUEEN STREET
GREAT WILD STREET
Portugal Street
St Clements Burial Ground

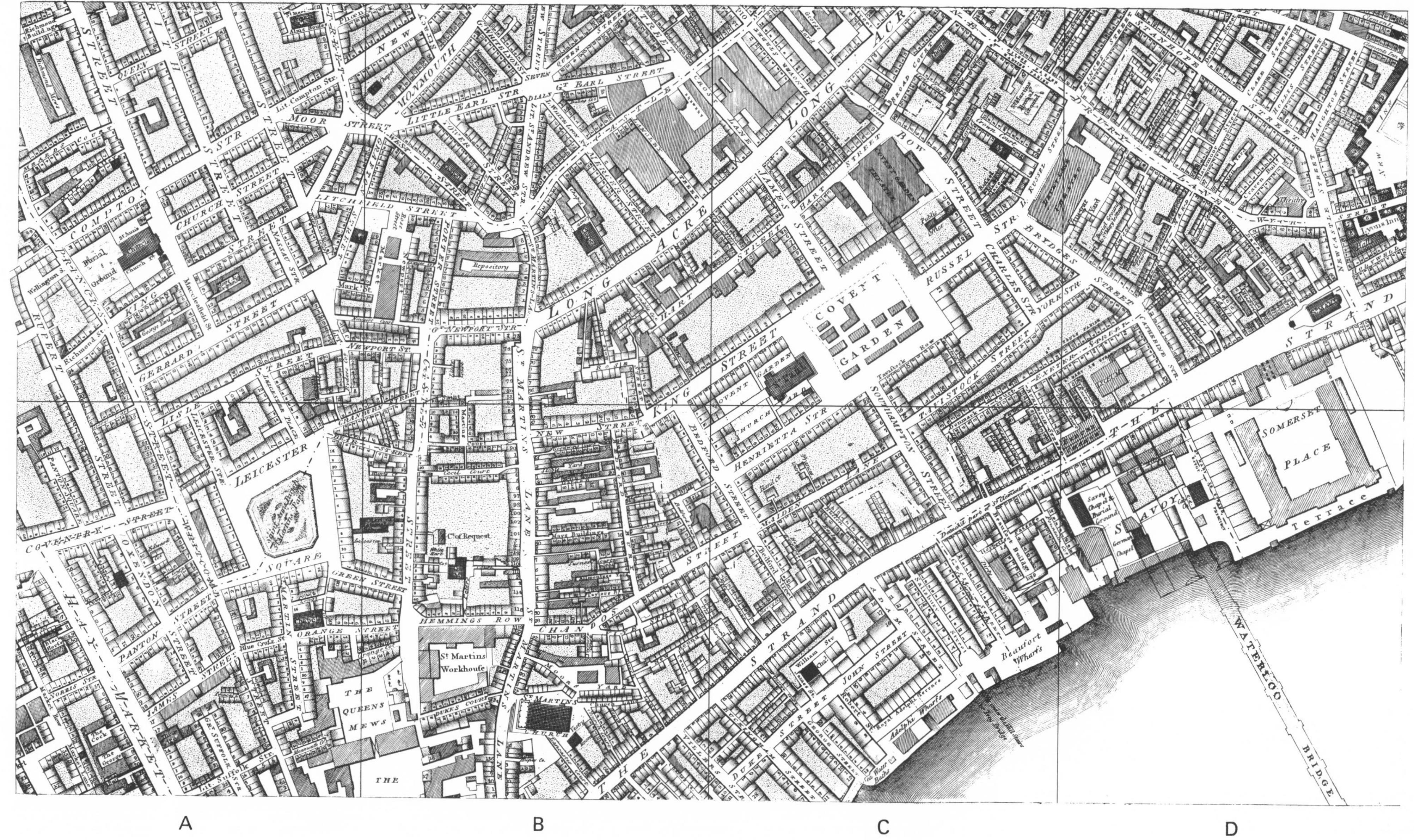
SOMERSET PLACE
Terrace
WATERLOO BRIDGE
STRAND
COVENT GARDEN
BOW STREET
RUSSEL STREET
CHARLES STR
YORK STR
SOUTHAMPTON STREET
HENRIETTA STR
JAMES STREET
HART STREET
KING STREET
LONG ACRE
BEDFORD STREET
MAIDEN LANE
NEW STREET
St MARTINS LANE
CHANDOS ST
HEMMINGS ROW
Repository
Ct of Request
Cecil Court
Mark St
Market
LITCHFIELD STREET
NEWPORT ST
LEICESTER SQUARE
LEICESTER
LISLE STREET
GERRARD STREET
KING STREET
COMPTON STREET
CHURCH STREET
MOOR STREET
LITTLE EARL STR
GT EARL STREET
SEVEN DIALS
NEW MONMOUTH
Lit. Compton Str.
Burial Ground
RUPERT
Richmond St
Wellington St
COVENTRY STREET
OXENDON
PANTON STREET
JAMES STREET
HAY MARKET
ORANGE STREET
GREEN STREET
St Martins Workhouse
THE QUEENS MEWS
St MARTINS CHURCH
DUKES COURT
ADAM STREET
JOHN STREET
William Str
Adelphi Wharfs
Beaufort Wharfs
SAVOY
German Chapel
Savoy Chapel & Burial Ground
DUKE STREET
VILLERS STREET
STANHOPE
DRURY LANE
Lyons Inn
Theatre

c

d

A

B

C

D

13

14

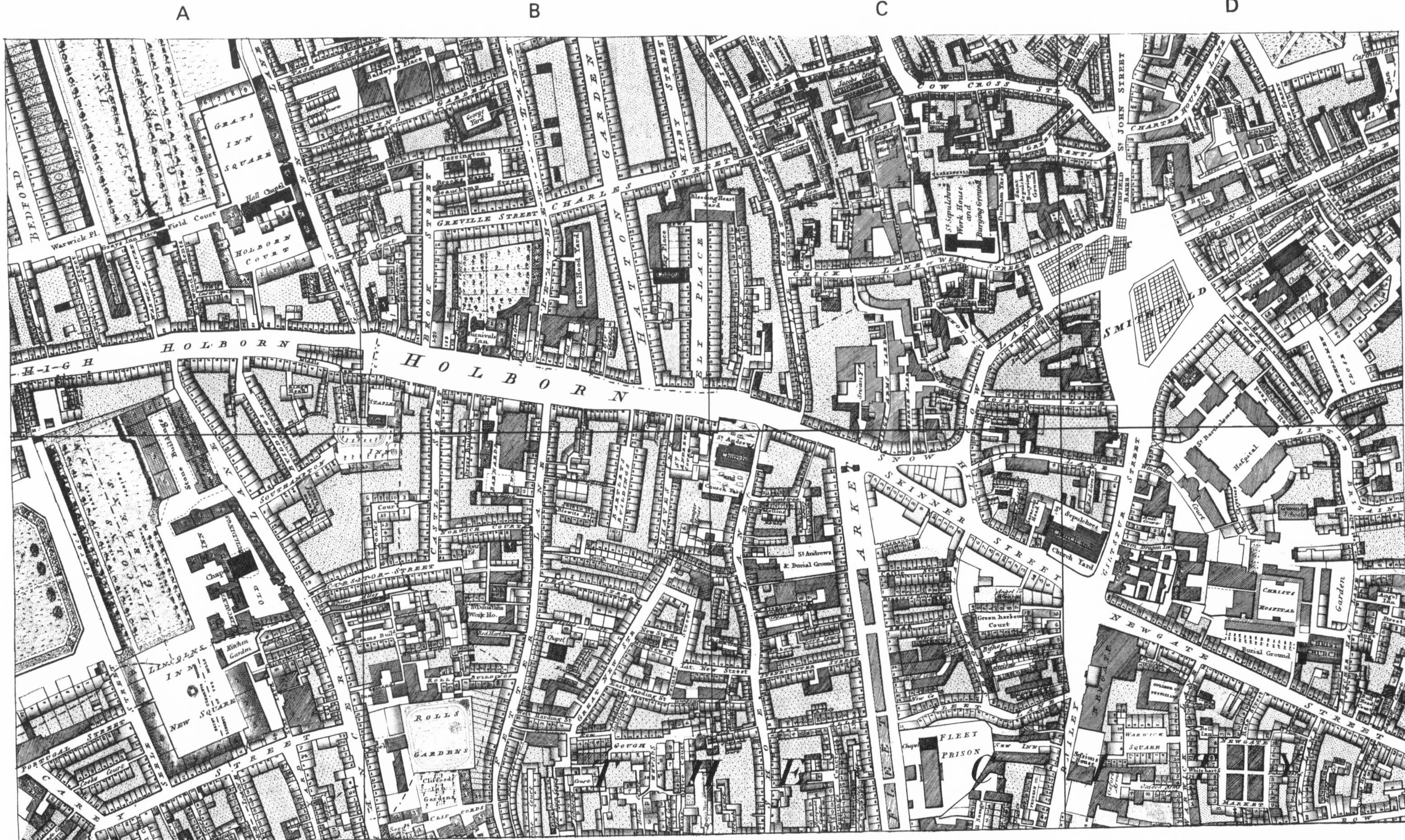

A
B
C
D
a
b
BEDFORD
Warwick Pl.
GRAYS INN SQUARE
Field Court
Hall Chapel
HOLBORN COURT
HIGH HOLBORN
HOLBORN
Borrington Street
GREVILLE STREET
BROOK STREET
Robin Hood Yard
CHARLES STREET
HATTON GARDEN
KIRBY STREET
ELY PLACE
Bleeding Heart Yard
COW CROSS STREET
St Sepulchre Work House and Burying Ground
Durham Yard
CHICK LANE or WEST STREET
St JOHN STREET
CHARTER HOUSE LANE
LONG LANE
SMITHFIELD
St Bartholomew Hospital
LITTLE BRITAIN
SNOW HILL
SKINNER STREET
St Andrews Church
St Andrews & Burial Ground
St Sepulchre Church Yard
GILTSPUR STREET
NEWGATE STREET
CHRISTS HOSPITAL
Garden
Burial Ground
Green harbour Court
FLEET PRISON
Chapel
WARWICK SQUARE
NEWGATE MARKET
CASTLE STREET
SOUTHAMPTON
Stone Buildings
LINCOLNS INN
NEW SQUARE
OLD
Chapel
Kitchen Garden
ROLLS GARDENS
Cliffords Inn Garden
PORTUGAL STREET
CAREY STREET
28

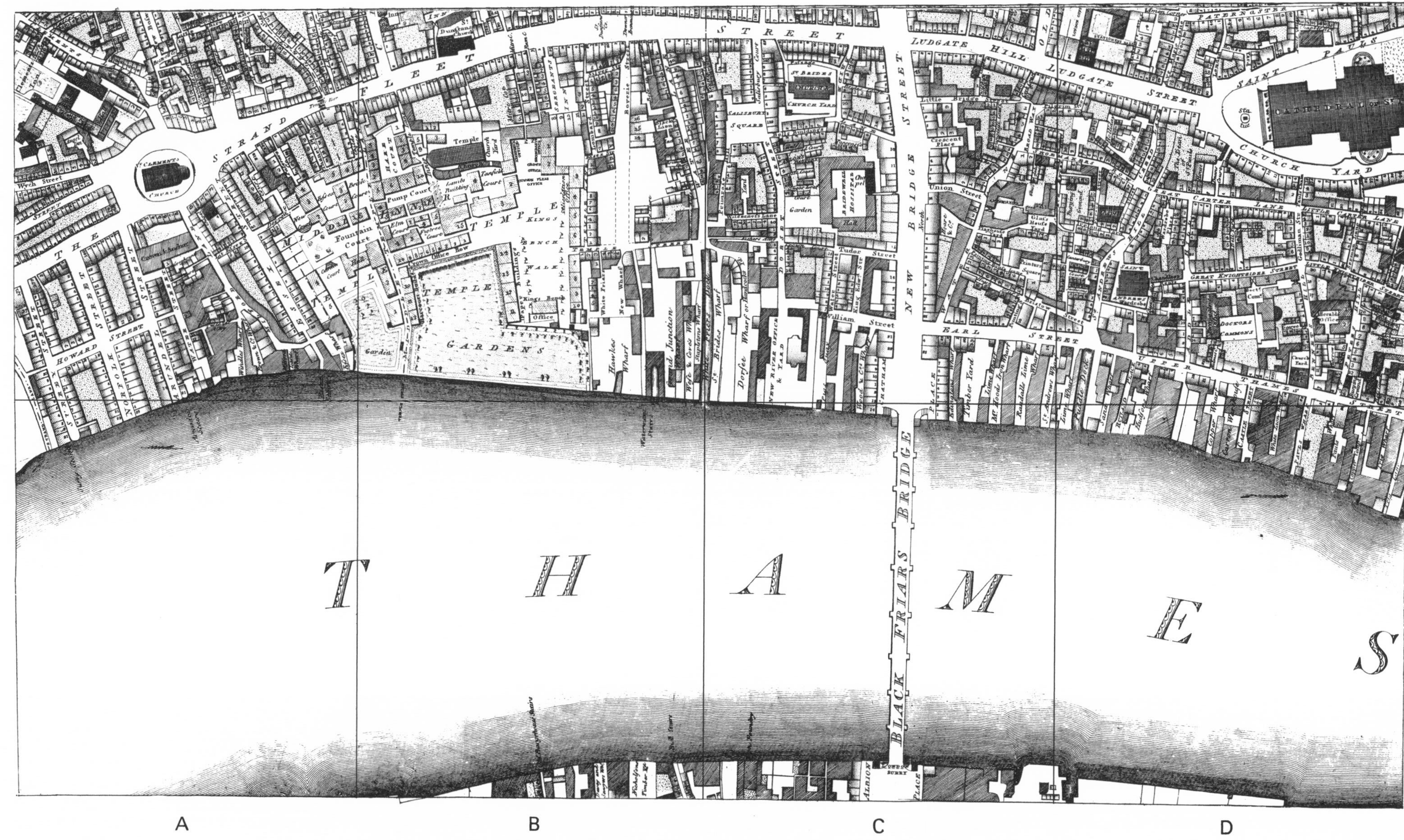
c
c
d
d
A
B
C
D
14
THAMES
BLACK FRIARS BRIDGE
NEW BRIDGE STREET
FLEET STREET
STRAND
LUDGATE HILL
LUDGATE STREET
OLD
SAINT PAULS CHURCH YARD
PATERNOSTER
GREAT CARTER LANE
GREAT KNIGHTRIDER STREET
DOCTORS COMMONS
EARL STREET
UPPER THAMES STREET
TEMPLE GARDENS
KINGS BENCH WALK
Pump Court
Fountain Court
Elm Court
Temple
Garden
St. CLEMENTS CHURCH
St. BRIDES CHURCH YARD
SALISBURY SQUARE
BRIDEWELL HOSPITAL
Tudor Street
William Street
Union Street
Crescent Place
Hawkes Wharf
New Wharf
White Friars
Grand Junction Wharf
St. Brides Wharf
Dorset Wharf
NEW RIVER OFFICE & YARD
Timber Yard
Puddle Dock
CHATHAM PLACE
ALBION PLACE
HOWARD STREET
NORFOLK STREET
ARUNDEL STREET
Wych Street

15

A B C D

a b

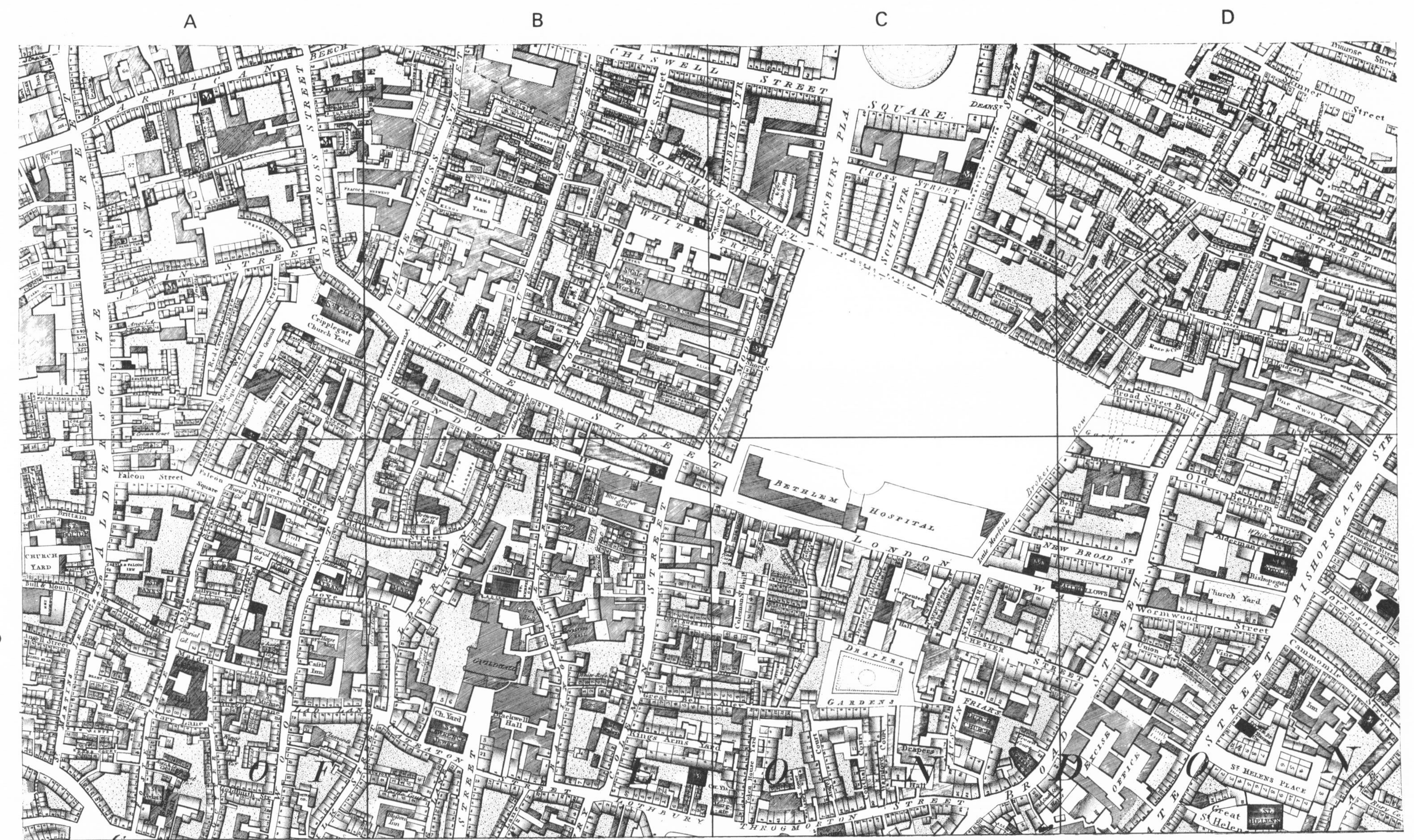

CHISWELL STREET
FINSBURY SQUARE
CROWN STREET
SUN STREET
ROPE MAKERS STREET
WHITE CROSS STREET
RED CROSS STREET
JEWIN STREET
FORE STREET
LONDON WALL
BETHLEM HOSPITAL
Cripplegate Church Yard
Falcon Square
Silver Street
ALDERSGATE STREET
NEW BROAD ST
BISHOPSGATE STREET
Wormwood Street
Church Yard
DRAPERS GARDENS
THROGMORTON STREET
LOTHBURY
Blackwell Hall
Kings Arms Yard
EXCISE OFFICE
St HELENS PLACE
Great St Helen
O F L O N D O N

a b

CHEAPSIDE
POULTRY
Mansion House Street
THE BANK
PRINCES STREET
Royal Exchange
Threadneedle Street
Merchant Taylors Hall
CORNHILL
LEADENHALL STREET
INDIA HOUSE
SKIN MARKET
BISHOPSGATE
GRACECHURCH STREET
FENCHURCH STREET
The Mansion House
Charlotte Row
George Yard
Great Eastcheap
Little Eastcheap
Church Yard
FISH STREET HILL
LOWER THAMES STREET
THAMES STREET
Water Works
BRIDGE
Dyers Hall
Dyers Hall Wharf
Steel Yard
St. Dunstans
Burial Ground
c
d
A
B
C
D

15

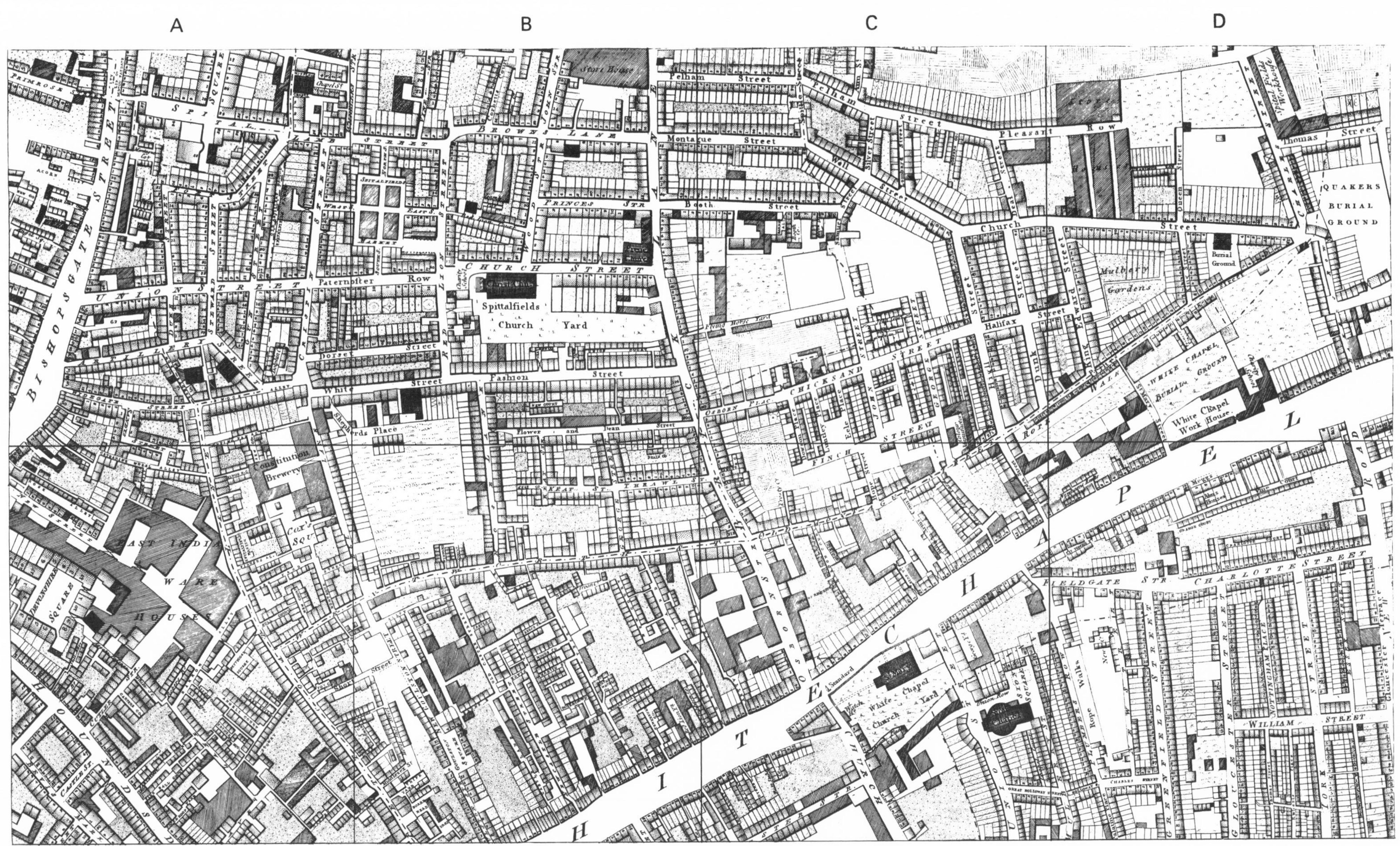
A
B
C
D
a
b
Pelham Street
Montague Street
Booth Street
Browns Lane
Princes Str
Church Street
Pleasant Row
Thomas Street
Spital Fields Workhouse
QUAKERS BURIAL GROUND
Burial Ground
Queen Street
Mulberry Gardens
Halifax Street
Dunk Street
King Edward Street
White Chapel Burial Ground
White Chapel Work House
Spittalfields
Church Yard
Paternoster Row
Union Street
Bishopsgate Street
Dorset Street
White Street
Fashion Street
Flower and Dean Street
Shepherds Place
Constitution Brewery
Cox's Squ
East India Ware House
Devonshire Square
Chicksand Street
John Street
Finch Street
Osborn Plac
Fieldgate Str
Charlotte Street
Rope Walks
White Chapel Church Yard
William Street
Gloucester Street
Greenfield Street
WHITE CHAPEL

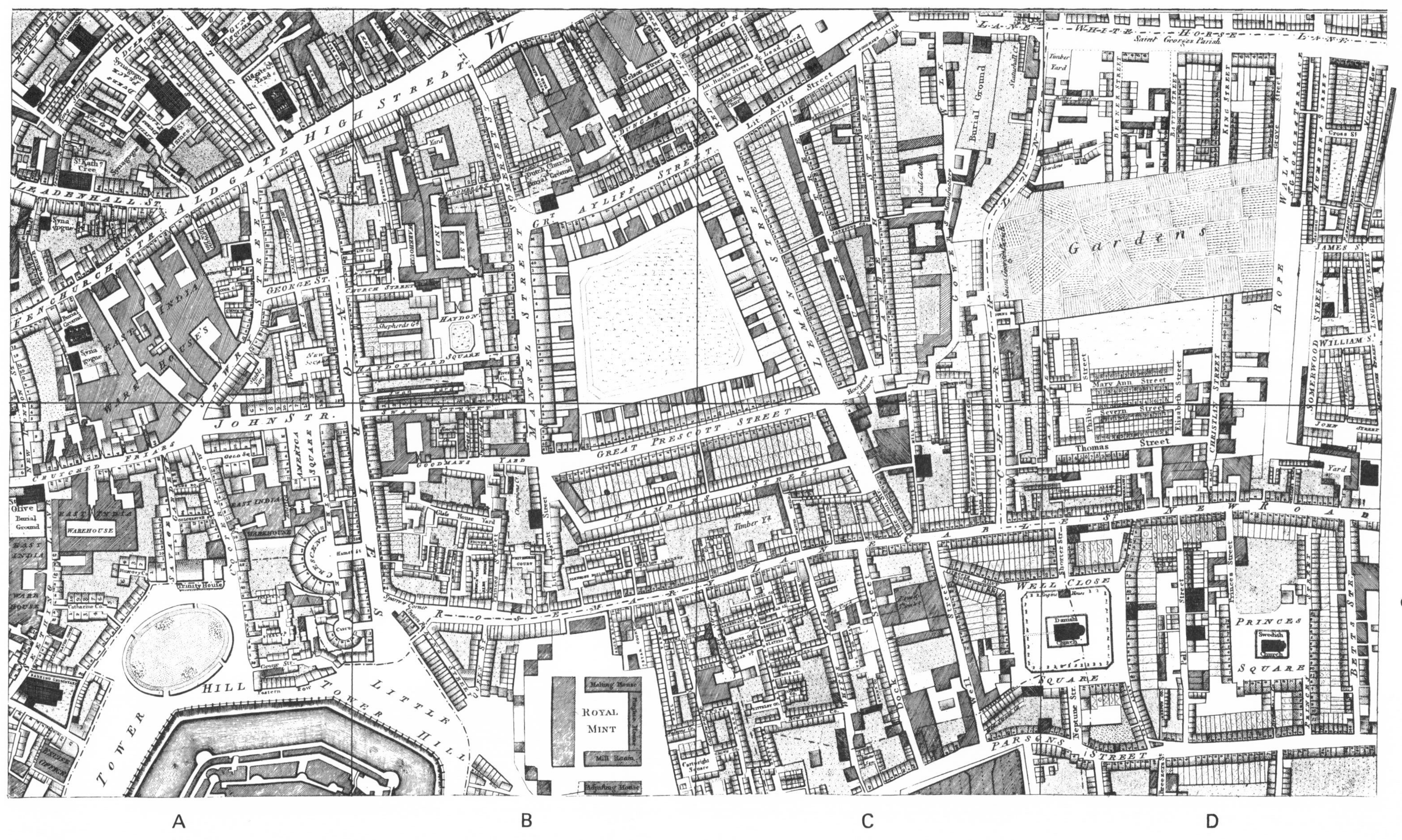
c
d
A
B
C
D
WHITE HORSE LANE
Saint Georges Parish
ROPE WALK
Gardens
Burial Ground
Timber Yard
KING STREET
SOMERWOOD STREET
WILLIAM ST
JAMES ST
CHRISTIAN STREET
Elizabeth Street
Mary Ann Street
Severn Street
Philip Street
Thomas Street
NEW ROAD
WELL CLOSE SQUARE
Danish Church
PRINCES SQUARE
Swedish Church
Princes Street
Shorter Str.
Neptune Str.
PARSONS STREET
Dock Street
LEMAN STREET
GREAT PRESCOTT STREET
CHAMBERS STREET
Timber Yd
MANSEL STREET
GT AYLIFF STREET
Lit Ayliff Street
Dutch Church
Nelson Street
ALDGATE HIGH STREET
LEADENHALL ST.
FENCHURCH STR.
St. Kath. Cree
Synagogue
EAST INDIA WAREHOUSES
EAST INDIA WAREHOUSE
HAYDON SQUARE
HAYDON YARD
Shepherds Ct.
GEORGE ST.
CHURCH STREET
JOHN STR.
AMERICA SQUARE
CRESCENT
GOODMANS YARD
Champions Ct.
Glass House Yard
CRUTCHED FRIARS
SAVAGE GARDENS
COOPERS ROW
Trinity House
Olive Burial Ground
ROYAL MINT
Melting House
Mill Room
Assaying House
TOWER HILL
LITTLE TOWER HILL
Cartwright Square
BETTS STR.

17

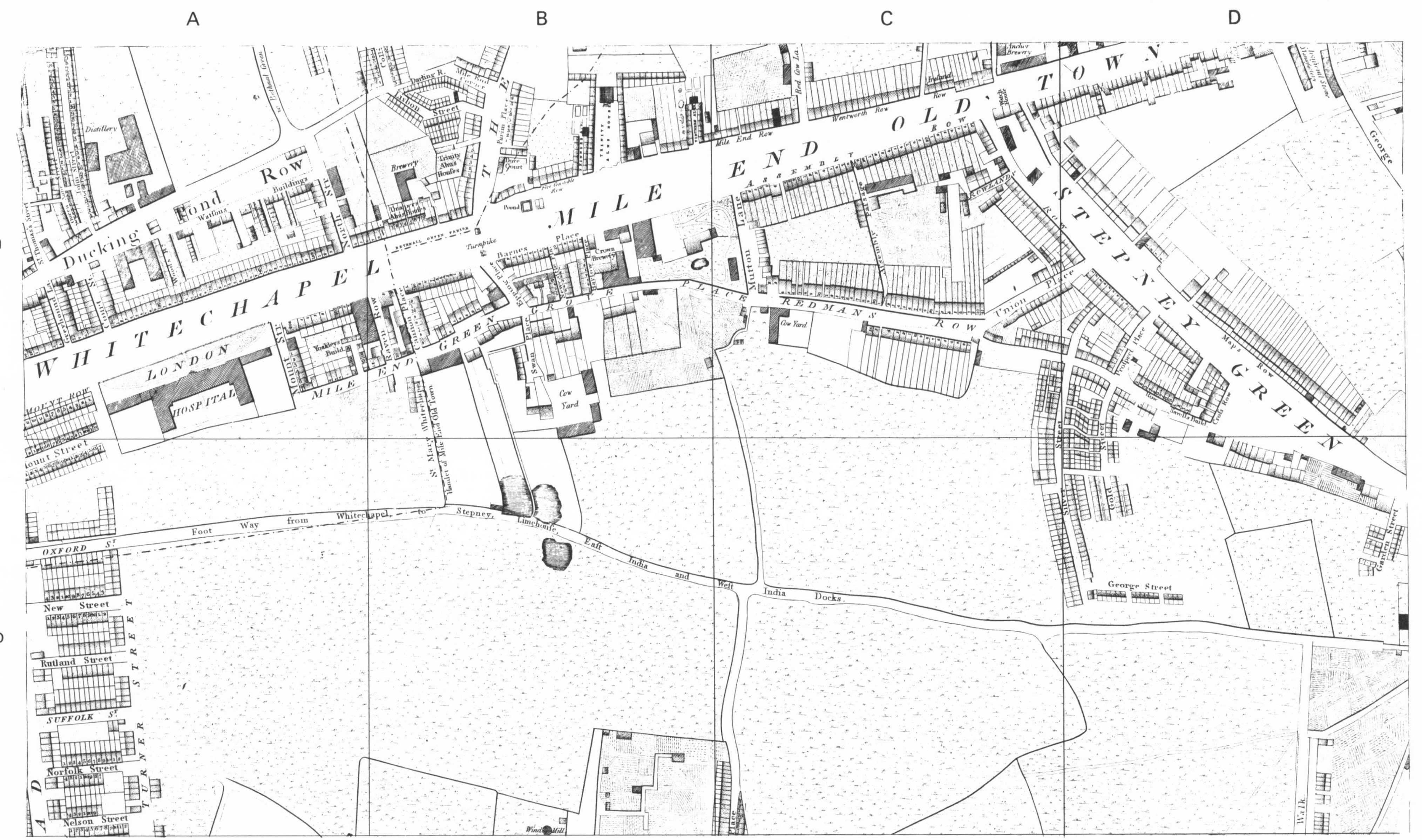

A
B
C
D
a
b
WHITECHAPEL
MILE END
OLD TOWN
STEPNEY GREEN
LONDON HOSPITAL
Ducking Pond Row
Mile End Row
Wentworth Row
Redmans Row
Mutton Lane
Cow Yard
Swan Place
Turnpike
Trinity Alms Houses
Brewery
Distillery
Anchor Brewery
Maps Row
George Street
Foot Way from Whitechapel to Stepney
Limehouse
East India and West India Docks
Oxford St.
New Street
Rutland Street
Suffolk St.
Norfolk Street
Nelson Street
Turner Street
Mount Str.
Wind Mill

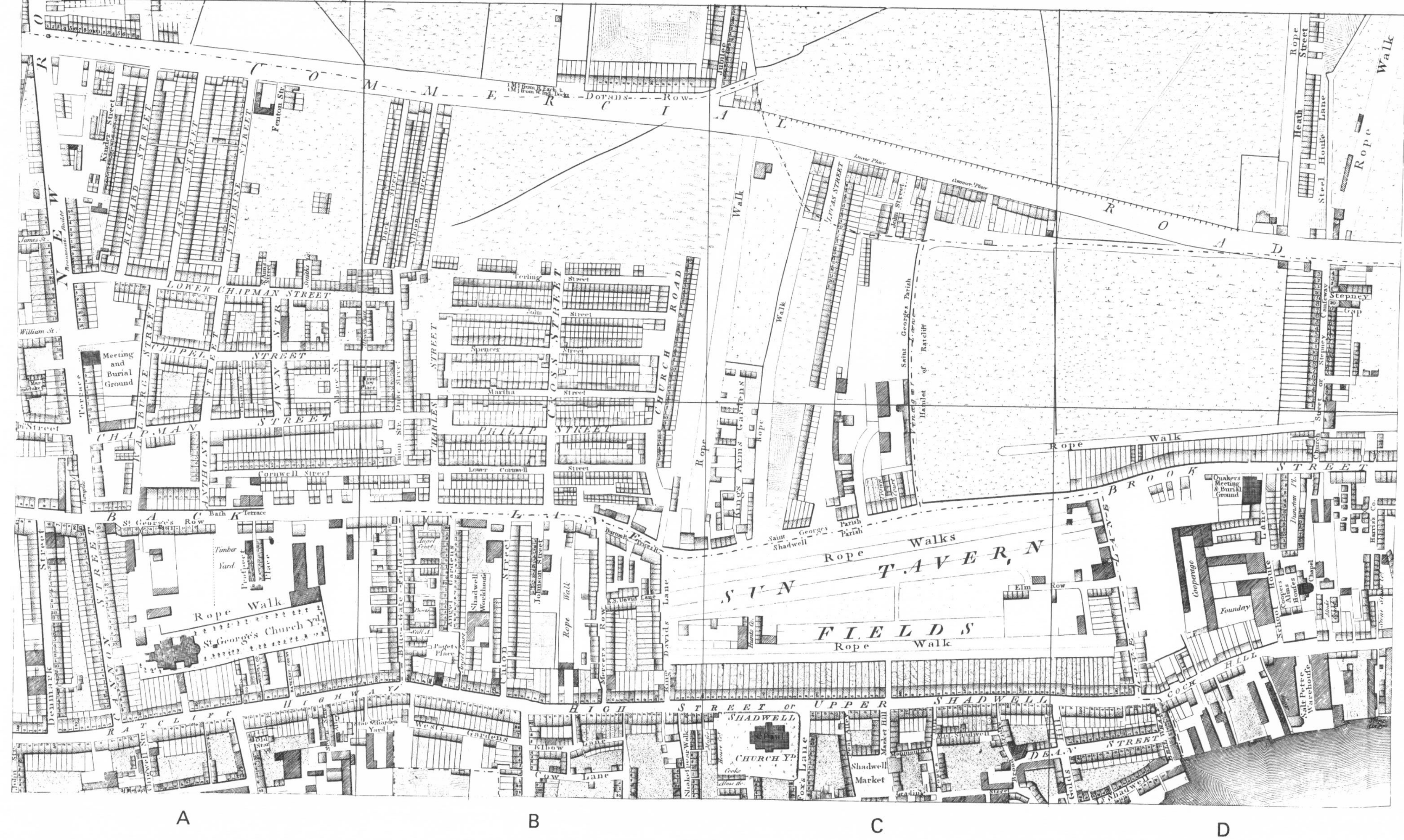
COMMERCIAL ROAD
NEW ROAD
Dorans Row
Jubilee
Fenton St.
Kinder Street
RICHARD STREET
JANE STREET
CATHERINE STREET
Dock Street
Albion Street
LOWER CHAPMAN STREET
CHAPEL STREET
ANN STREET
ALBURGE STREET
CHAPMAN STREET
ANTHONY STREET
Meeting and Burial Ground
Cornwell Street
CHARLES STREET
PHILIP STREET
CROSS STREET
CHURCH ROAD
Terling Street
John Street
Spencer Street
Martha Street
Lower Cornwell Street
Lucas Street
John Street
Saint Georges Parish
Hamlet of Ratcliff
Kings Arms Gardens
Rope Walk
BACK LANE
St. George's Row
Bath Terrace
Timber Yard
Prospect Place
Rope Walk
St. George's Church Yd.
Shadwell Workhouse
Johnson Street
Rope Walk
Mercers Row
Davids Lane
Saint Georges Parish
Shadwell Parish
Rope Walks
SUN TAVERN FIELDS
Rope Walk
Elm Row
BROOK STREET
Quakers Meeting & Burial Ground
Cooperage
Foundery
School House Lane
Coopers Alms Houses
Chapel
Harris's Co.
Heath Street
Steel House Lane
Rope Walk
Stepney Gap
Church Street or Stepney Causeway
CANNON STREET
RATCLIFF HIGHWAY
HIGH STREET or UPPER SHADWELL STREET
SHADWELL CHURCH Yd.
Shadwell Market
Market Hill
Fox's Lane
Shakespear Walk
Cow Lane
Elbow Lane
Wests Gardens
DEAN STREET
COCK HILL
Salt Petre Warehouse
Denmark Street
A
B
C
D
c
d
17

A
B
C
D
a
b
ROPE WALK
BOW
Maritime Alms Houses
The Parish of Bromley
Hamlet of Mile End Old Town
COMMON
Cow House
ROPE WALK
John Street
Street
TRAFALGAR
SQUARE
STREET
EDWARD
OCEAN STREET
WHITE HORSE LANE
to Bow
RHODES WELL COMMON
Rhodes Well
LANE
Place
CHURCH ROW
STEPNEY
STEPNEY
CHURCH YARD
BULL LANE
ROPE WALK
ROPE WALK
CATHARINE STREET
ROSETTA ST
VINE ST
RICHARD
Yard
STREET
STREET
Hamlet of Mile End Old Town
The Parish of Limehouse
TORY
Rope Walk

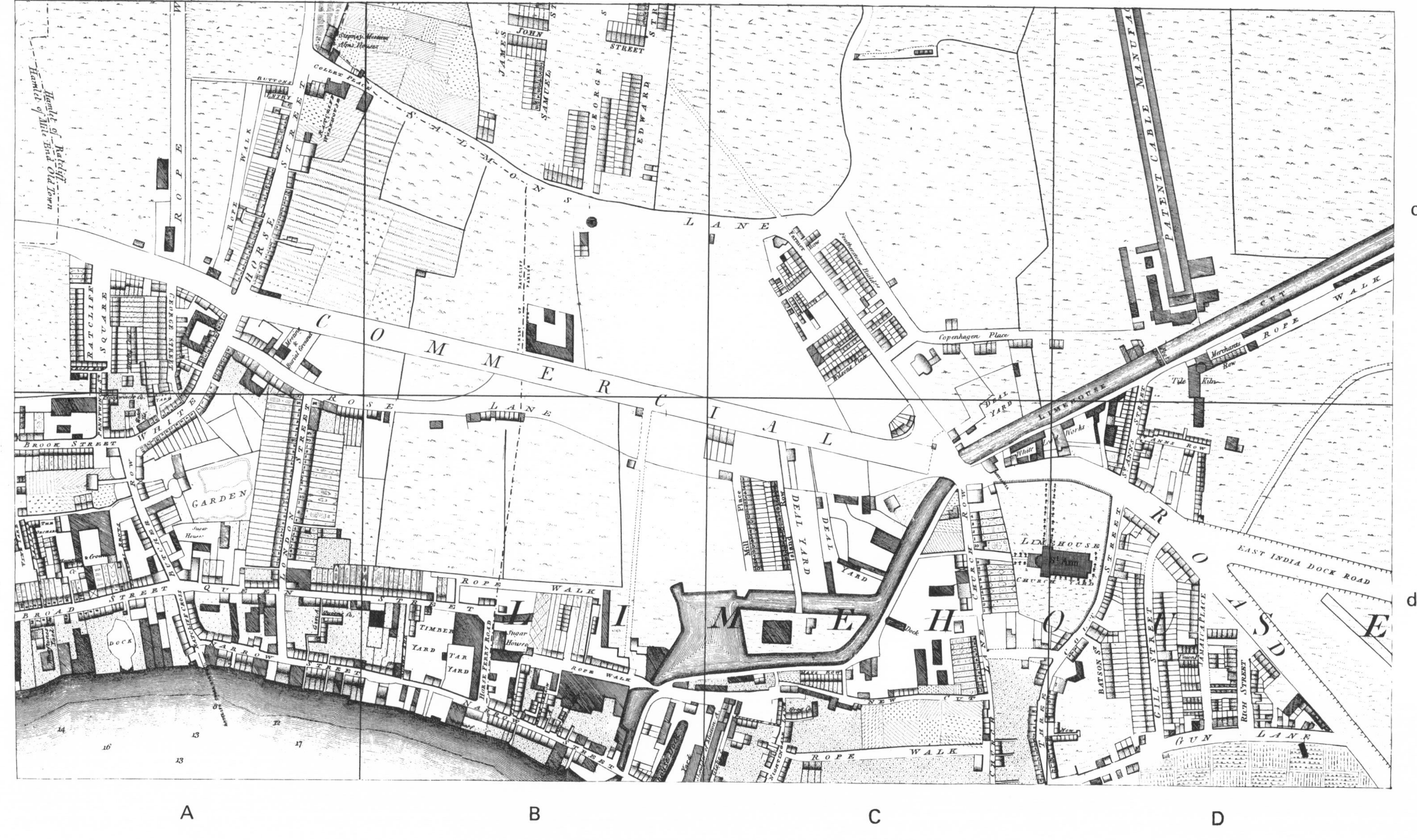

c
d
A
B
C
D
18
Hamlet of Ratcliff
Hamlet of Mile End Old Town
COMMERCIAL ROAD
LIMEHOUSE
PATENT CABLE MANUFAC
EAST INDIA DOCK ROAD
LIMEHOUSE CUT
ROPE WALK
SALMONS LANE
ROSE LANE
DEAL YARD
Mill Place
TIMBER YARD
TAR YARD
HORSE FERRY ROAD
Sugar Houses
GARDEN
HORSE STREET
GEORGE STREET
RATCLIFF SQUARE
BROOK STREET
WHITE ROW
BROAD STREET
QUEEN STREET
NARROW STREET
LONDON STREET
DOCK
Copenhagen Place
Featherstone Build.gs
Merchants Row
Tile Kiln
EDWARD STREET
GEORGE STREET
SAMUEL STREET
JOHN STREET
JAMES ST
CHURCH ROW
St. Ann
NEW CUT
BATSON ST
GILL STREET
JAMAICA PLACE
RICH STREET
GUN LANE

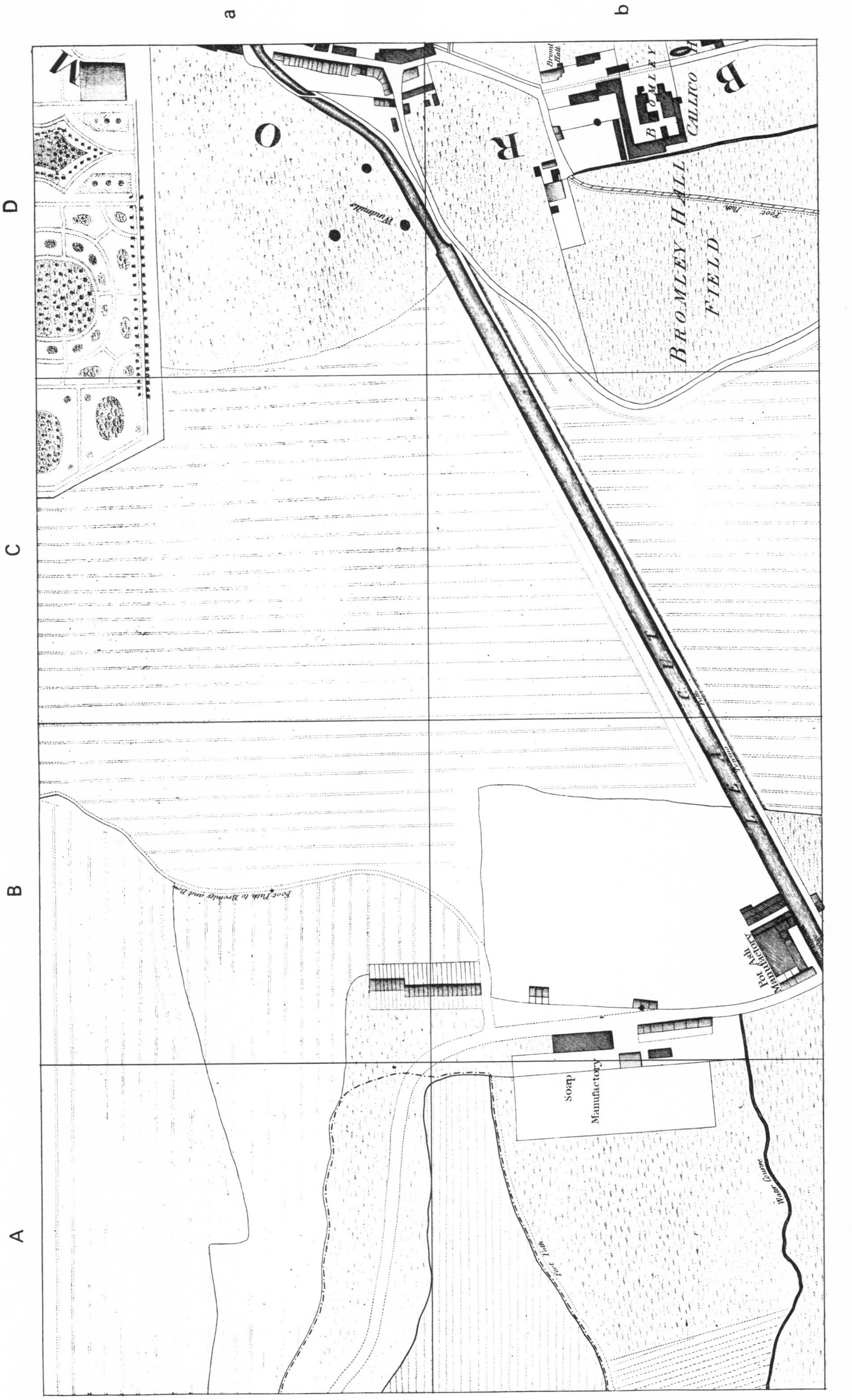

19

A B C D

a b

O R B

Windmills

Foot Path to Bromley and Bow

Foot Path

Water Course

Soap Manufactory

Pot Ash Manufactory

LEA CUT

Bromley Hall

BROMLEY

CALLICO

BROMLEY HALL FIELD

c
d
A
B
C
D
19
Lime Kiln
Rope Walk
Pearl Ash
Manufactory
Common Sewer
North Street
GARDENS
Bow Lane
East India Dock Road
E. India Alms-houses
Union Street
Ashton Street
Rope Walk

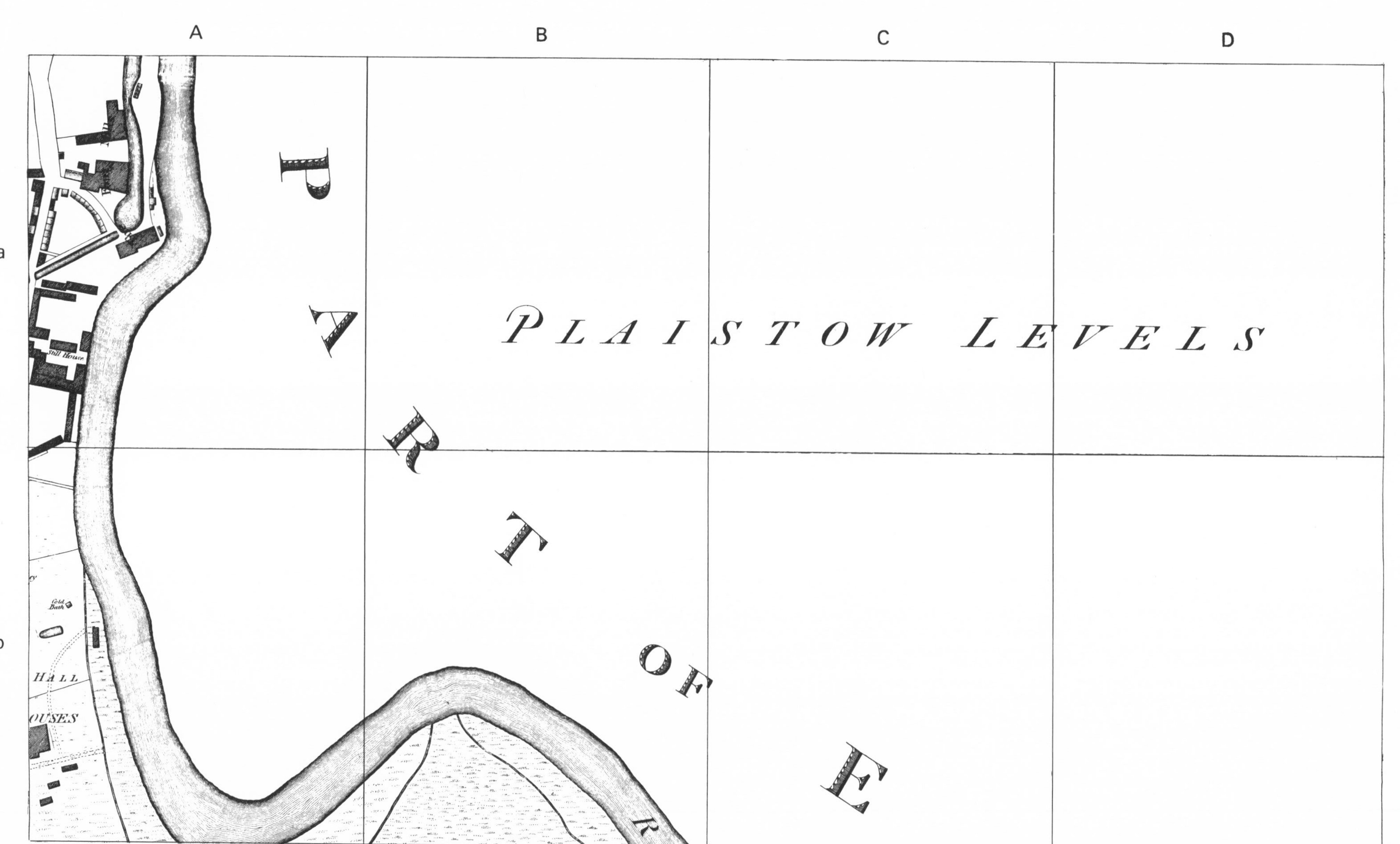

A
B
C
D
a
b
PLAISTOW LEVELS
PART OF E
R
Still House
Cold Bath
HALL
OUSES

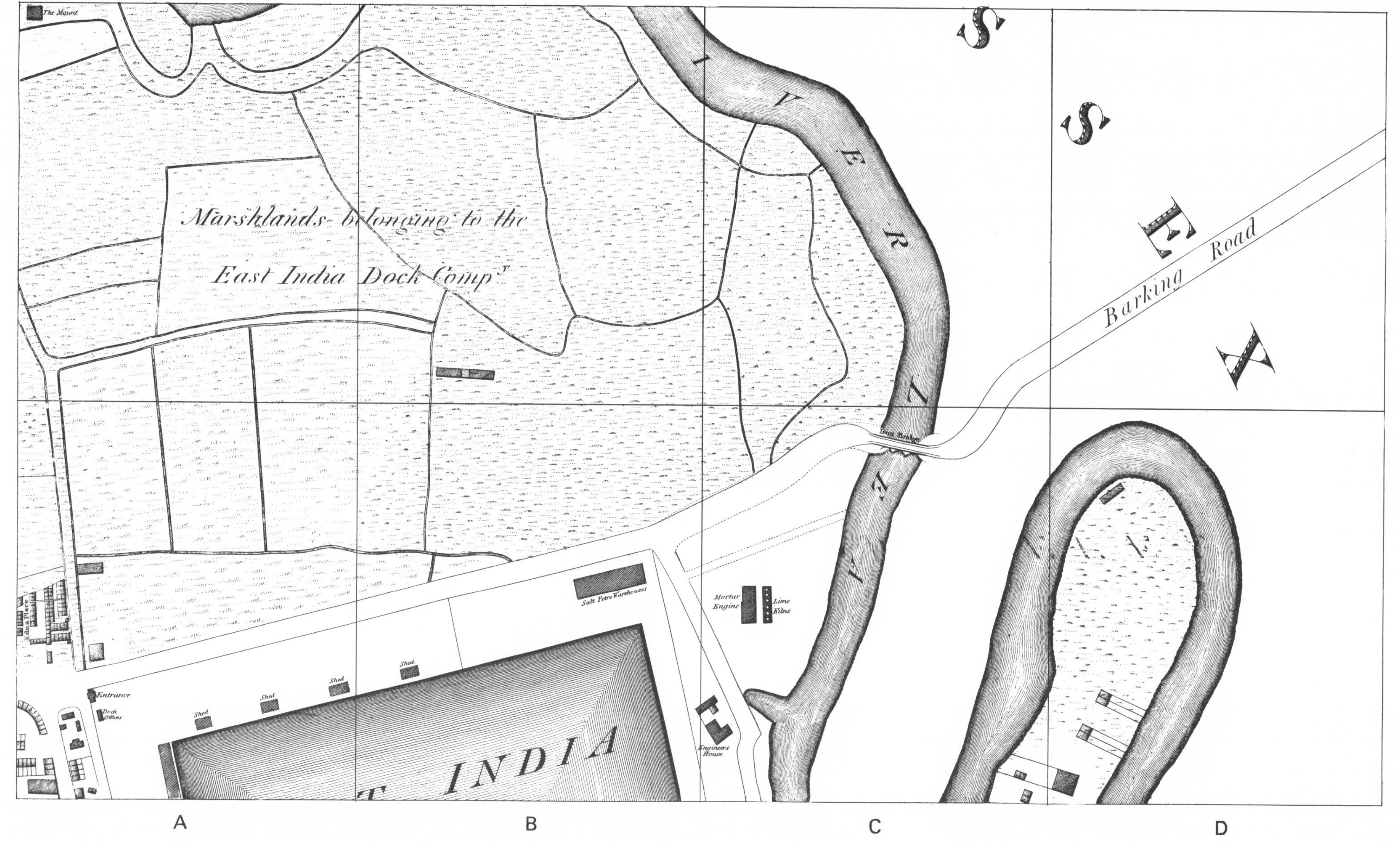
The Mount
Marshlands belonging to the
East India Dock Compy.
S S E X
Barking Road
R I V E R L E A
Iron Bridge
Mortar Engine
Lime Kilns
Salt Petre Warehouses
Engineers House
Edna Place
Entrance
Dock Offices
Shed
Shed
Shed
Shed
INDIA
A
B
C
D
c
d
c
d

21

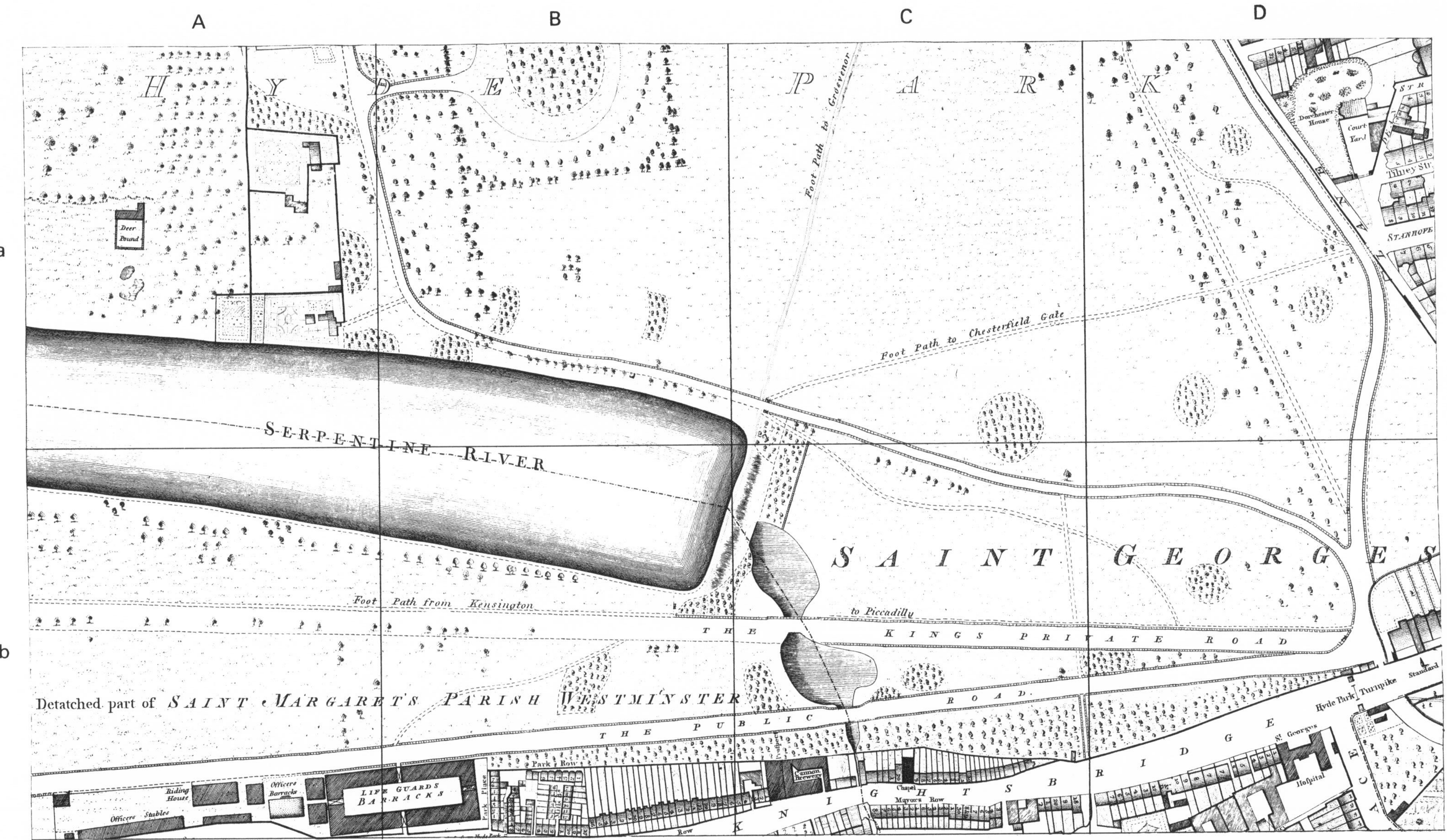

A
B
C
D
a
b
HYDE PARK
SAINT GEORGES
S-E-R-P-E-N-T-I-N-E R-I-V-E-R
Foot Path to Chesterfield Gate
Foot Path to Grosvenor
Foot Path from Kensington
to Piccadilly
THE KINGS PRIVATE ROAD
THE PUBLIC ROAD.
Detatched part of SAINT MARGARET'S PARISH WESTMINSTER
KNIGHTSBRIDGE
LIFE GUARDS BARRACKS
Officers Barracks
Riding House
Officers Stables
Deer Pound
Dorchester House
Court Yard
Tilney Str
STANHOPE
Park Row
Park Place
Cannon Brewery
Chapel
Mayors Row
Hyde Park Turnpike
Standard
St. Georges Hospital

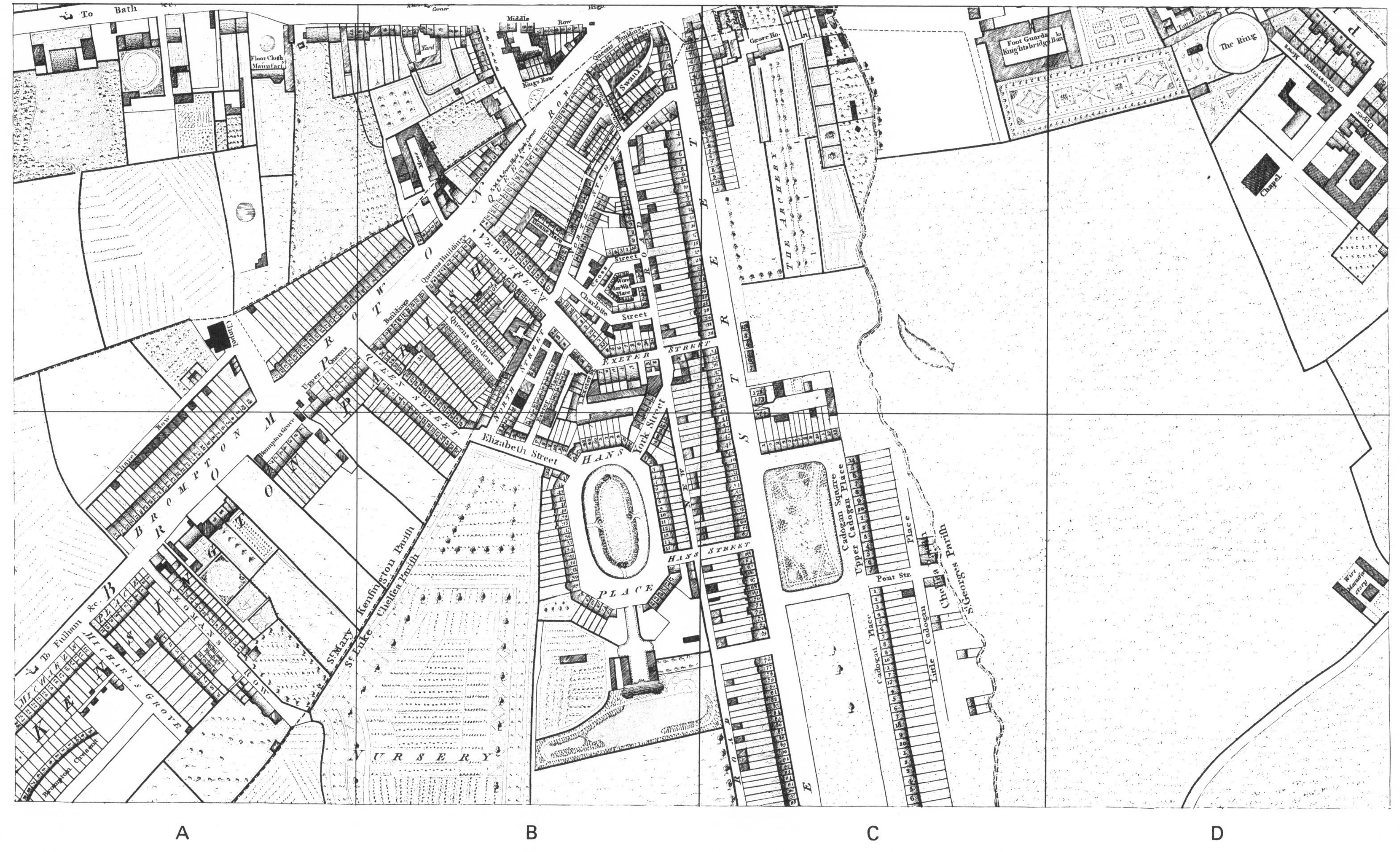

A
B
C
D
c
d
To Bath
Floor Cloth Manufacty
Middle Row
Kings Row
Yard
Foot Guards Knightsbridge Barracks
The Ring
Grosvenor Mews
Chapel
The Archery
Queens Buildings
Swan
Cross Street
Charlotte Street
Exeter Street
North Street
Queen Street
Queens Gardens
New Street
York Street
Elizabeth Street
Hans Place
Hans Street
New Street
Upper Queens Buildings
Brompton Grove
Chapel Row
Brompton Row
Brompton
Knightsbridge
Yeomans Row
Michaels Grove
Michaels Place
Brompton Crescent
To Fulham &c.
St. Mary Kensington Parish
St. Luke Chelsea Parish
Nursery
Cadogan Square
Upper Cadogan Place
Cadogan Place
Little Cadogan Place
Pont Str.
Chelsea Parish
St. Georges Parish
Wire Manufactory
Road
Street
Sloane
21

22

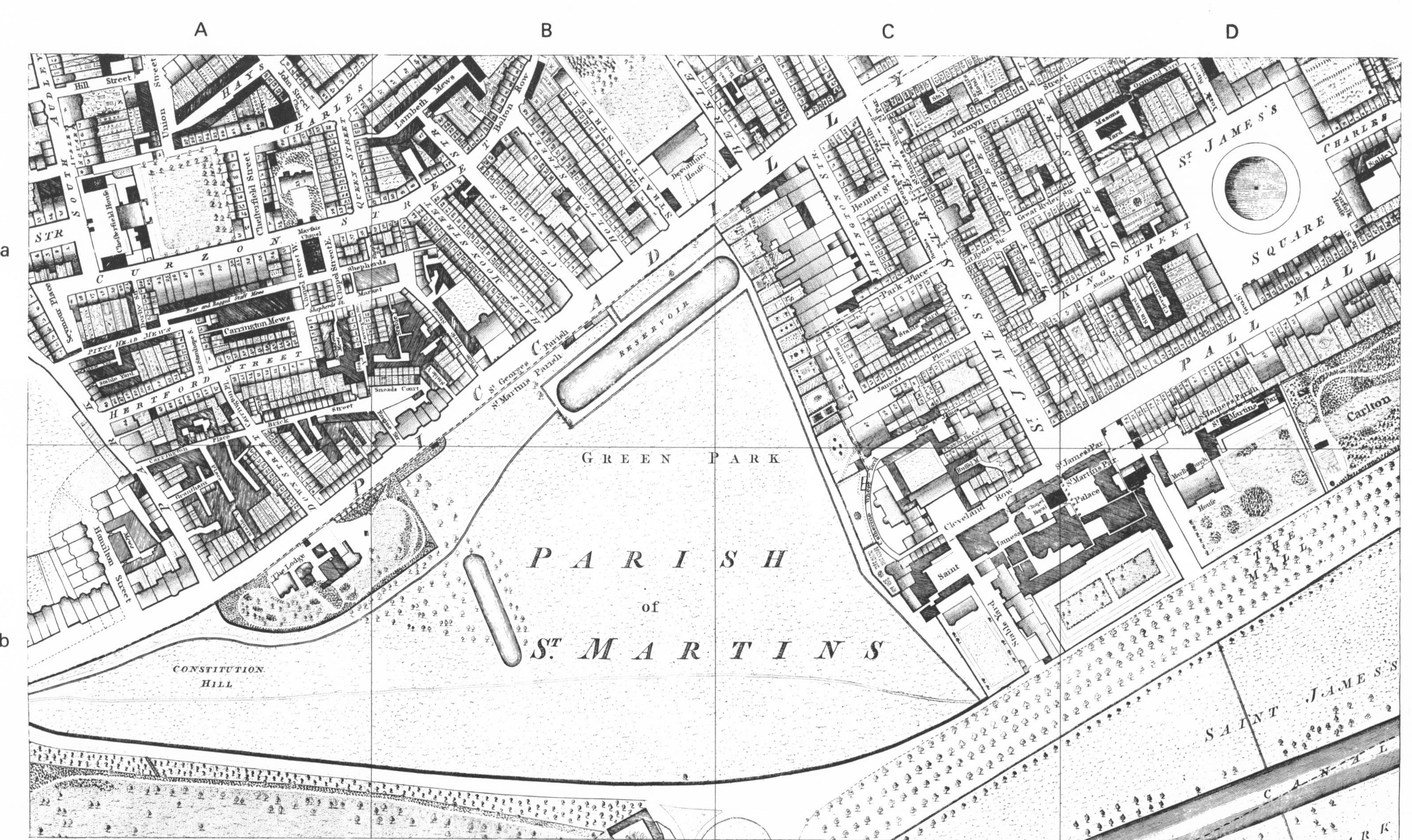

A
B
C
D
a
b
ST. JAMES'S SQUARE
PALL MALL
ST. JAMES'S STREET
KING STREET
Jermyn Street
Great Ryder Str.
Bennet St.
Park Place
Stable Yard
Masons Yard
Ormond Yard
CHARLES
York Street
Cleveland Row
St. James's Palace
Chapel Royal
Marlborough House
Carlton
THE MALL
SAINT JAMES'S PARK
CANAL
St. James's Par.
St. Martins Par.
Stable Yard
Saint James's
PICCADILLY
Devonshire House
STRATTON STREET
BERKELEY
Bolton Row
HALF MOON STREET
CLARGES STREET
Lambeth Mews
CHARLES STREET
John Street
HAYS
QUEEN STREET
Union Street
Hill Street
SOUTH AUDLEY STR
Chesterfield House
Chesterfield Street
CURZON STREET
Mayfair Chapel
Chapel Street W.
Chapel Street E.
Shepherds Market
Shepherds St.
Carrington Mews
Bear and Ragged Staff Mews
PITTS HEAD MEWS
Seymour Place
HERTFORD STREET
Lit. Stanhope St.
Sneads Court
Brick Street
DOWN STREET
Carrington Place
Brantham Place
Hamilton Street
St. Georges Parish
St. Martins Parish
RESERVOIR
GREEN PARK
PARISH of ST. MARTINS
The Lodge
CONSTITUTION HILL

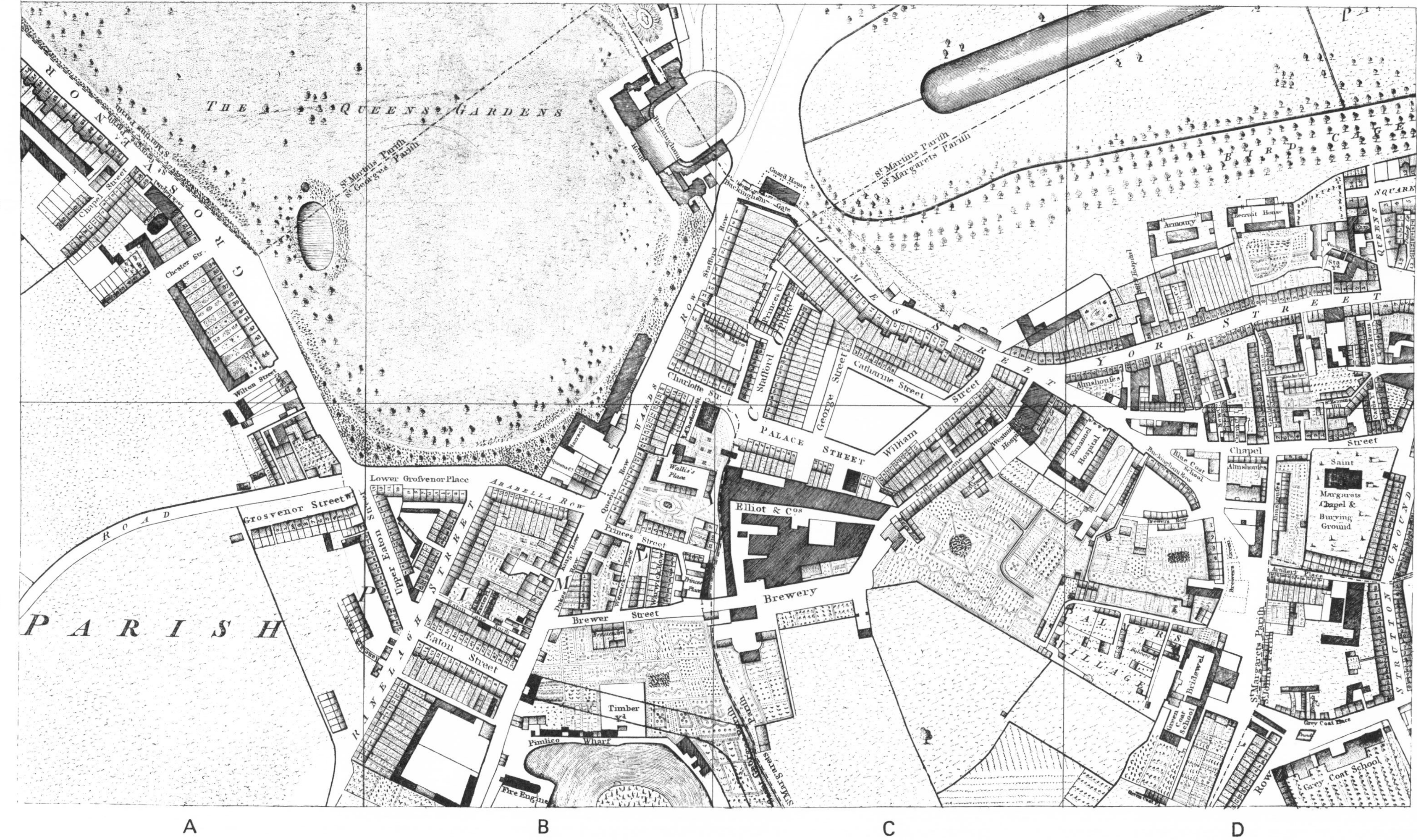
THE QUEENS GARDENS
St Martins Parish
St Georges Parish
St Margarets Parish
BIRD CAGE
Buckingham House
Buckingham Gate
Guard House
Armoury
Recruit House
QUEENS SQUARE
JAMES STREET
YORK STREET
Stafford Row
Stafford Place
Princes Ct
Charlotte St.
Stafford
George Street
Catharine Street
PALACE STREET
William Street
Almshouses
Westminster Hospital
Emanuel Hospital
Blue Coat School
Buckingham Row
Chapel Street
Chapel
Saint Margarets Chapel & Burying Ground
Artillery Place
Brewers Row
Elliot & Cos
Brewery
Brewer Street
Wallis's Place
Princes Street
Queens Row
ARABELLA ROW
Lower Grosvenor Place
Grosvenor Street
Upper Eaton Street
RANELAGH STREET
Eaton Street
Chester Str.
Wilton Street
Timber yd
Pimlico Wharf
Fire Engine
TOTHILL FIELDS
VILLAGE
Bridewell
Green Coat School
Grey Coat Place
Grey Coat School
STRUTTON GROUND
ROAD
PARISH
A
B
C
D
c
d

A
B
C
D
a
b
Kings Mews
Phoenix Fire Engine
Cockspur Street
Charing Cross
Pall Mall
Carlton House
House Gardens
Spring Garden
New Street
The Admiralty
Northumberland Gardens
Northumberland Street
Craven Street
Hungerford Market
Villiers Street
Craigs Court
Gr. Scotland Yard
Middle Scotland Yard
Lt. Scotland Yard
Whitehall Place
Whitehall Stairs
The Horse Guards
Parade
Chapel
White Hall
The Treasury
Privy Gardens
Treasury Yard
Downing Street
Fludyer Street
Charles Street
Wharf
White Hall Timber Yard
R
E
Lambeth Water Works
Barge Builder
Timber Yard
Brewery
College Street
Tan Yard
Timber Yard
Narrow Wall

c d

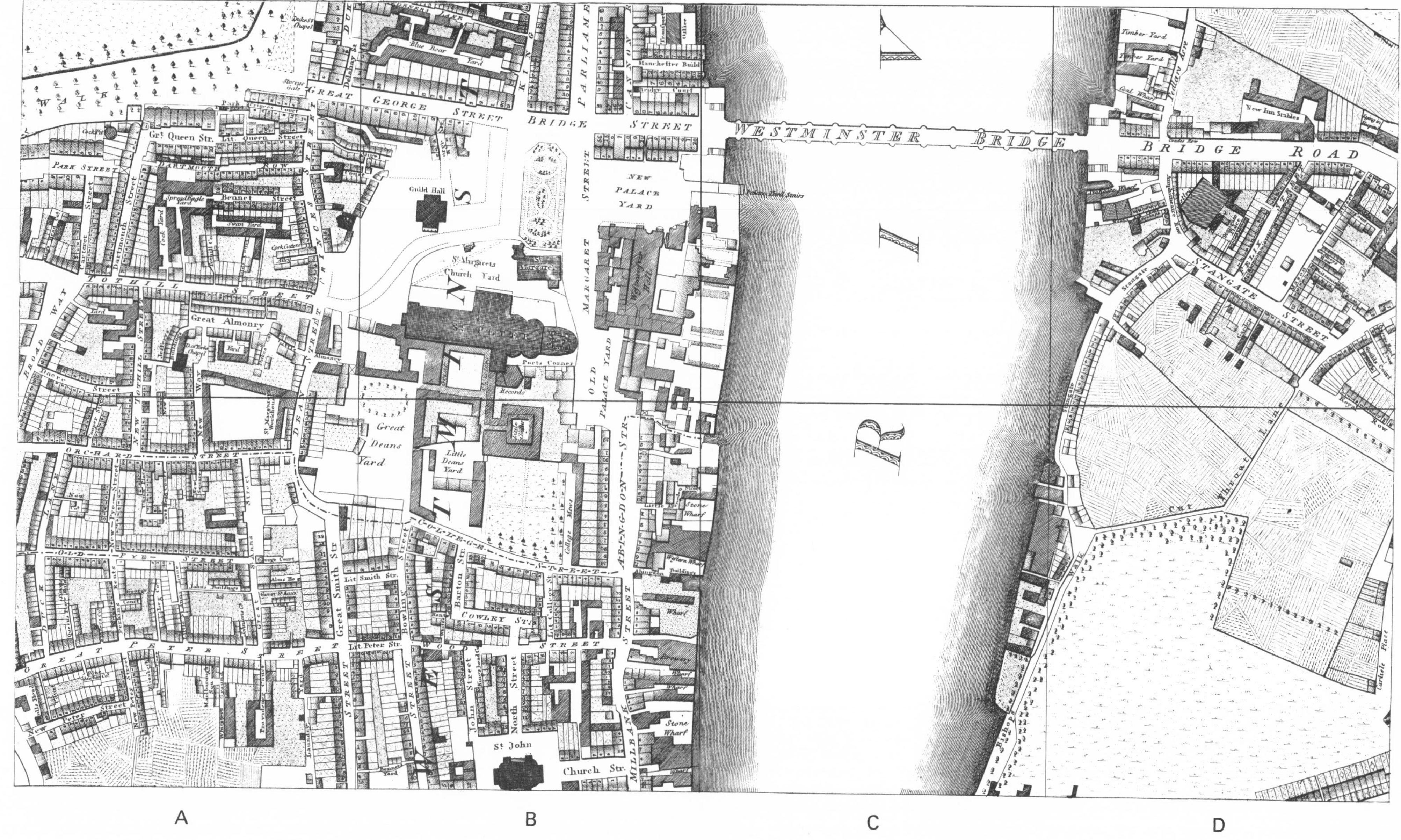

WESTMINSTER BRIDGE
BRIDGE ROAD
STANGATE STREET
Amphitheatre Row
New Inn Stables
Timber Yard
Bishops Walk
RIVER
NEW PALACE YARD
Westminster Hall
OLD PALACE YARD
MARGARET STREET
PARLIAMENT STREET
BRIDGE STREET
GREAT GEORGE STREET
Guild Hall
St. Margarets Church Yard
ST. PETER
Great Deans Yard
Little Deans Yard
ABINGDON STR
MILLBANK
Stone Wharf
COLLEGE STREET
COWLEY STR.
Barton Str.
North Street
John Street
Church Str.
St. John
Bowling Street
Great Smith Str.
GREAT PETER STREET
TOTHILL STREET
NEW TOTHILL STREET
Great Almonry
ORCHARD STREET
Dartmouth Street
PARK STREET
Gt. Queen Str.
Dukes Chapel
Storeys Gate
BROAD WAY

c d

A B C D

23

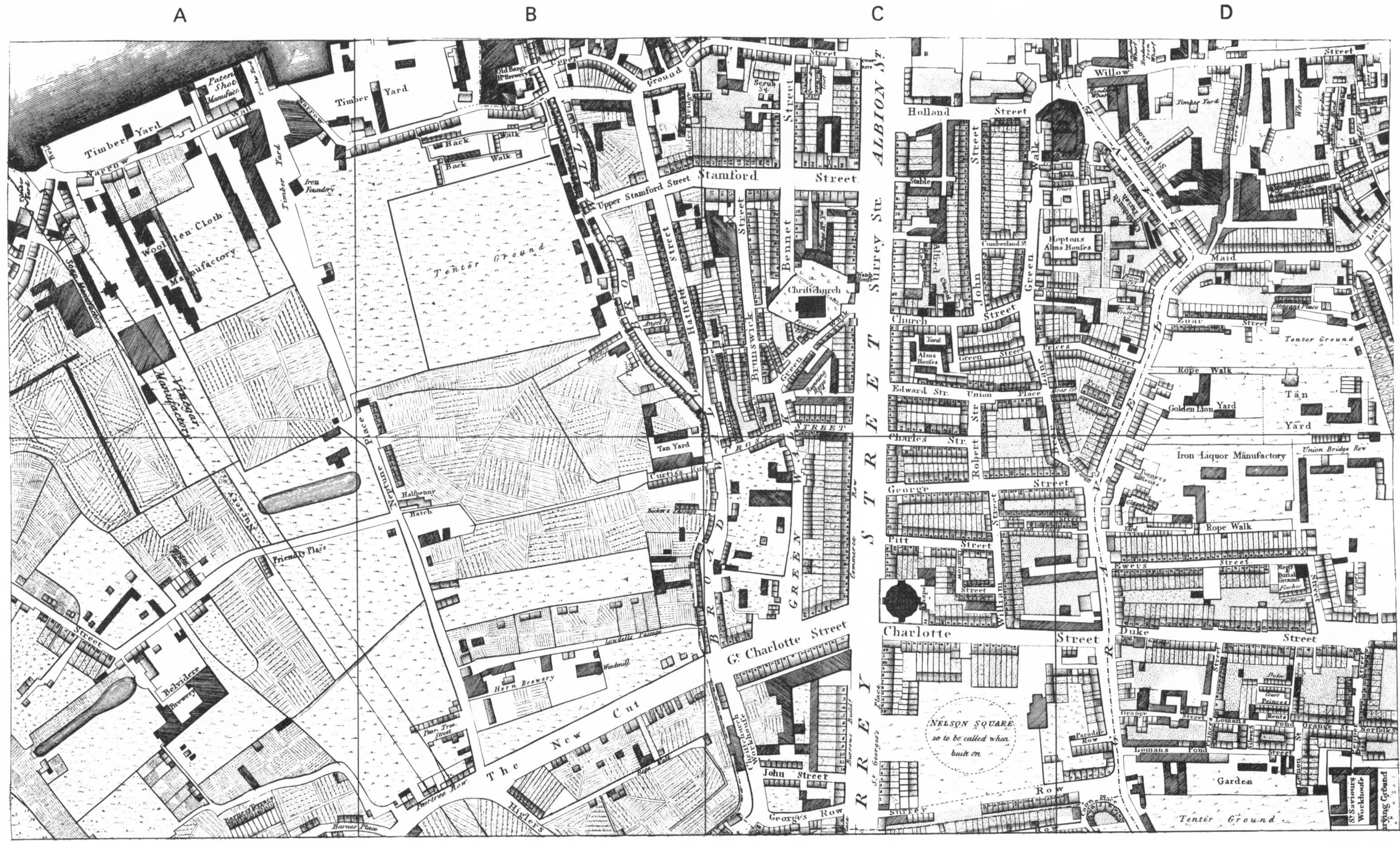

A
B
C
D
a
b
Timber Yard
Narrow Wall
Paten Shot Manufacty
Iron Foundery
Woollen Cloth Manufactory
Vinegar Manufactory
Tenter Ground
Back Walk
Upper Stamford Street
Stamford Street
Hatfield Street
Brunswick Street
Bennet Street
Christchurch
Surrey Str.
Albion St.
Holland Street
John Street
Green Walk
Hoptons Alms Houses
Cumberland St.
Church Yard
Alms Houses
Edward Str.
Union Place
Charles Str.
Robert Str.
George Street
Pitt Street
William Street
Charlotte Street
Gt. Charlotte Street
Nelson Square so to be called when built on
Neptune Place
Halfpenny Hatch
Friendly Place
Nursery
Tan Yard
Curtiss Row
Herm Brewery
Windmill
The New Cut
Belvidere Brewery
Pear Tree Street
Partree Row
Barnes Place
Hidlers
John Street
Georges Row
Christchurch Workhouse
Maid Lane
Zoar Street
Tenter Ground
Rope Walk
Golden Lion Yard
Tan Yard
Iron Liquor Manufactory
Union Bridge Row
Duke Street
Ewers Street
Gardens
Tenter Ground
St. Saviours Workhouse
Willow Street
Timber Yard
Wharf

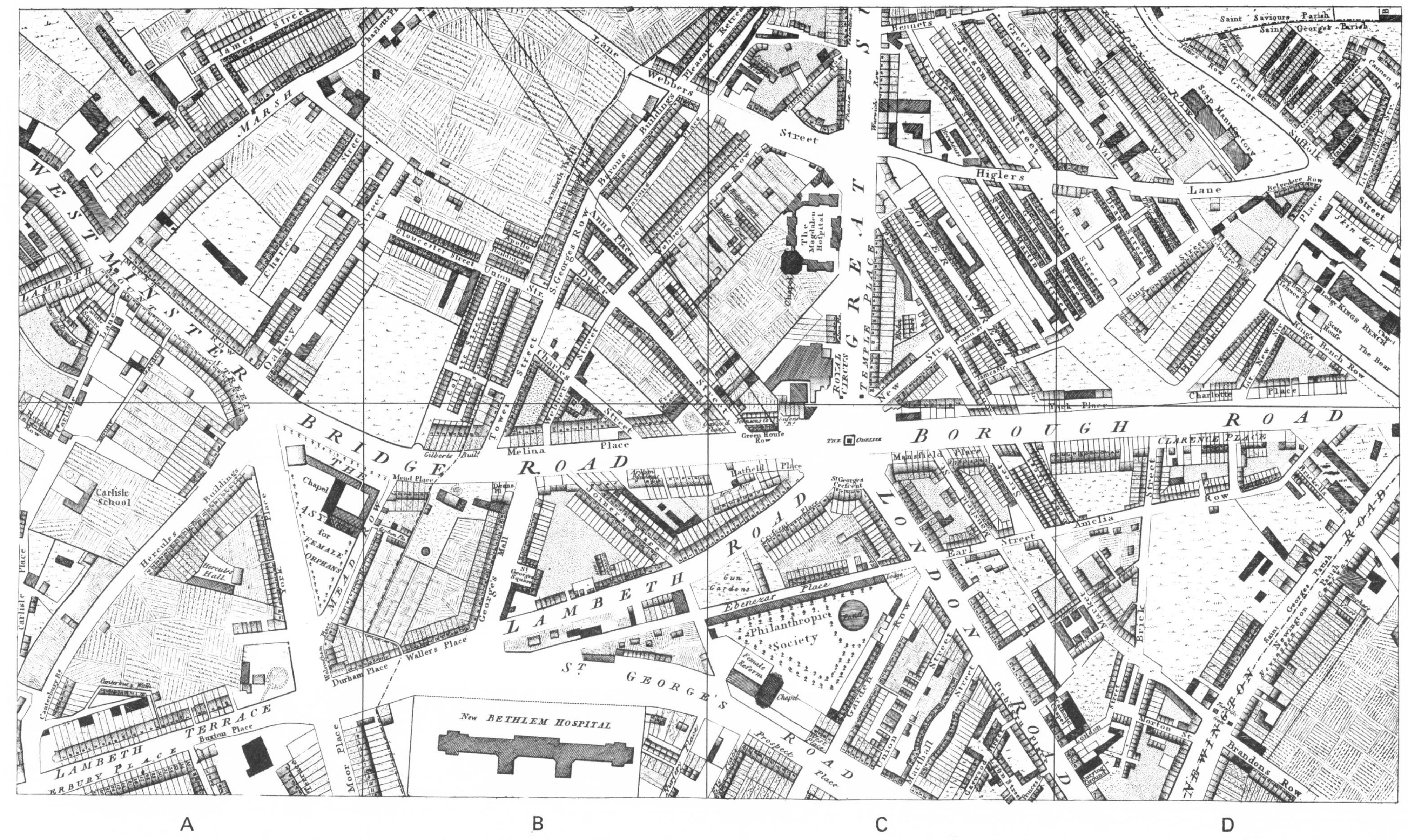
c
d
A
B
C
D
BOROUGH ROAD
LONDON ROAD
ST. GEORGE'S ROAD
LAMBETH ROAD
BRIDGE ROAD
WESTMINSTER STREET
NEWINGTON ROAD
MARSH
TEMPLE PLACE
DOVER STREET
ROYAL CIRCUS
THE OBELISK
The Magdalen Hospital
Chapel
Philanthropic Society
Female Reform
New BETHLEM HOSPITAL
THE ASYLUM for FEMALE ORPHANS
Carlisle School
Hercules Hall
Soap Manufactory
KINGS BENCH
Kings Bench Row
The Bear
Great Suffolk Street
Higlers Lane
Jetsom Street
Green Street
Melina Place
Mansfield Place
Clarence Place
Charles Street
Gloucester Street
Oakley Street
Brandons Row
Moor Place
LAMBETH TERRACE
Buxton Place
Gun Gardens
Ebenezar Place
St. Georges Crescent
Hatfield Place
Wallers Place
Durham Place
Mead Place
Webbers
Pleasant Retreat
Barons Buildings
St. Georges Row
Anns Place
Union Str.
Tower Street
Amelia
Earl Street
Brick
Morton St.
Saint Saviours Parish
Saint Georges Parish
Belvedere Row

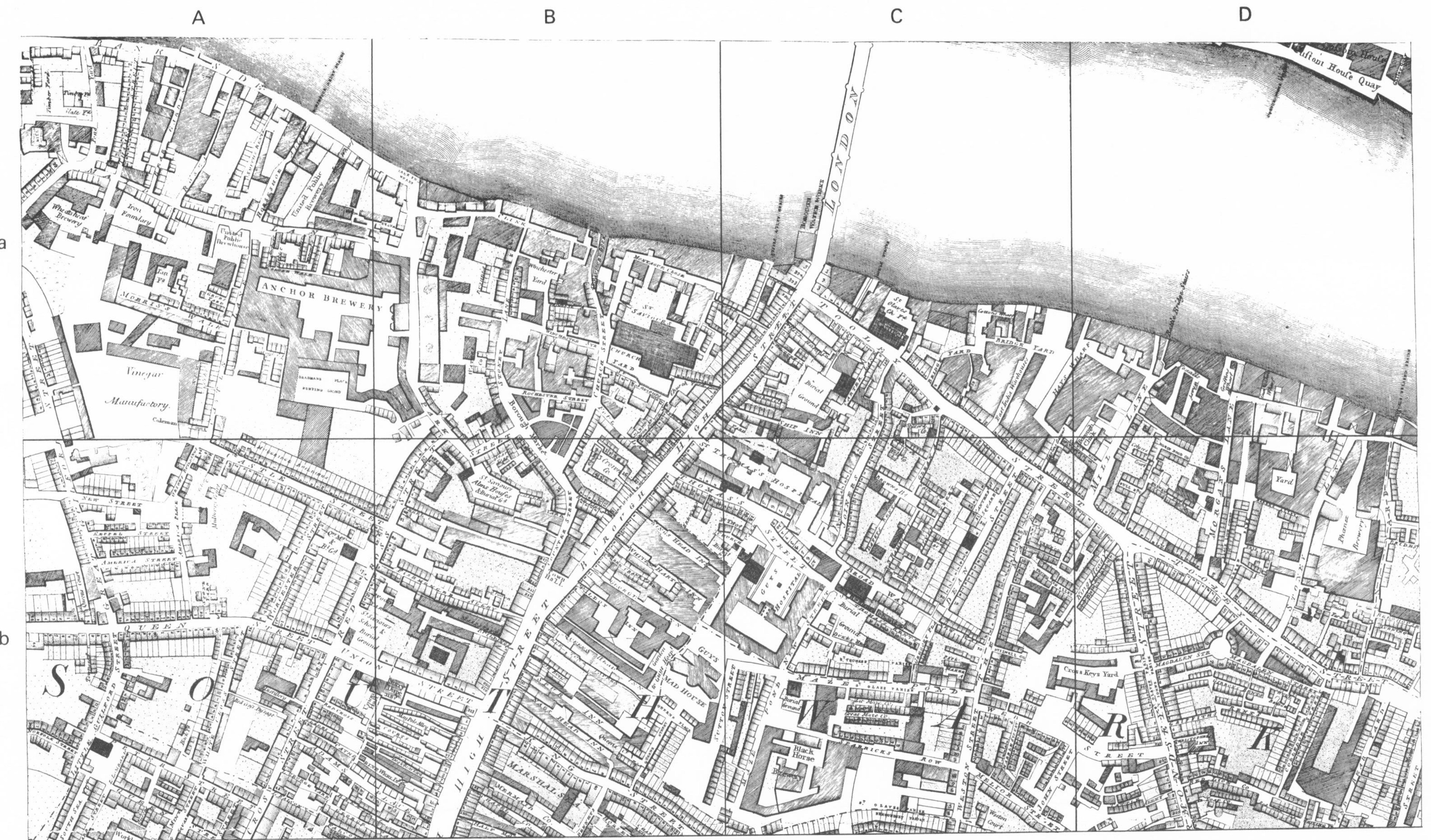
A
B
C
D
a
b
LONDON
ANCHOR BREWERY
Vinegar Manufactory
Iron Foundery
Custom House Quay
St. Saviours
Church Yard
Burial Ground
Guys Hospital
Guys
Mad House
Cross Keys Yard
Black Horse
High Street
Borough Market
Queen Street
Union Street
New Street
America Street
Maze Pond
Tooley Street
Morgans Lane
Mill Lane
Phoenix Brewery
Yard
Bridge Yard
S
O
U
T
H
W
A
R
K

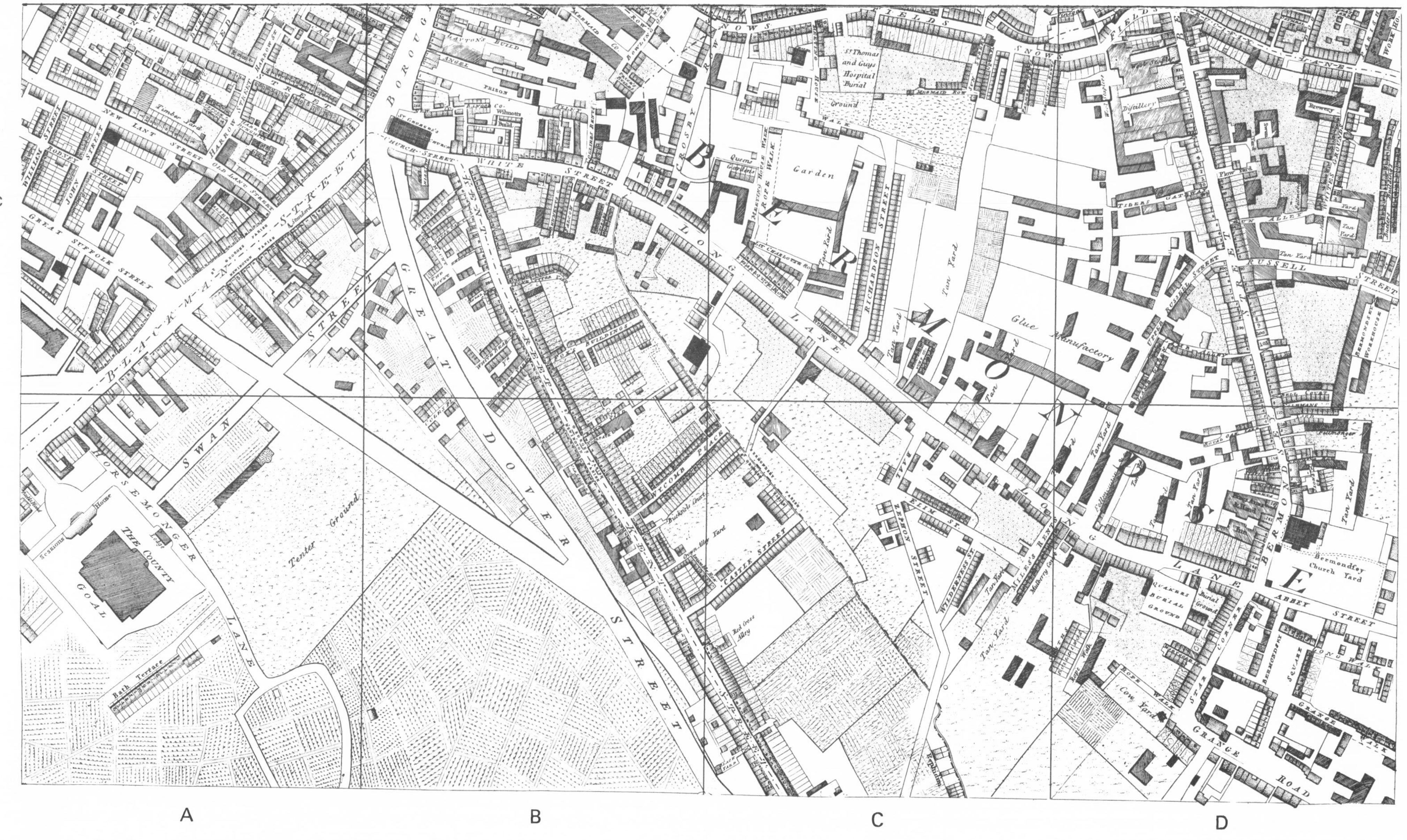
c
d
A
B
C
D
BERMONDSEY
LONG LANE
KENT STREET
GREAT DOVER STREET
HORSEMONGER LANE
THE COUNTY GOAL
Sessions House
SWAN STREET
BLACKMAN STREET
Tenter Ground
Bath Terrace
RICHARDSON STREET
Garden
Glue Manufactory
Tan Yard
Bermondsey Church Yard
Bermondsey Workhouse
ABBEY STREET
GRANGE ROAD
GRANGE WALK
BERMONDSEY SQUARE
Cow Yard
ROPE WALK
STAR CORNER
ZEPHON STREET
ELIM ST.
WILDERNESS ST.
CASTLE STREET
Red Cross Alley
CROSBY ROW
St. Thomas and Guys Hospital Burial Ground
QUAKERS BURIAL GROUND
Queens Gardens
ROPE WALK
RUSSELL STREET
Distillery
Brewery
NEW LANT STREET
OLD LANT STREET
GREAT SUFFOLK STREET
JOHN STREET
WILLIAM STREET
RODNEY STREET
Timber Yard
St. George's Church
CHURCH STREET
WHITE STREET
ANGEL
PRISON
MERMAID ROW
SNOWS FIELDS
BOROUGH

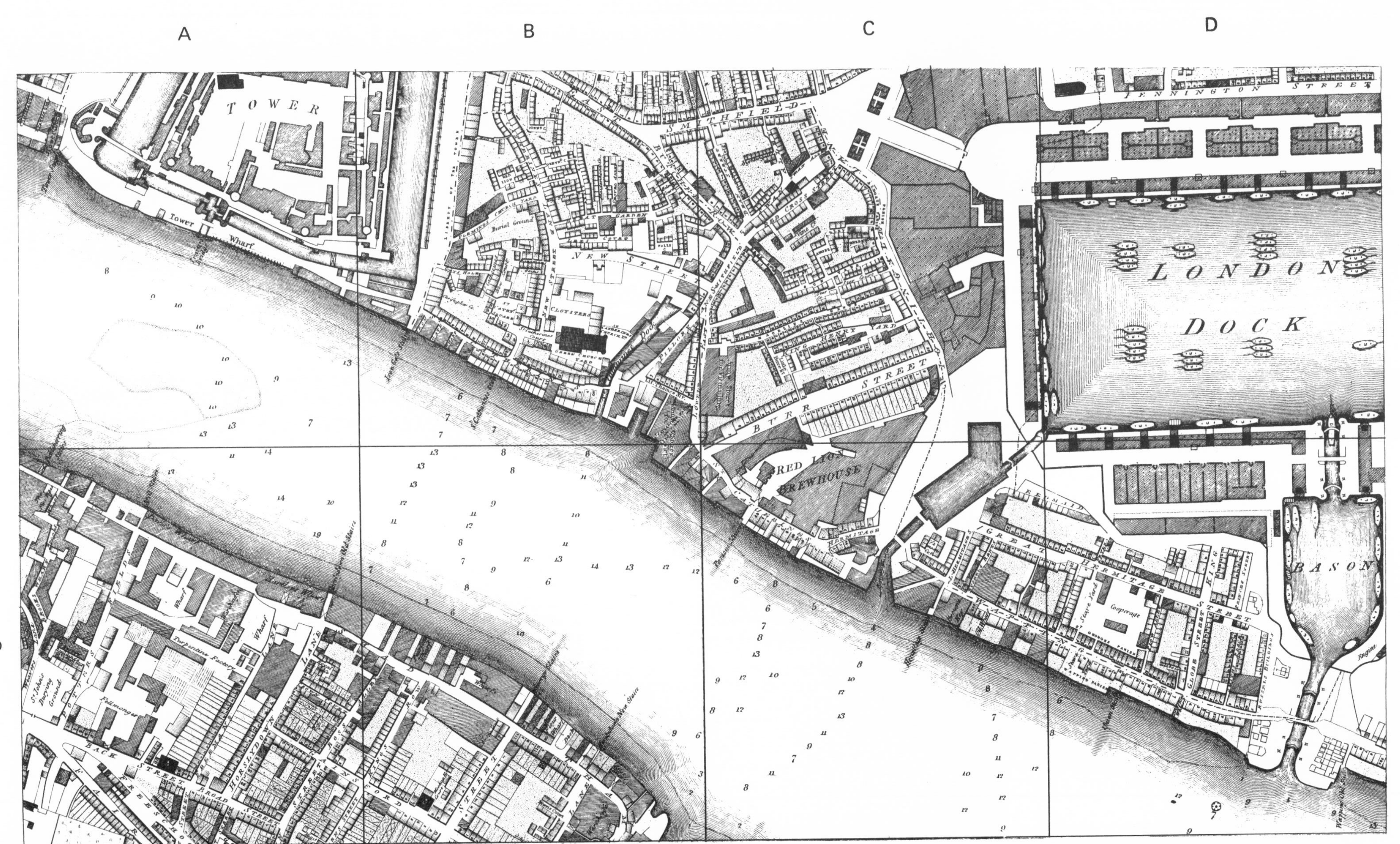
A
B
C
D
a
b
TOWER
Tower Wharf
NEW STREET
BURR STREET
SMITHFIELD
PENNINGTON STREET
LONDON DOCK
RED LION BREWHOUSE
GREAT HERMITAGE
KING STREET
GLOBE STREET
Cooperage
Stave Yard
BASON
Turpentine Factory
Wharf
HORSLYDOWN
BACK STREET
BROAD STREET
St Johns Burying Ground
Burial Ground

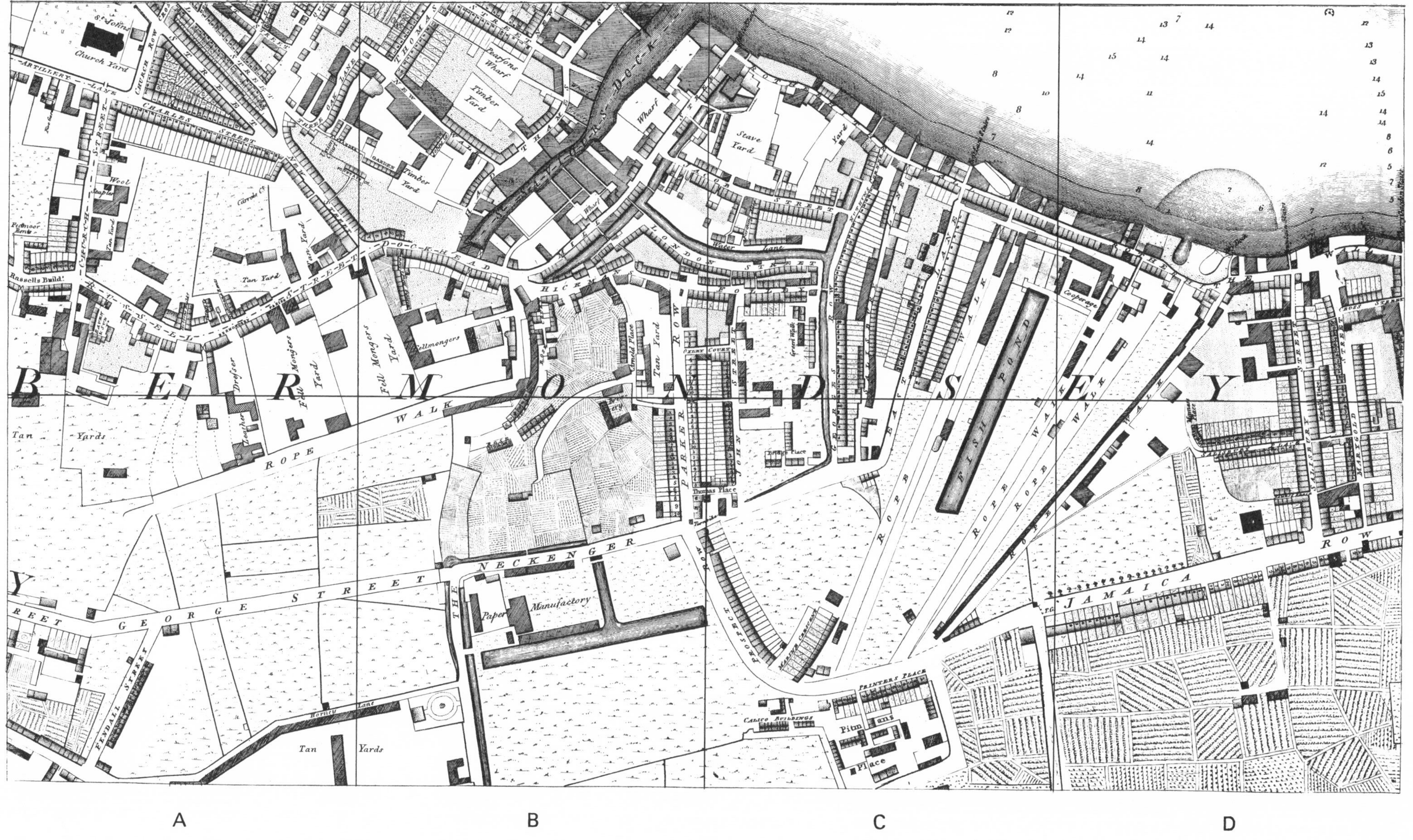
BERMONDSEY
St. John's
Church Yard
CHURCH ROW
ARTILLERY LANE
CHARLES STREET
CHURCH STREET
Rassells Build.
Wool Staplers
Tan Yard
Tan Yards
Fell Mongers Yard
Fellmongers
Leather Dresser
Pearsons Wharf
Timber Yard
Wharf
Stave Yard
Yard
THOMAS STREET
NEW STREET
DOCK HEAD
HICKMANS FOLLY
LONDON STREET
Water Lane
PARKER ROW
JOHN STREET
Thomas Place
Green Walk
GEORGES ROW
EAST LANE
FISH POND
ROPE WALK
Cooperage
JAMAICA ROW
MARYGOLD STREET
SALISBURY STREET
THE NECKENGER
GEORGE STREET
Paper Manufactory
PROSPECT ROW
PRINTERS PLACE
CALICO BUILDINGS
Pitts Place
FENDALL STREET
Horney Lane
c
d
A
B
C
D
26

27
A
B
C
D
a
b
Pennington Street
Keppel Street
Gravel Lane
Broad Str
Worcester Str
Charles St.
Johnson Str
Tench Street
Bird Str
Church Str
Wapping
Farmer Street
Milk Yard
Store House
Shadwell Dock
Lower Turning
Cinnamon Street
Brewhouse Lane
New Market Str
Woolcombes Yard
Halfpenny Hatch to Deptford
Draw Bridge
Wharf
T H E
G R A N D S
I S L A N
O U T

c
d
A
B
C
D
R O T H E R H
Rotherhithe Church Yard
Timber Yard
Burial Ground
PRINCES STREET
Neptune Str.
ADAM STREET
ALBION STREET
New Street
Kennings Buildings
CLARENCE STREET
YORK STREET
Regent Street
Maling Place
Morrison Str.
Hawley Place
UPPER CLARENCE STREET
KINGS ROAD
Kings Row
PARADISE STREET
PARADISE ROW
LUCAS STR.
Mill Pond Br.
Mill Pond Street
Calanders Gardens
DEPTFORD Lower ROAD
Bedford Place
Rope Walk
ER DOCK

A
B
C
D
a
b
R
I
V
E
R
ROPE MAKERS FIELDS
LIMEHOUSE CAUSEWAY
Park Row
Phoebe St.
Timber Yard
GILL STREET
PARK STREET
Rope & Sail Cloth Manufactory
LIMEKILN DOCK
YARD
Limehouse Hole
Dry Dock
Dry Dock
Dry Dock
Dry Dock
Entrance to the West India
ROTHERHITHE
Timber Yd
Essex Place
Lavender Lane
YARD
YARD
YARD
Cuckolds' Point
Garden
Ground
Towing
Path
URRY
BO

c
d
COMMERCIAL DOCK
No. 5. 13¼ Acres.
Foot Bridge
COMMERCIAL DOCK
No. 4. 9 Acres.
GRAND SURRY INNER DOCK
NDING YARDS AND QUAYS
COW LANE
Rope
LOWER
Brewery
Wharf
STREET
TRINITY
Wharf
STREET
TRINITY
Mr. WELLS'S YARD
Swing Bridge
ROAD
BONDING
Buckley Row
YORK STREET
STREET
STREET
Canal Iron Works
Ord Street
Varnish Manufactory
Oil
DEPTFORD AND GREENWICH ROAD
Mill Wall Stairs
Iron Foundry
Wind Mill
A
B
C
D
c
d

29

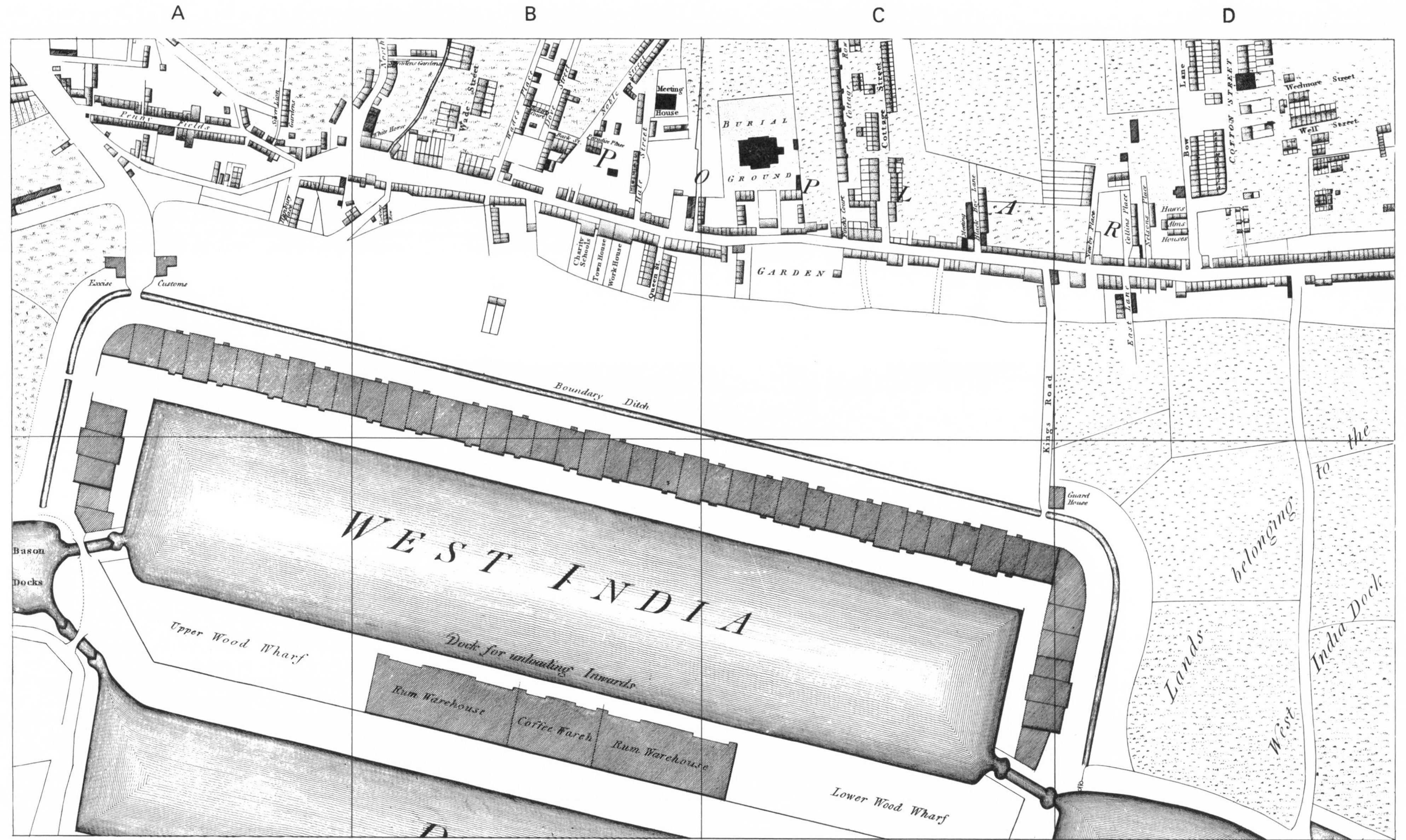
A
B
C
D
a
b
WEST INDIA
Dock for unloading Inwards
Upper Wood Wharf
Lower Wood Wharf
Rum Warehouse
Coffee Wareh
Rum Warehouse
Boundary Ditch
Kings Road
Guard House
Lands belonging to the West India Dock
BURIAL GROUND
GARDEN
Meeting House
Work House
Town House
Charity Schools
Queen St
Cottage Street
Cotton Street
Bow Lane
East Lane
Customs
Excise
Bason Docks
P O P L A R
Wade Street
Well Street
Wetmore Street

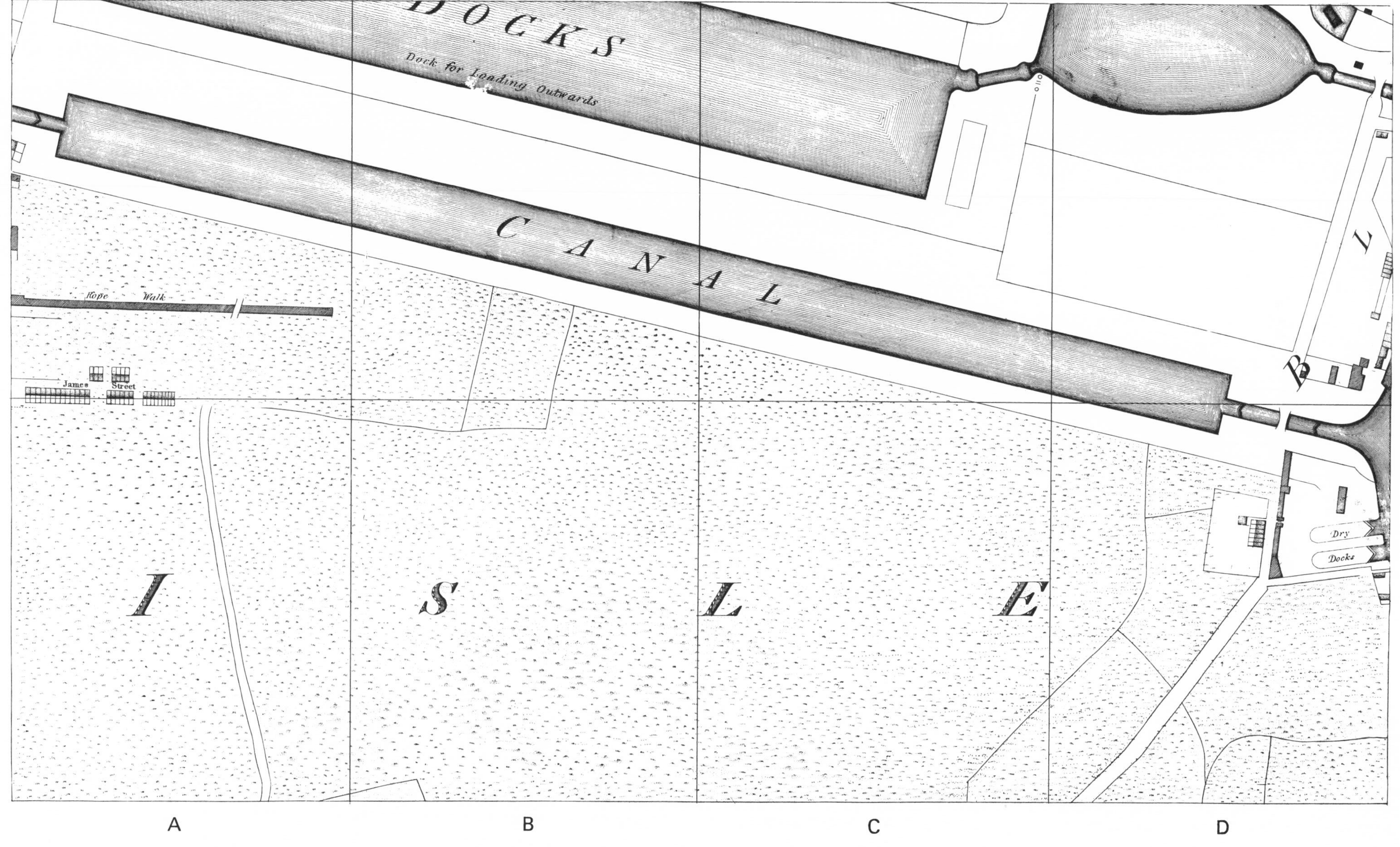
DOCKS
Dock for Loading Outwards
CANAL
Rope Walk
James Street
Dry Docks
ISLE
A
B
C
D
c
d

A
B
C
D
a
b
EAST
Dock for unloading inwards
Waggon Shed
DOCKS
Dock for Loading Outwards
Entrance Bason
Engine
Dock Masters Ho.
Quay
Cooperage
Orchard House
Trinity Bouy House
Bow Creek
Old Dock
Naval Row
Robin Hood Lane
White Hart Place
Ship Alley
Rope Walk
Rope Walk
Rope Walk
Causeway
Blackwall
Blackwall Stairs
Rock

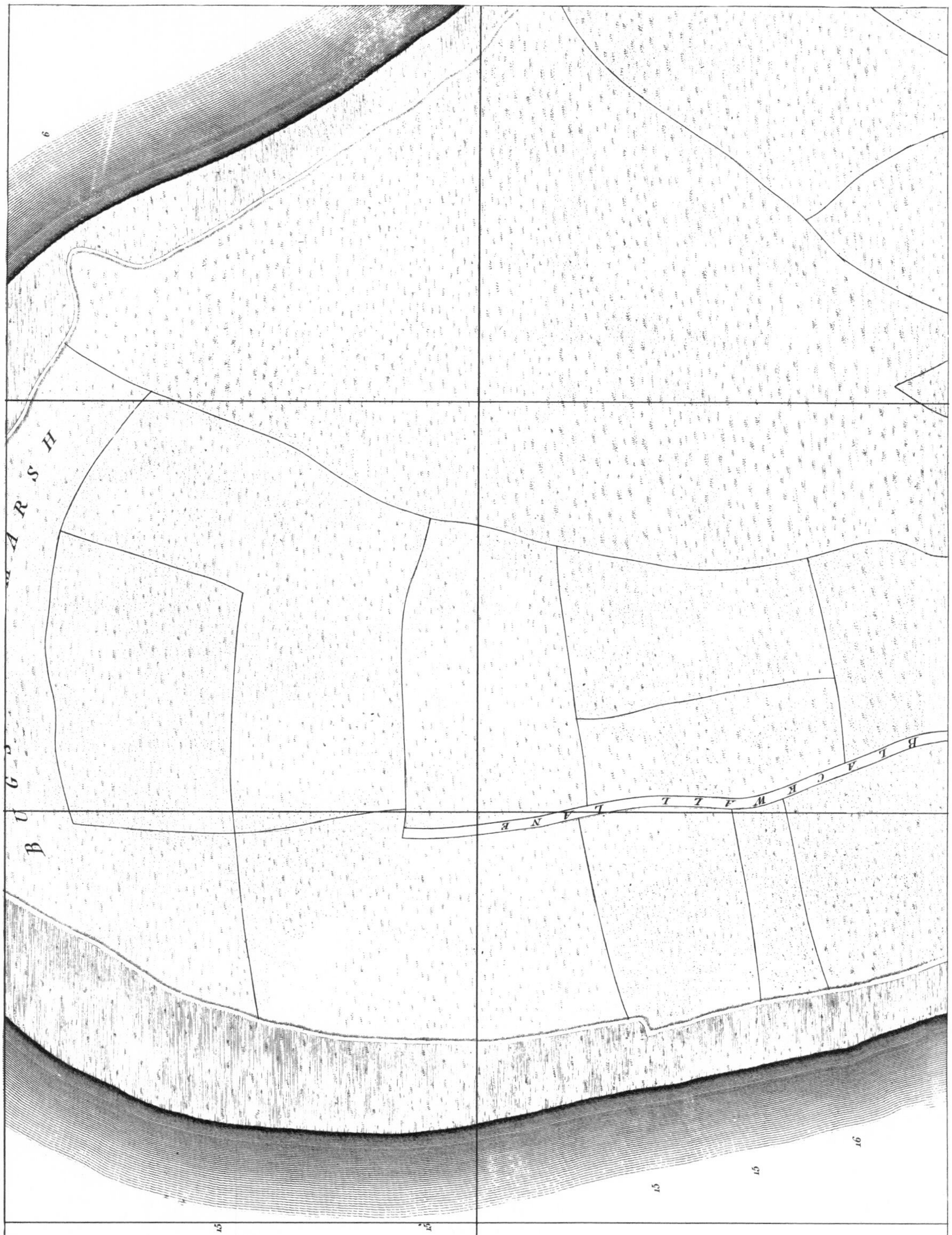

BUGS[illegible] MARSH

BLACKWALL LANE

REACH

c

d

A

B

C

D

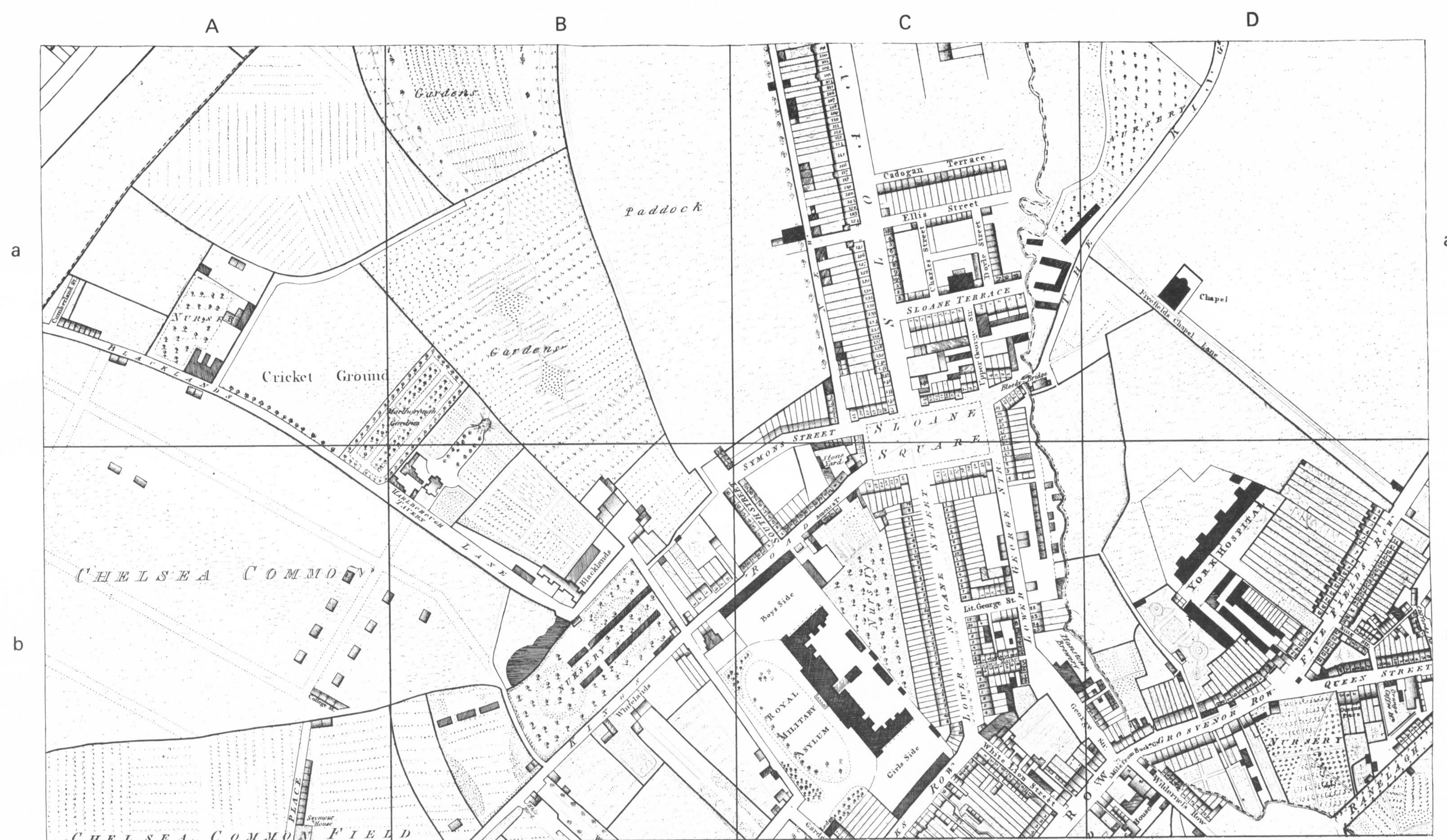
31
A
B
C
D
a
b
Gardens
Paddock
Gardens
Cricket Ground
Marlborough Gardens
Marlborough Tavern
BLACKLANDS
LANE
Blacklands
NURSERY
Whitelands
CHELSEA COMMON
CHELSEA COMMON FIELD
PLACE
Seymour House
Cadogan Terrace
Ellis Street
Charles Street
Doyle Street
SLOANE TERRACE
Upper George St.
Bloody Bridge
SLOANE SQUARE
SYMONS STREET
Stone Yard
SOUTH STREET
ROAD
Nursery
Boys Side
ROYAL MILITARY ASYLUM
Girls Side
LOWER SLOANE STREET
LOWER GEORGE STR.
Lt. George St.
White Lion Street
Hanstown Brewery
George St.
GROSVENOR ROW
Wilderness Row
YORK HOSPITAL
FIVE FIELDS ROW
QUEEN STREET
NURSERY
RANELAGH
Fivefields Chapel Lane
Chapel

CHELSEA
Botanic Garden
Swan Walk
Timber Yard
Chapel
Drying Ground
Stable Yard
Gardens
Kitchen Garden
Hospital Garden
Canal
Meadow
Governors Gardens
Terrace
Osier Beds
Smith Street
Little Smith Street
Durham Place
Greens Row
Franklins Row
Jews Hospital Burying Ground
Jubilee
Manor Terrace
Manor Row
Manor Buildings
Manor Street
Cheyne Walk
Paradise Row
Garden Ground
Paddock
Winchester House
A
B
C
D
c
d

31

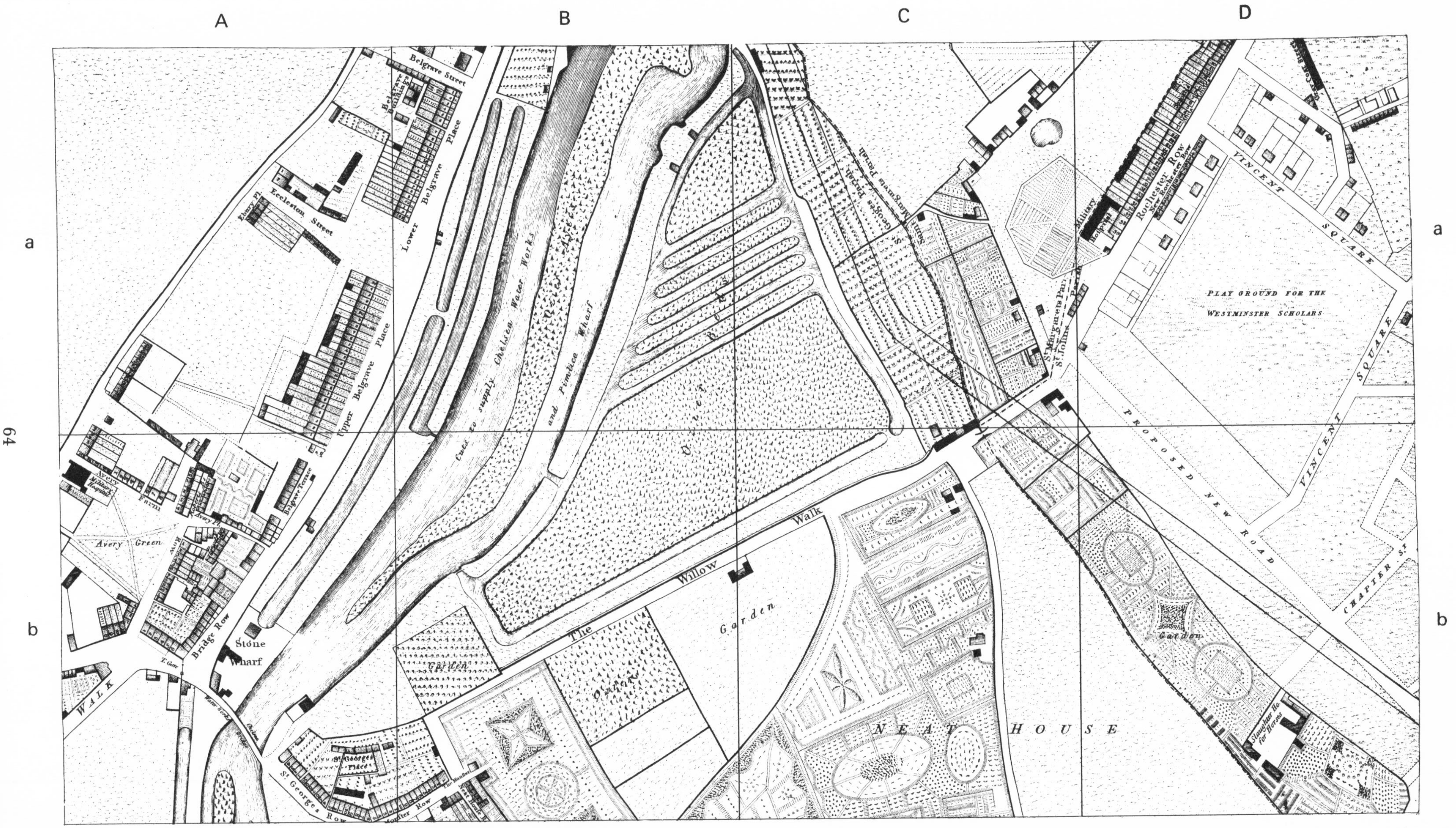
A
B
C
D
a
b
Belgrave Street
Belgrave Buildings
Lower Belgrave Place
Ebury Pl.
Eccleston Street
Upper Belgrave Place
Belgrave Terrace
Cut to supply Chelsea Water Works
and Pimlico Wharf
Avery Farm
Avery Green
Bridge Row
Stone Wharf
Walk
The Willow Walk
Garden
Neat House
St. Georges Place
St. Georges Row
St. Georges Parish
St. Margarets Parish
St. Johns Parish
Military Hospital
Rochester Row
New Rochester Row
Vincent Square
Play Ground for the Westminster Scholars
Proposed New Road
Chapter St.
Slaughter Ho. for Horses

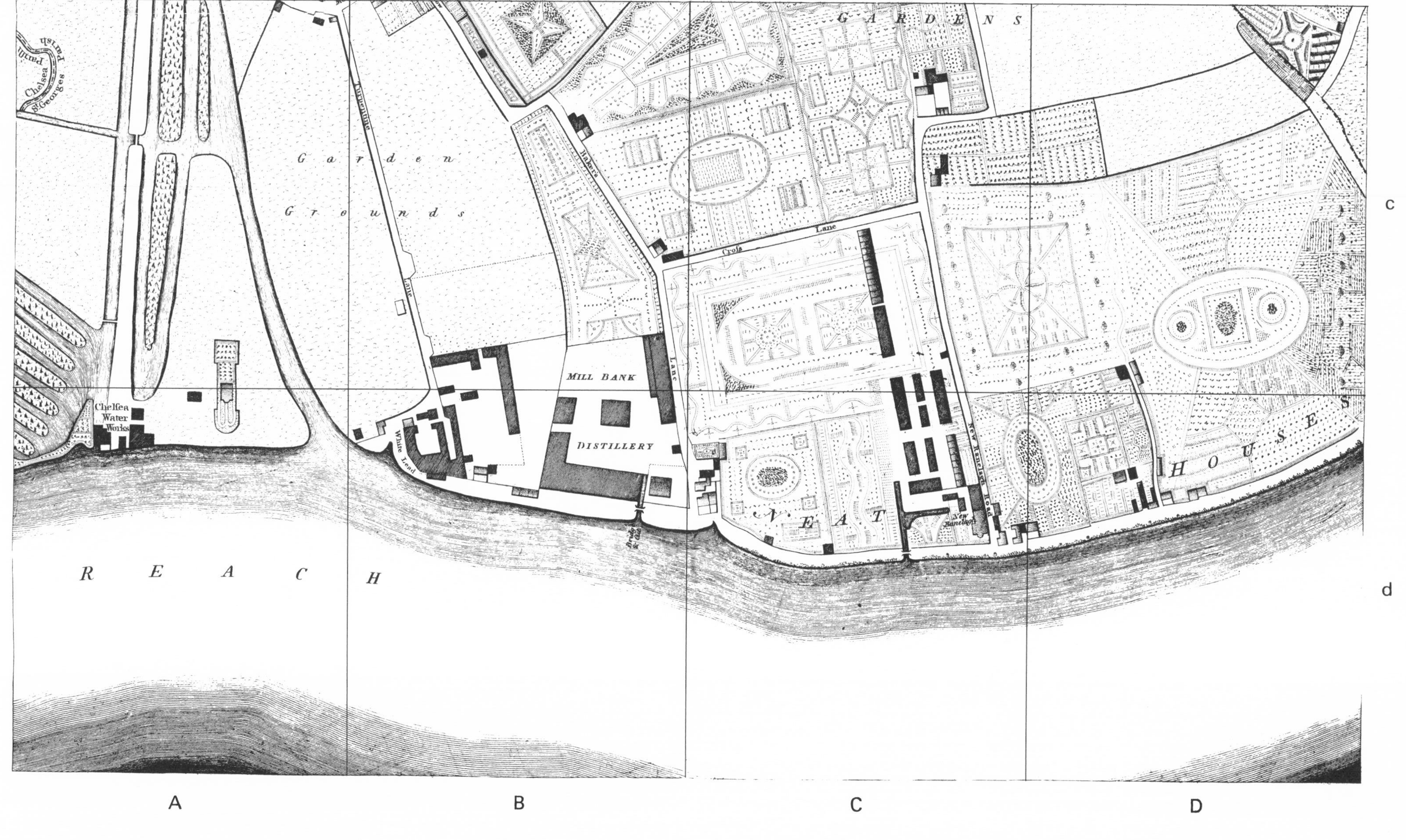
Chelsea Parish
St Georges Parish
Chelsea Water Works
Garden Grounds
Turpentine Lane
White Lead
MILL BANK
DISTILLERY
Baker's Lane
Cross Lane
Lane
GARDENS
NEAT HOUSES
New Ranelagh Road
New Ranelagh
REACH
c
d
A
B
C
D
32

33

A
B
C
D
a
b
Medway Street
Allington Str.
Romney Street
VINE STREET
CHURCH Yd.
Masons Yard
Grub St.
FERRY ROAD
MILL BANK ROW
Mr. Coplands Yard
Yard
Grosvenor Street
VINCENT STREET
REGENT STREET
THE NEW PENITENTIARY
Pest Houses
Distillery
E
Lambeth Rectory House
Dolly Court
Lambeth Palace
Stable Yard
Lambeth Church Yard
Lawn
CHURCH STREET
PRATT STREET
Berkeley Street
Ferry Street
PARADISE ROW
Wind Mill
Harpurs Walk
Bear Yard
Burial Ground
B
Pond
Mustard Manufactory
BROAD STREET
Lambeth Butts
WORKHOUSE LANE
Lambeth Work House
King Street
TYERS
Andersons Street
WOOD STREET
BARRETT STREET
Margaret Str.
Gloucester Street
A

c
d
A
B
C
D
VAUXHALL BRIDGE
Timber Yard
Thomas Bank Wharf
GLASSHOUSE STREET
George Street
Intended Brick Field
VAUXHALL SQUARE
VAUXHALL ROW
VAUXHALL WALK
VAUXHALL GARDENS
Vinegar Manufactory
Vinegar Yard
Cumberland Gardens
VAUXHALL
New Bridge Street
KENNINGTON LANE
KENNINGTON PLACE
DEVONSHIRE PLAC
VAUXHALL STREET
ROGERS STREET
New Street
SOUTH LON
WATER WOR
SOUTH LAMBETH
VAUXHALL PLACE
The Retreat
The Lawn
Belmont House
Kingston Road
Timber Yard
Road from Battersea
HAMLET OF NINE ELMS
KENNINGTON

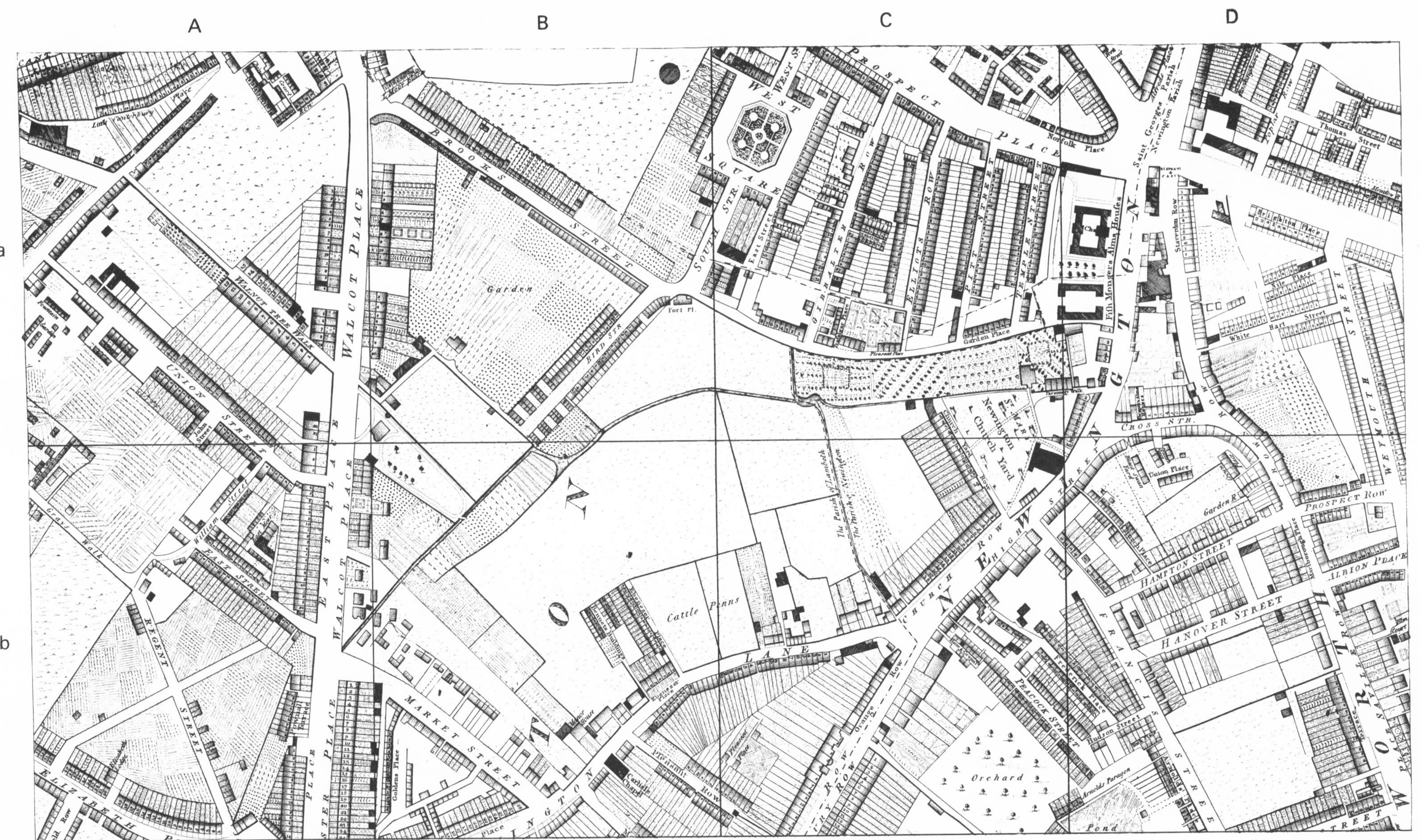
A
B
C
D
a
b
WALCOT PLACE
EAST PLACE
BROOKS STREET
WEST SQUARE
SOUTH STR.
PROSPECT PLACE
Norfolk Place
TEMPLE STREET
PITT STREET
ELLIOTS ROW
GIBRALTER ROW
East Street
Garden Place
Pleasant Place
Fort Pl.
BIRD STR
WALNUT TREE WALK
UNION STREET
EAST STREET
William Street
Grays Walk
REGENT STREET
MARKET STREET
Goldens Place
Garden
Fish Mongers Alms Houses
Saint Georges Parish
Newington Parish
Starvdon Row
Brighton Place
Nile Place
White Hart Street
WEYMOUTH STREET
Thomas Street
CROSS STR.
PROSPECT ROW
ALBION PLACE
Union Place
HAMPTON STREET
HANOVER STREET
FRANCIS STREET
PEACOCK STREET
Hudson Street
Arnolds Paragon
Pond
Orchard
St. Mary Newington Church Yard
Church Yard Row
HIGH STREET
CHURCH ROW
The Parish of Lambeth
The Parish of Newington
Cattle Penns
LANE
Orange Row
Pleasant Place
Carlisle Chapel
ELIZABETH

A
B
C
D
c
d
Kennington Common
Princes Square
Pond
Pond
Newington Parish
Lambeth Parish
Kennington Lane
Kennington Row
Kennington Cross
Kennington Green
Clayton Street
Devonshire Street
Park Street
Princes Road
Canterbury Place
Manor House Farm
Francis Str.
Amelia Street
Penton Place
Penton Street
Manor Place
White Hart Row
Cleaver Street
Clayton Place
Newington Place
South Place
New Street
Back Lane
Queens Place
Queens Row
Brooks Place
Marlborough Pla.
Cumberland Row
Harford
May Buildings
Poplar Place
William Street
Bowling Green
Bowling Green Place
from Croydon & Epsom
Newton Terrace
Montpelier Gardens
Garden
Oil of Vitriol Manufactory

34

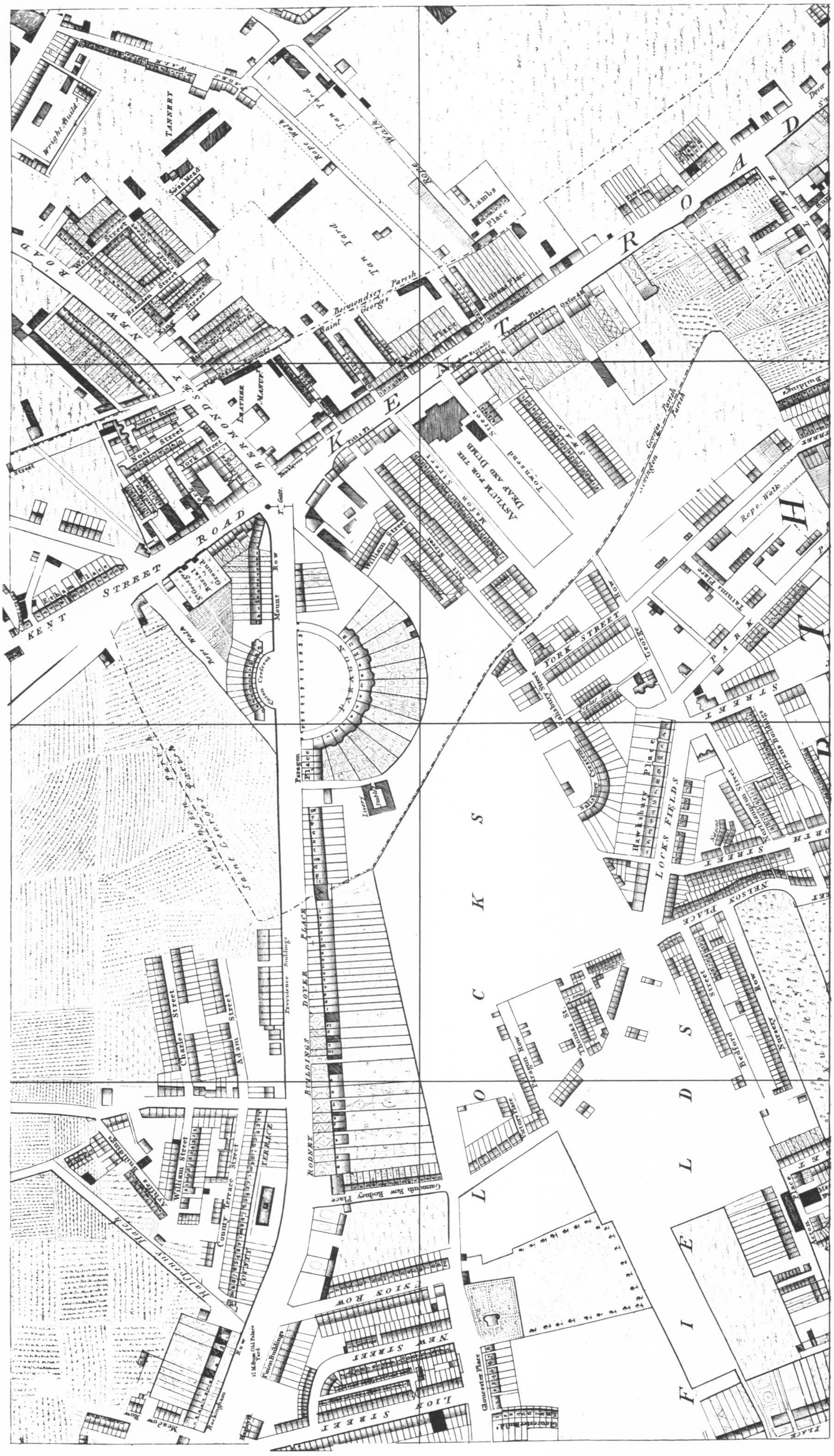
a
b
A
B
C
D
KENT STREET ROAD
BERMONDSEY NEW ROAD
KENT ROAD
ASYLUM FOR THE DEAF AND DUMB
Townsend Street
Mason Street
York Street
Noel Street
Potters Street
Webb Street
Brandon Street
TANNERY
Tan Yard
Rope Walk
Lambs Place
Bermondsey Parish
Saint Georges
Paragon
Mount Row
Union Crescent
Providence Buildings
DOVER PLACE
RODNEY BUILDINGS
Gainsborough Row
Rodney Place
Charles Street
Adam Street
William Street
County Terrace Street
COUNTY TERRACE
Halfpenny Hatch
Meadow Row
Rockingham Row
New Street
Lion Street
Gloucester Place
LOCKS FIELDS
LOCKS FIELDS
Hawkesbury Place
Salisbury Crescent
York Street
George Row
Park Street
Rope Walk
Nelson Place
Bedford Row
Nursery Row
Thomas St.
Lyon Row
Livery Stables
Saint Georges Parish
Newington Parish

c
d
A
B
C
D
WALWORTH
FIELDS
WALWORTH COMMON
APOLLO BUILDINGS
PRIOR PLACE
RICHMOND PLACE
Little Richmond Place
Belgrade Place
Phœnix Street
EAST STREET
TRAFALGAR STREET
George Street
Trafalgar Street
CAMDEN STREET
KING STREET
Cross Street
YORK STREET
NURSERY
SURREY SQUARE
Kings Row
Mount Street
QUEENS ROW
PORTLAND STREET
Portland Place
Charles St.
Providence St.
CHARLOTTE ROW
Walworth Workhouse
Montpelier
T. Gate
Camberwell
NEW ALBANY ROAD
Albany Place
Newington Parish
Camberwell Parish

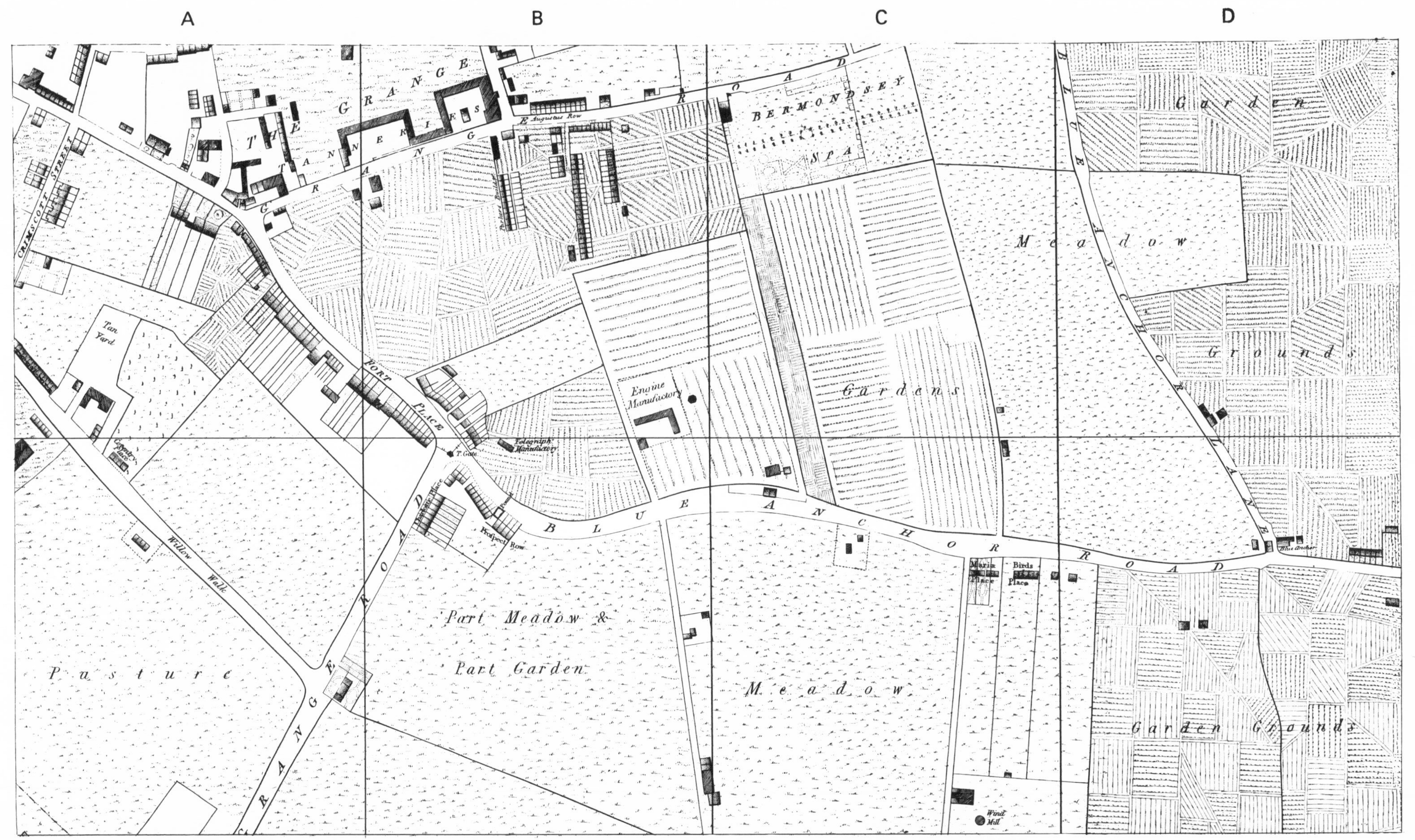
A
B
C
D
a
b
THE GRANGE
TANNERIES
GRANGE ROAD
Augustus Row
BERMONDSEY SPA
CRIMSCOTT STREET
Tan Yard
PORT PLACE
T. Gate
Telegraph Manufactory
Engine Manufactory
Prospect Row
BLUE ANCHOR ROAD
BLUE ANCHOR LANE
Blue Anchor
Maria Place
Birds Place
Wind Mill
Willow Walk
Pasture
Part Meadow &
Part Garden
Meadow
Gardens
Garden Grounds
Garden
Grounds

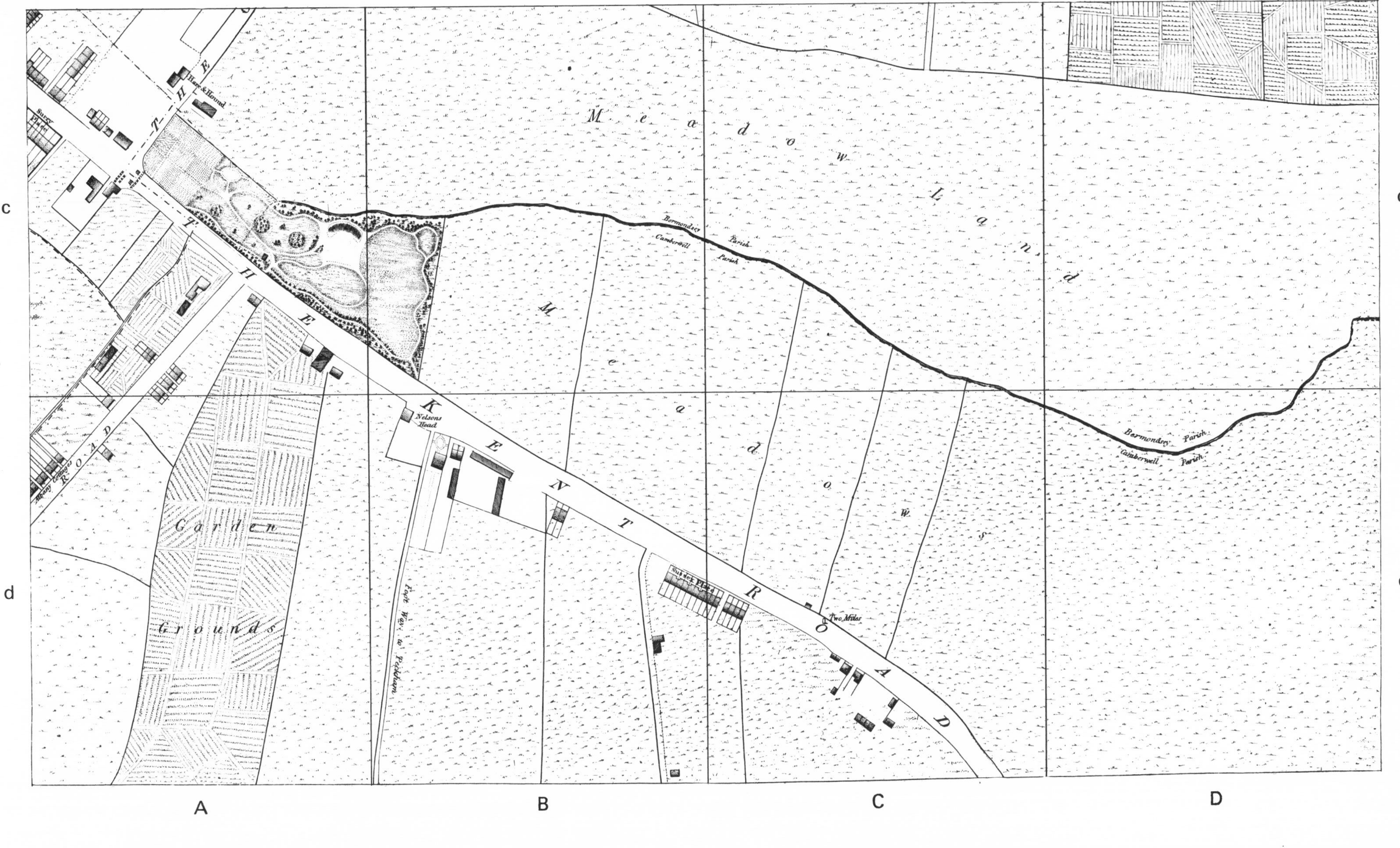
Meadow Land
Bermondsey Parish
Camberwell Parish
Meadows
THE KENT ROAD
Hare & Hound
Surry Place
Nelsons Head
Foot Way to Peckham
Sussex Place
Two Miles
Garden Grounds
c
d
A
B
C
D
36

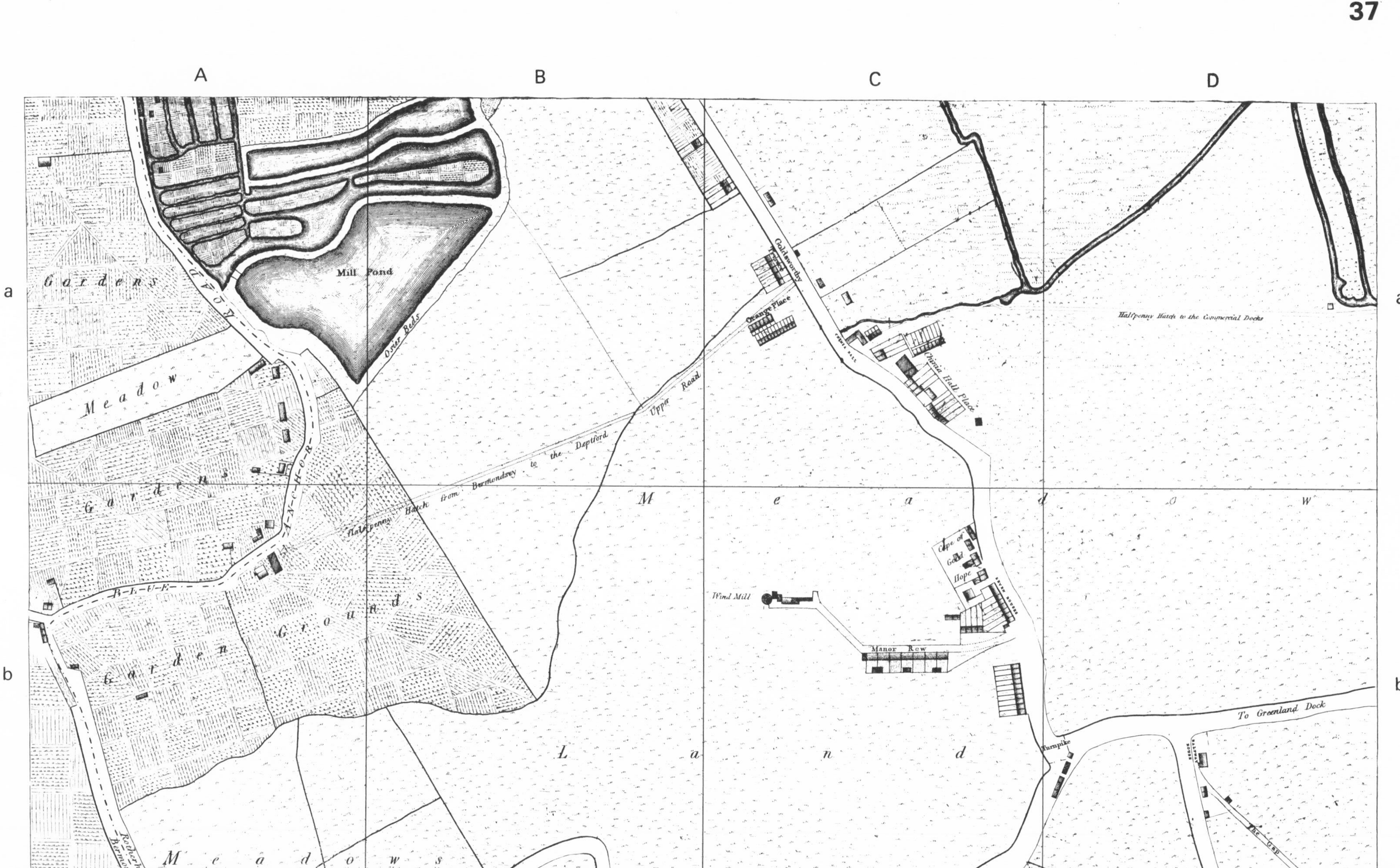
A
B
C
D
a
b
Gardens
Meadow
Gardens
Garden Grounds
Blue Anchor Road
Mill Pond
Osier Beds
Halfpenny Hatch from Bermondsey to the Deptford Upper Road
Orange Place
Goldsworthy
China Hall Place
Halfpenny Hatch to the Commercial Docks
Meadow Land
Cape of Good Hope
Wind Mill
Manor Row
Turnpike
To Greenland Dock
The Gap
Meadows

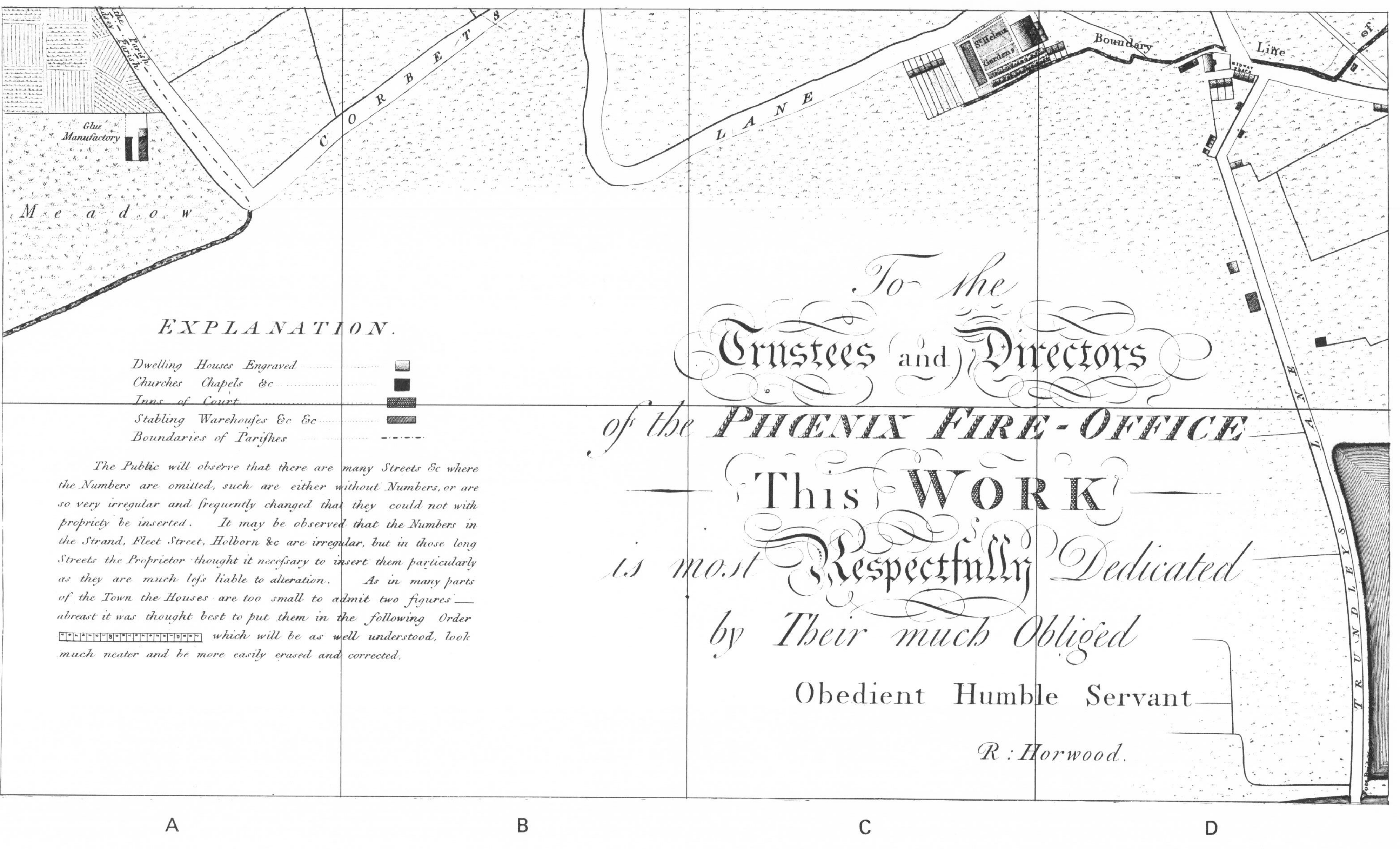

To the Trustees and Directors of the PHŒNIX FIRE-OFFICE — This WORK — is most Respectfully Dedicated by Their much Obliged Obedient Humble Servant

R: Horwood.

EXPLANATION.

Dwelling Houses Engraved	
Churches Chapels &c	
Inns of Court	
Stabling Warehouses &c &c	
Boundaries of Parishes	

The Public will observe that there are many Streets &c where the Numbers are omitted, such are either without Numbers, or are so very irregular and frequently changed that they could not with propriety be inserted. It may be observed that the Numbers in the Strand, Fleet Street, Holborn &c are irregular, but in those long Streets the Proprietor thought it necessary to insert them particularly as they are much less liable to alteration. As in many parts of the Town the Houses are too small to admit two figures — abreast it was thought best to put them in the following Order [sample] which will be as well understood, look much neater and be more easily erased and corrected.

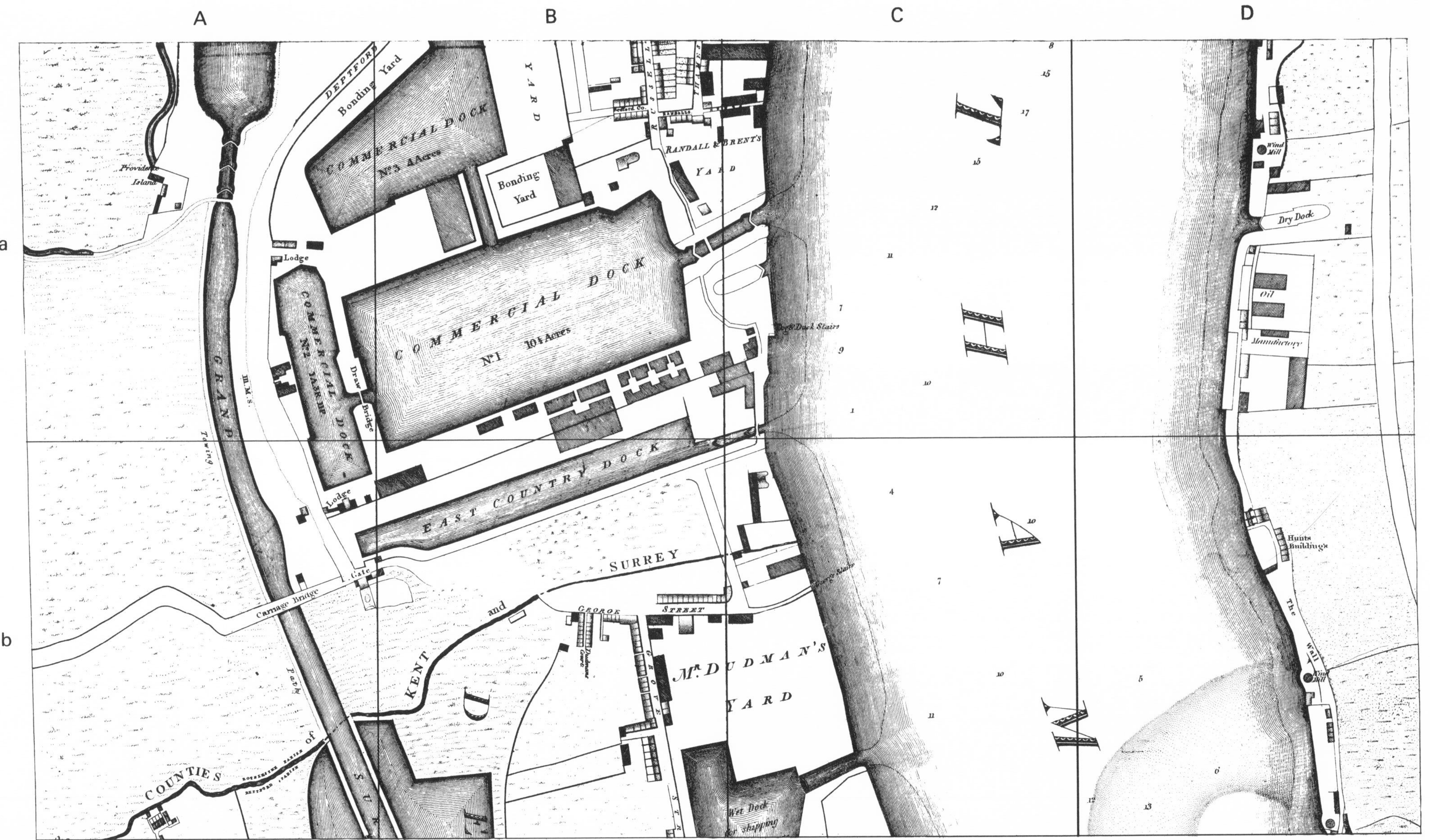
A
B
C
D
a
b
T H A M
DEPTFORD
Bonding Yard
COMMERCIAL DOCK
N.º 3 4 Acres
YARD
Bonding Yard
RANDALL & BRENT'S YARD
Providence Island
Lodge
COMMERCIAL DOCK
N.º 1 10½ Acres
COMMERCIAL DOCK
N.º 2
Draw Bridge
Lodge
EAST COUNTRY DOCK
GRAND
Towing
Path
Gate
Carriage Bridge
SURREY
and
KENT
COUNTIES
GEORGE
STREET
GROVE
Dudmans Court
Mr DUDMAN'S YARD
Wet Dock for shipping
Wind Mill
Dry Dock
Oil
Manufactory
Hunts Buildings
The Wall

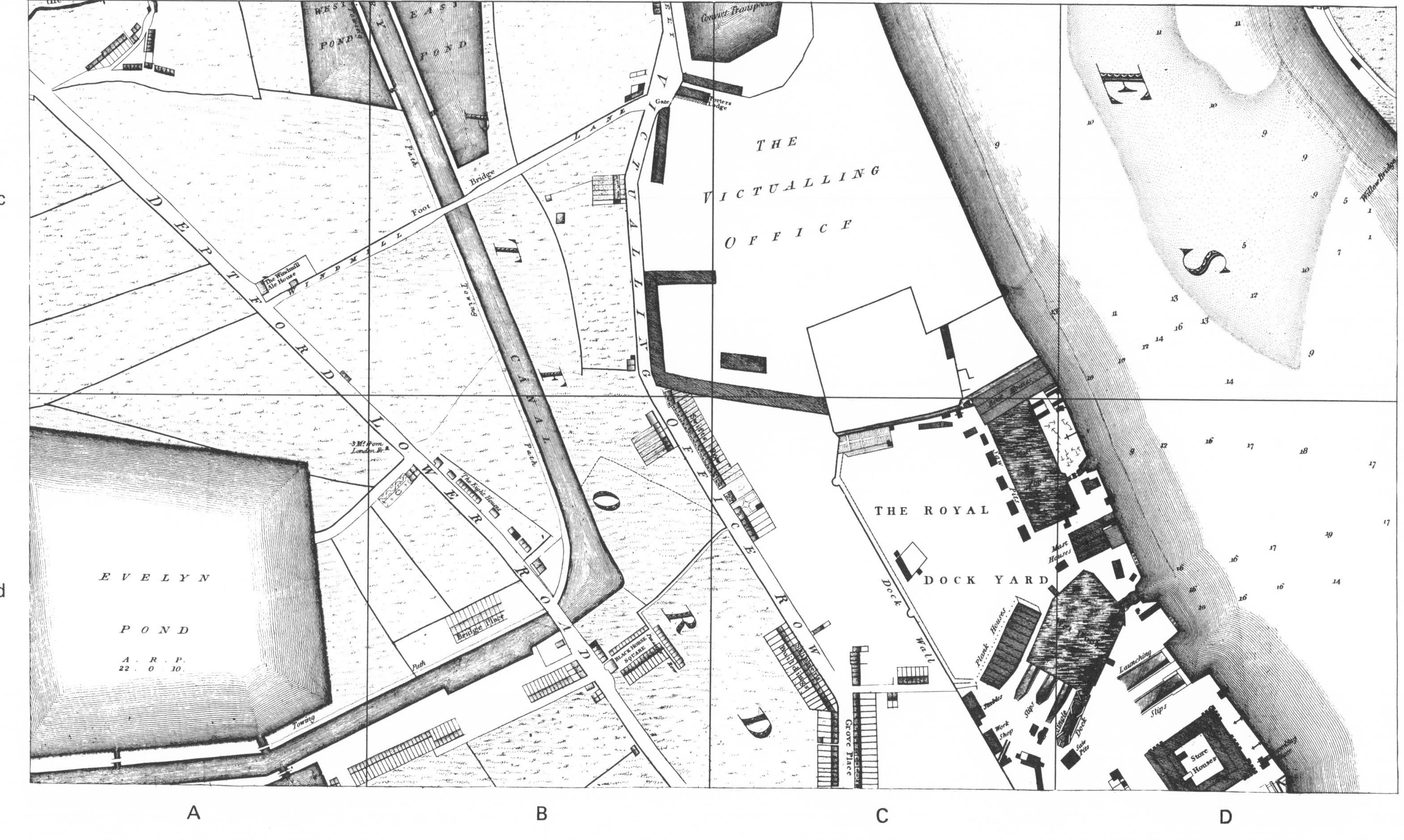
THE VICTUALLING OFFICE
THE ROYAL DOCK YARD
Dock Wall
Grove Place
VICTUALLING OFFICE ROW
DEPTFORD LOWER ROAD
WINDMILL LANE
The Windmill Ale House
Foot Bridge
CANAL
Towing Path
The Eight Houses
Bridge Place
BLACK HORSE SQUARE
3 M. from London Br.
EVELYN POND
A. R. P.
22. 0. 10.
WEST POND
EAST POND
Gate
Porters Lodge
Convict Transport
Plank Houses
Mast Houses
Launching
Slips
Store Houses
Stables
Work Shop
Dock
Saw Pits
Willow Bridge
T F O R D
E S
A
B
C
D
c
d
38

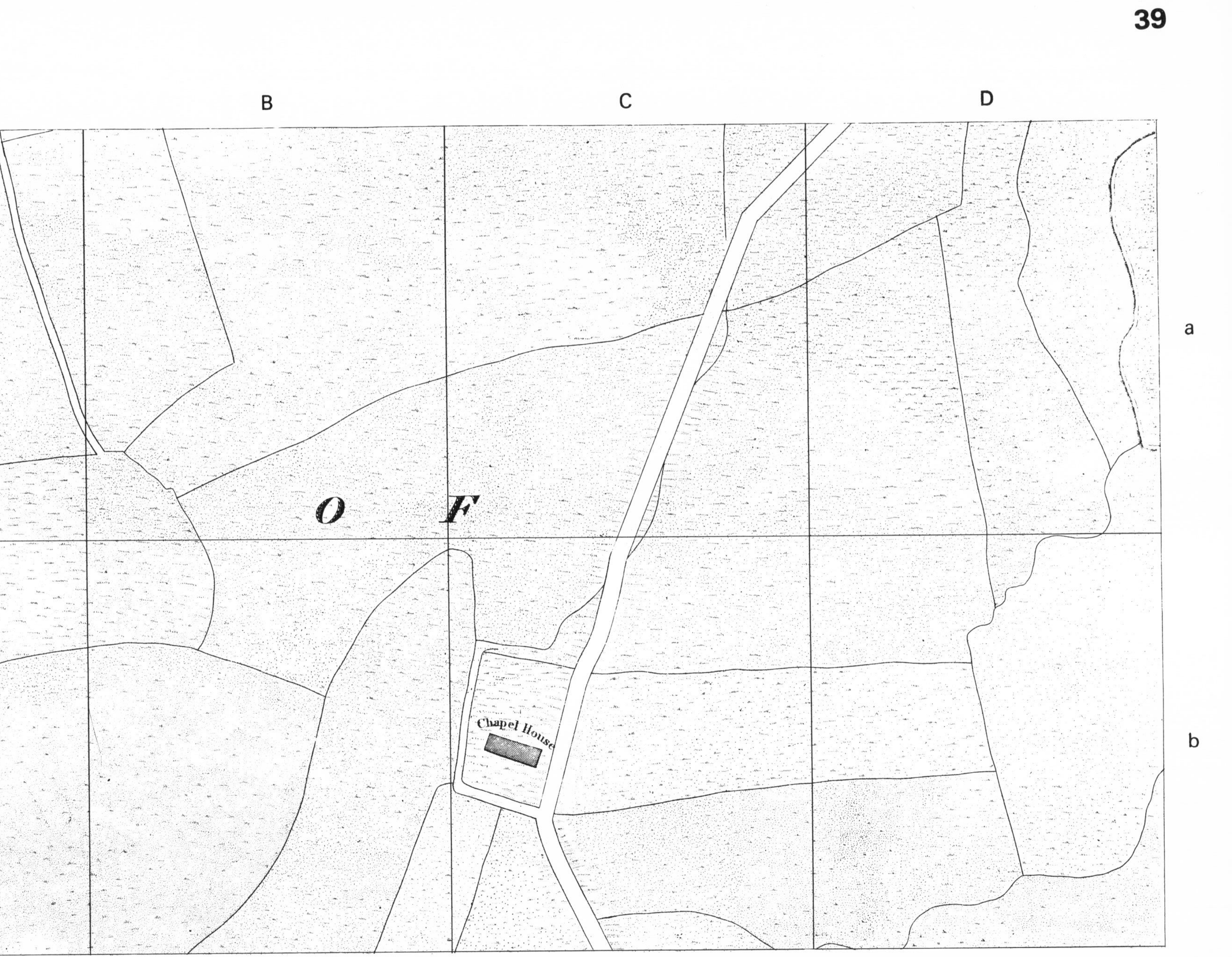
A
B
C
D
a
a
b
b
O F
Chapel House
DEPTFORD AND GREEN

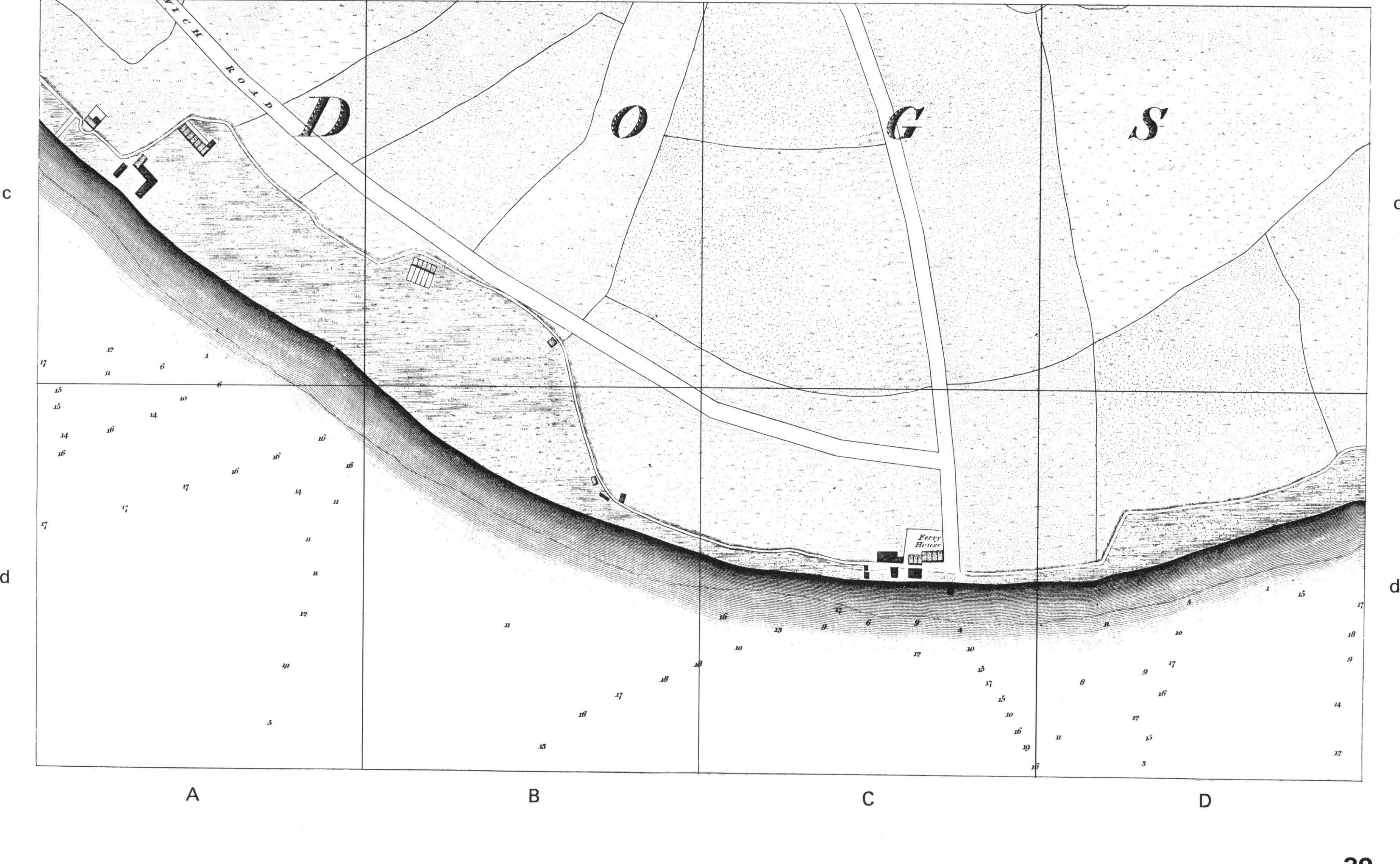
WICH ROAD
D O G S
Ferry House
c
d
A
B
C
D

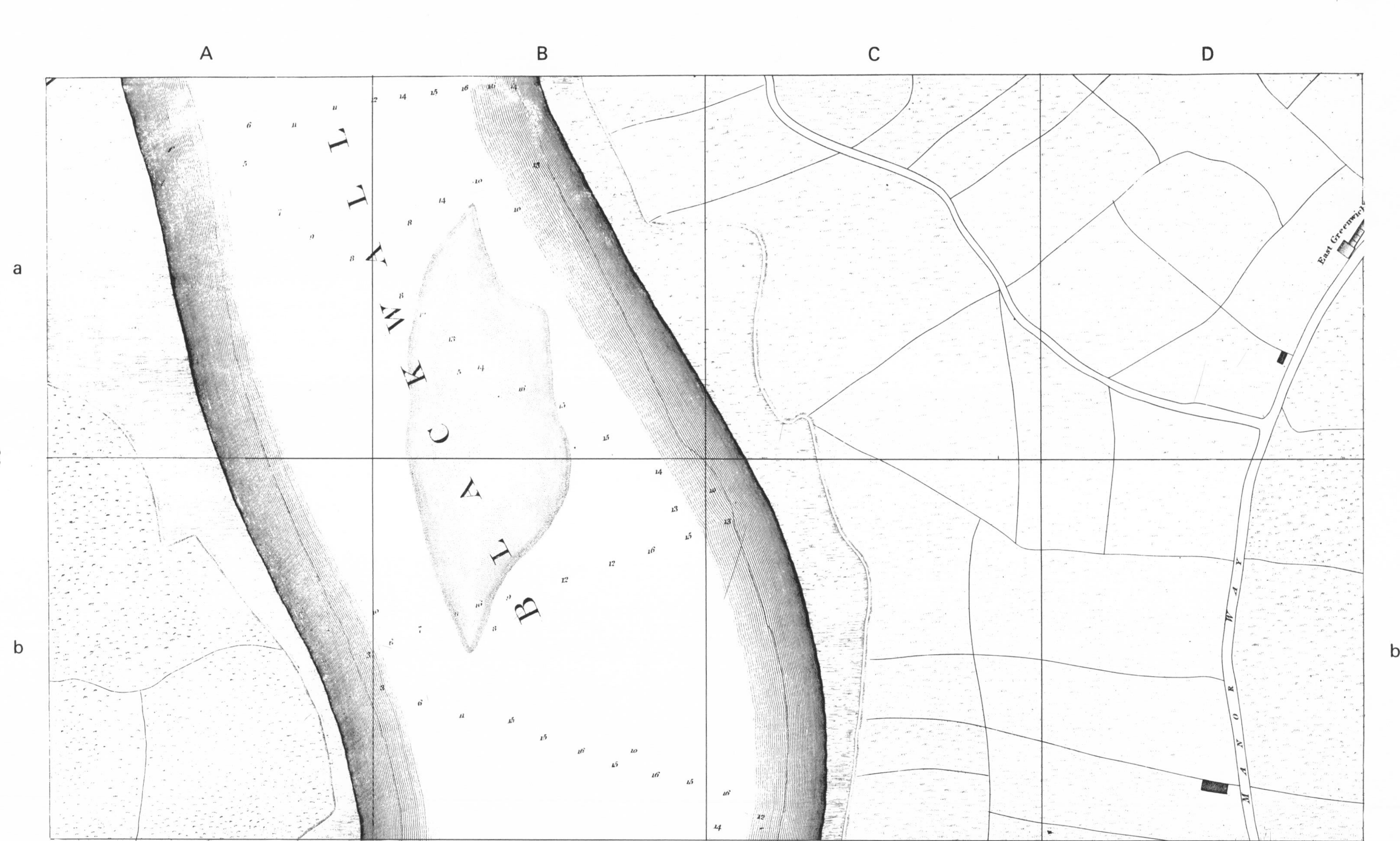
A
B
C
D
a
b
BLACKWALL
MANOR WAY
East Greenwich

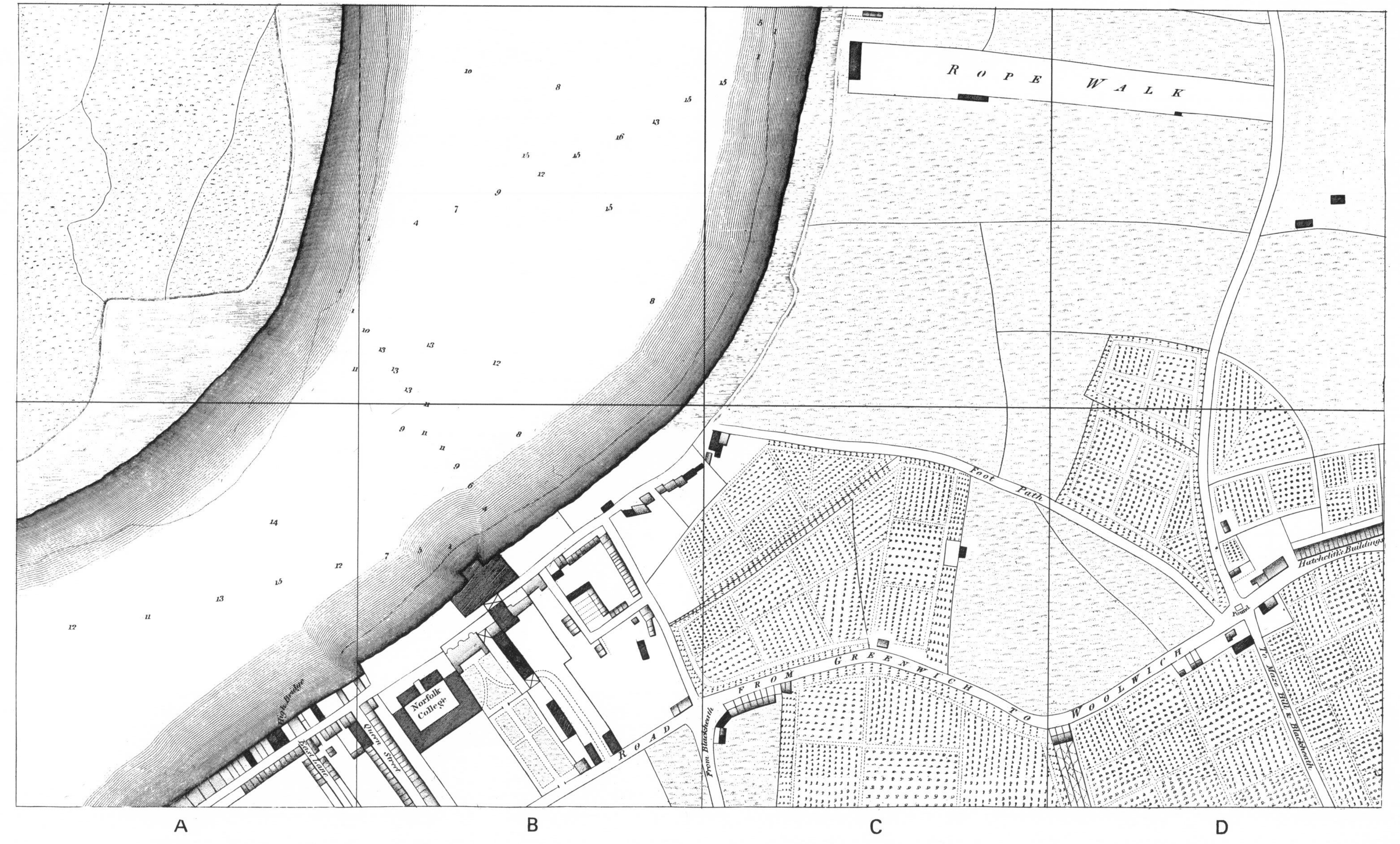
c
d
ROPE WALK
Foot Path
Hatchcliffs Buildings
Pound
FROM GREENWICH TO WOOLWICH
To Maze Hill & Blackheath
From Blackheath
ROAD
Norfolk College
Queen Street
East Lane
High Bridge
A
B
C
D
40

EXPLANATION OF INDEX

The index has been designed for use in conjunction with the key map on pp. 16–17. When the index lists several streets with identical names the required street can often be identified by referring first to the key map. For example, to find the Bennet Street in St. James's one turns to the key map from the four index entries for streets of that name. Entries in 12Da and 24Ca can be eliminated immediately, and one can see that the street in 23Ac must lie south of St. James's Park, leaving only the entry in 22Ca.

Horwood's spelling has been retained even when it differs from that in Lockie[1] or modern usage. In a few cases, where the spelling on the map is unconventional, added entries have been made using Horwood's more usual spelling. Where Horwood's spelling might lead to difficulty in finding an index entry an added entry has been made using the modern form of name. Both types of added entry are marked with an asterisk.

Names preceded by North, South, East, West, Old, New, Great, Little, Lower and Upper, have been inverted to file under the second element, e.g. King St., Little. In a few exceptional cases entry has been made under the first element, e.g. Old Bailey.

The names of churches appearing on the map have been expanded or qualified to differentiate between churches with the same dedication.

Generic terms such as warehouse, rope walk, etc., have been omitted.

J.J.W.

[1] J. Lockie, *Topography of London, or Street Directory*, 2nd edn (London: Sherwood, 1816).

PLACE NAME INDEX

Abbey St. **6Dc**
Abbey St. **25Dd**
Abchurch La. **15 Cd** **15Cc**
Abingdon Bldgs **23Bd**
Abingdon St. **23Bd**
Abingdon St., Little **23Bd**
Acorn Alley **16Aa**
Acorn Ct. **14Bb**
Acton Pl. **35Ab**
Acton St. **3Db**
Adam & Eve Ct. **5Bd**
Adam St. **13Cd**
Adam St. **27Bc** **27Cc**
Adam St. **35Ba**
Adams Ct. **15Cb** **15Cc**
Adams Mews **11Dd** **12Ad**
Adams Mews **11Bb**
Adams Pl. **25Ab** **25Bb**
Adams Pl. **27Bc**
Adams St. **11Bb**
Adams St. **11Db**
Addle Hill **14Dc**
Addle St. **15Ab** **15Bb**
Adelphi Wharf **13Cd**
Admiralty **23Ba**
Aggats Pass. **16Ab**
Air St. **12Dd**
Albans Ct. **15Ab**
Albany **12Cd**
Albany Cottages **36Ad**
Albany New Rd. **35Cd** **35Dd** **36Ad** **36Ac**
Albany Pl. **35Dd**
Albany St. **2Bc** **2Bb**
Albany Ter. **1Dd**
Albermarle St. **4Dd** **4Cd**
Albermarle St. **22Ca** **12Cd** **12Bd**
Albion Pl. **14Cd**
Albion Pl. **17Bc**
Albion Pl. **34Db**
Albion St. **17Bc**
Albion St. **24Ca**
Albion St. **27Bc** **27Cc**
Albions Bldgs **15Aa**
Aldermanbury **15Bb**
Aldermanbury Postern **15Ba**
Aldermans Walk **15Db**
Aldersgate Bldgs **5Ad**
Aldersgate St. **15Ba** **15Aa**
Aldgate Churchyard **16Ac**
Aldgate High St. **16Ac**
Alexander Garden **26Ac** **26Bc**
Alfred Ct. **15Aa**
Alfred Mews **2Dd**
Alfred Pl. **4Ca**
Alfred Pl. **24Ca**
Alfreds Bldgs **5Cd**
Alfreds Pl. **34Da**
Alienation Office **14Bc**
All Hallows Barking Church **16Ad**
All Hallows Church, Bread St. **15Ac**
All Hallows Church, Lombard St. **15Cc**
All Hallows La. **15Bd**
All Hallows Staining Church, Mark La. **15Dc** **15Dd**
All Hallows Stairs **15Bd**
All Hallows The Great Church, Upper Thames St. **15Bd**
Allen St. **4Dc**
Allens Bldgs **4Bc**
Allens Ct. **12Db**
Allens Ct. **16Ab**
Allerton St. **5Cb** **5Ca**
Allington St. **33Aa**
Allmontree Yd. **13Bd**
Almacks **22Da**
Allsops Bldgs **1Cd**
Allsops Mews **1Cd**
Allsops Pl. **1Cc**
Almonry, Great **23Ac**
Almonry, Little **23Ac**
Alpha Cottages **1Ac**
Alpha Rd. **1Ac**
Amelia Row **24Dd**
Amelia St. **34Dc** **34Db**
Amen Corner **14Dc**
America Mews **16Ad**
America Pl. **25Ab**
America Sq. **16Ad**
America Sq. **25Ab**
America Terr. **31Cb**
Amicable Row **25Bd** **25Cd**
Amphitheatre Row **23Dc**
Anchor and Hope Alley **27Ab**
Anchor Brewery **17Ca**
Anchor Brewery **25Aa**
Anchor St. **6Ad** **6Bd**
Anchor St., Little **6Bc**
Andersons Bldgs **4Da**
Andersons St. **33Cb** **33Db**
Andersons Walk **33Cb**
Angel **4Ca**
Angel **12Dd**
Angel Alley **15Aa**
Angel Alley **15Ba**
Angel Alley **15Bd**
Angel Alley **15Da**
Angel Alley **16Bb** **16Cb**
Angel Alley **17Ad**
Angel Alley **25Bc**
Angel Alley **26Ca**
Angel Ct. **5Ad** **5Bd**
Angel Ct. **13Dc**
Angel Ct. **14Cb**
Angel Ct. **15Ac**
Angel Ct. **15Ba**
Angel Ct. **15Cb**
Angel Ct. **16Ab**
Angel Ct. **16Ac**
Angel Ct. **16Cd**
Angel Ct. **17Bd**
Angel Ct. **22Da**
Angel Ct. **23Ac** **23Bc**
Angel Ct. **25Bb**
Angel Gdns **17Bd**
Angel Inn **14Ac**
Angel Inn **14Db**
Angel Pass. **15Da**
Angel Pl. **24Ba**
Angel Sq. **16Aa**
Angel St. **14Db** **15Ab**
Ann St. **4Aa**
Ann St. **6Dc** **7Ac**
Ann St. **7Cc**
Ann St. **16Ca**
Ann St. **17Ad** **17Ac**
Anns Ct. **27Ab**
Anns Pl. **24Bc**
Ansels Rents **28Da**
Anthony St. **17Ad** **17Ac**
Apollo Bldgs **24Bc**
Apollo Bldgs **35Bc** **35Cc**
Apollo Ct. **14Ac**
Apothecaries Hall **14Cc**
Appletree Yd. **12Dd**
Arabella Row **22Bd**
Arch Row **13Db**
Archer St. **12Dc**

Archery, The 21Cc
Argyll St. 12Cc 12Cb
Argyll St., Little 12Cb
Ariss Row 4Bc
Arklow St. 1Bc
Arlington St. 22Ca
Armagh St. 1Bb
Arneld Pl. 26Bc
Arnolds Paragon 34Db
Arnolds Pl. 34Db
Arthur St., Great 5Ad
Arthur St., Little 5Ad
Artillery Ground 5Cd
Artillery La. 26Ac
Artillery Pl. 5Cd
Artillery Pl. 22Dd
Artillery St. 16Aa
Artillery St. 24Cc
Arundel Stairs 14Ac
Arundel St. 14Ab
Ashby St. 4Cc 4Cb
Ashby St., Upper 4Db
Ashentree Ct. 14Bc
Ashfield Pl. 18Ab
Ashton St. 19Dd
Aske Ter. 5Db
Assembly Pass. 17Ca
Assembly Row 17Ca
Astleys Theatre 23Dc
Asylum Bldgs 24Bd
Asylum for Female Orphans 24Ad
Asylum for the Deaf and Dumb 35Cb
Asylum Pl. 24Bd
Auction Mart 15Cb 15Cc
Audley Sq. 22Aa
Audley St., North 11Dc
Audley St., South 22Aa 11Dd
Augustus Row 36Ba
Augustus St. 2Ca
Austin Friars 15Cb
Austin St. 6Ab 6Bb
Ave Marie Lane 14Dc
Avery Farm Row 32Ab
Avery Green 32Ab
Avery Pl. 32Ab
Avery Row 12Bc
Aylesbury St. 4Cd
Ayliff St., Great 16Bc 16Cc
Ayliff St., Little 16Cc
Ayliffes Bldgs 35Aa

Baal Zephon St. 25Cd
Babmays Mews 12Dd
Baches Row 5Cb
Back Alley 26Ba
Back Change 16Bd
Back Hill 4Bd
Back La. 7Cb
Back La. 17Ad 17Bd
Back La. 34Bd 34Bc 34Cc
Back Roll Ct. 15Da
Back St. 26Ab
Back St. 29Ba
Back Walk 24Ba
Back Yd. 25Ab
Bacon St., Great 6Bc
Bacon St., Little 6Bc
Badger Yd. 4Cd
Badgers and Drapers Alms Houses 6Ab
Badgers Ct. 6Ad
Bagnigge Pl. 4Ab
Bagnigge Wells 4Ac
Bagnio Ct. 14Db
Baileys Ct. 6Ad
Baileys Ct. 14Ab
Bainbridge St. 13Ab 13Bb
Baker St. 11Db 11Da 11Ca
Baker Street North 1Cd
Bakers Alley 9Cc
Bakers Alley 25Db
Bakers Bldgs 15Db 15Da
Bakers Ct. 6Bb
Bakers Ct. 14Ba
Bakers Ct. 15Da
Bakers Ct. 16Ca
Bakers Hall 15Dd
Bakers La. 32Bd 32Bc
Bakers Mews 11Db
Bakers Rents 6Bb
Bakers Row 4Bd 4Bc
Bakers Row 16Da
Baldwin St. 5Ac
Baldwins Ct. 15Bc
Baldwyns Gdns 14Aa 14Ba
Baldwyns Pl. 14Ba
Ball Alley 15Da
Ball Yd. 5Ad
Ball's pond, Road to 5Ca
Banbury Ct. 13Bc
Bancroft's Almshouses* 8Ad
Bancroft's Pl.* 8Bd
Bangor Ct. 14Bb 14Cb
Bangor Ct. 25Bc
Bangor House 14Bb
Bank Bldgs 15Cc
Bank End Wharf 25Ba
Bank of England 15Bc 15Cc
Bank Side 25Aa
Bank St. 15Cc
Banks Ct. 5Bd
Banner Sq. 5Bc
Banner St. 5Bc
Baptist Head Ct. 15Ba
Barbers Hall 15Aa
Barbican 15Aa
Barbican Ct. 15Aa
Barebinder La. 9Aa
Barge House Alley 24Ba 14Bd
Barge House Stairs, Old 14Bd
Barge Yd. 15Bc
Barking Churchyard 17Ad
Barking Rd. 20Dc
Barleymow Ct. 16Bb
Barleymow Pass. 14Da
Barlow Mews 12Bd
Barlow St., Great 11Da
Barlow St., Little 11Da
Barnards Inn 14Bb
Barnes Ct. 4Ac 4Bc
Barnes Pl. 17Ba
Barnes Pl. 24Ab 24Bb
Barnes St., Little 4Bc
Barnes's Ter. 24Ab
Barns Alley 16Ca
Barns Bldgs 16Bb
Barons Bldgs 24Bc
Barons Pl. 24Bc
Barret Ct. 12Ab
Barrett St. 33Db
Barron St. 4Ba
Barrosa Ter. 7Ba
Bartholomew Close 14Da
Bartholomew La. 15Cc 15Cb
Bartlets Ct. 14Bb
Bartlett Bldgs 5Dc
Bartletts Bldgs 14Bb
Bartletts Pass. 14Bb
Barton Ct. 6Aa
Barton St. 23Bd
Basing La. 15Ac
Basinghall St. 15Bb
Basinghall St., New 15Bb 15Ba
Basket Alley 5Ad
Bason 26Db
Batchelor Pl. 3Ca
Batemans Bldgs 13Ac 13Ab
Batemans Row 16Ac
Bath Bldgs 6Aa
Bath Ct. 4Bc 4Bd
Bath Pl. 2Cc
Bath Row 2Cc
Bath Row 4Bc
Bath St. 5Bc 5Bb
Bath St. 7Bc
Bath St., Great 4Bd 4Bc
Bath Ter. 17Ad
Bath Ter. 25Ad
Batson St. 18Dd
Battle Bridge Stairs 25Da
Batty St. 16Dc
Battys Gdns 16Dc
Bayles Ct. 16Cd
Bayleys Alley 13Cd
Baynes Row 4Ac 4Bc
Bear, The 24Dc
Bear Alley 14Cb
Bear Alley, Great 15Bb 15Cb
Bear and Ragged Staff Ct. 5Ad 5Bd
Bear and Ragged Staff Mews 22Aa
Bear Ct. 21Bb
Bear Ct. 24Da
Bear Garden 25Aa
Bear Inn Yd. 14Da
Bear La. 24Db 24Ca
Bear Quay 15Dd
Bear Quay, New 15Dd
Bear Quay Alley 15Dd
Bear St. 12Cc
Bear St. 13Ad 13Bd
Bear Yd. 13Db
Bear Yd. 33Ca
Bearbinder La. 15Bc 15Cc

For Key Map see p. 1

Beauchamp St. 14Ba
Beaufort Bldgs 13Cd
Beaufort Wharfs 13Cd
Beaumont Bldgs 16Cd
Beaumont Pl. 2Dc
Beaumont St. 2Ad
Beaumonts Bldgs 17Ac
Beckford Pl. 35Ac
Beckford Row 7Ac
Beckford Row 35Ac
Becks Rents 17Bd
Bedford Bury 13Bd
Bedford Chapel 13Bb
Bedford Ct. 13Bd
Bedford Ct. 13Da
Bedford House Yd. 13Ca
Bedford Mews, Upper 3Bd
Bedford Office 13Ba
Bedford Pass. 2Dd
Bedford Pl. 3Cd 13Ca
Bedford Pl. 27Bd
Bedford Pl. 34Da
Bedford Pl., Upper 3Bd
Bedford Row 14Aa 13Da
Bedford Sq. 13Aa
Bedford St. 4Bd
Bedford St. 13Aa
Bedford St. 13Bc 13Cc
Bedford St. 13Cd
Bedford St. 13Da
Bedford St. 35Bb
Beech La. 15Ba
Beech St. 15Aa 5Bd
Beer La. 15Dd
Belgrade Pl. 35Bc
Belgrave Bldgs 32Aa 32Ba
Belgrave Pl., Lower 32Ab
Belgrave Pl., Upper 32Aa
Belgrave St. 32Ba
Belgrave Ter. 32Ab
Bell 13Ad
Bell, Old 14Ba
Bell Alley 5Ad
Bell Alley, Little 15Cb
Bell and Crown 14Ba
Bell Brewery 6Ad
Bell Ct. 6Bd
Bell Ct. 14Aa 14Ba
Bell Ct. 14Dc
Bell Ct. 15Ab
Bell Ct. 15Da
Bell Ct. 25Dc
Bell Inn 14Da
Bell Inn 14Db
Bell Inn 15Ac
Bell La. 16Bb 16Ab 16Aa
Bell Savage Yd. 14Cb
Bell Sq. 15Ab
Bell Sq. 15Db
Bell St. 1Ad
Bell Wharf 17Dd
Bell Wharf La. 15Bd
Bell Yd. 14Ac 14Ab
Bell Yd. 14Dc
Bell Yd. 15Cc
Bell Yd. 15Cd
Bells Bldgs 14Cc
Belmont House 33Bd
Belmont Pl. 33Bd
Belton St., New 13Bb
Belton St., Old 13Cc 13Cb 13Bb
Belvedere Bldgs 24Dc
Belvedere Pl. 24Dc
Belvedere Row 24Dc
Belvidere 4Ba
Belvidere Brewery 24Ab
Bembers Rents 5Ad
Bencrofts Almshouses 8Ad
Bencrofts Pl. 8Bd
Benjamin St. 4Cd
Bennet Pl. 6Db
Bennet St. 12Da
Bennet St. 22Ca
Bennet St. 23Ac
Bennet St. 24Ca
Bennets Bldgs 34Bb
Bennets Ct. 6Cd
Bennets Ct. 13Dc
Bennets Hill 14Dc
Bennets Row 24Cc 24Cb
Bennets Yd. 23Bd
Bennetts Ct. 25Bc
Bentinck Chapel 11Aa
Bentinck Mews 12Aa
Bentinck St. 12Ab
Bentinck St. 12Dc
Beranders Almshouses 6Ab
Berkeley St. 22Ca 22Ba 12Bd
Berkeley St. 33Da
Berkley Ct. 4Cd
Berkley Mews 11Cb
Berkley Sq. 12Ad 12Bd
Berkley St. 4Cd
Berkley St. 11Db
Berkley St., Upper 11Bb 11Cb
Bermondsey Bldgs 35Da
Bermondsey Church Yd. 25Dd
Bermondsey New Rd. 35Ca 35Da 25Dd
Bermondsey Spa 36Ca
Bermondsey Sq. 25Dd
Bermondsey St. 25Dd 25Dc 25Da
Bermondsey Workhouse 25Dc
Bernard Mews 3Cc
Bernard St. 3Cd
Berner St. 16Dc
Berners Mews 12Da
Berners St. 12Db 12Da
Berry St. 4Dc
Berwick St. 12Dc 12Db
Bethlem, Old 15Da
Bethlem Hospital 15Cb
Bethlem Hospital, New 24Bd
Bethnal Green 7Bc 7Bb
Bethnal Green Rd. 6Dc 7Ac 7Bc
Bethnal Green Rd., Old 7Ab
Bethnal Green Workhouse 6Dd
Betts St. 16Dd
Bevis Marks 16Ab
Bickers Pass. 24Bb
Bidborough St. 3Bb
Bill Alley 4Cd
Billingsgate 15Dd
Billiter La. 15Dc
Billiter Sq. 15Dc
Bing St. 8Cc 8Cd
Birchin La. 15Cc
Bird Cage, The 6Cb
Bird Cage Alley 25Ac 25Bc
Bird Cage Walk 6Cb 6Ca
Bird Cage Walk 22Dc 22Ac
Bird in Hand Ct. 15Bc
Bird St. 12Ab 12Ac
Bird St. 27Ab
Bird St. 34Ba
Birds Ct. 15Bb
Birds Pl. 36Cb
Bishops Ct. 4Cd
Bishops Ct. 5Bc
Bishops Ct. 14Ab
Bishops Ct. 14Cb
Bishops Ct. 15Bb
Bishops Ct. 15Da
Bishops Head Ct. 14Aa
Bishops Walk 23Cd 23Dd
Bishops Yd. 12Ad
Bishopsgate St. 15Dc 15Db 16Aa
Bishopsgate Workhouse 15Da
Black Boy Alley 14Ca
Black Boy La. 29Ca
Black Bull 14Ba
Black Bull Yd. 12Dd
Black Dog 33Cc
Black Eagle St. 6Bd
Black Friars Bridge 14Cd
Black Horse 13Ad
Black Horse Alley 14Cb
Black Horse Brewery 25Cb
Black Horse Sq. 38Bd
Black Horse Yd. 13Ab 13Aa
Black Lion Ct. 25Db
Black Lion Inn 14Bc
Black Lion Yd. 16Cb
Black Raven Alley 15Cd
Black Raven Ct. 16Ad
Black Swan Alley 14Dc
Black Swan Alley 15Cb
Black Swan Ct. 5Ad
Black Swan Ct. 12Dd
Black Swan Ct. 15Dd
Black Swan Ct. 25Cb
Black Swan Yd. 34Db
Black Yd. 25Cd
Blackbird Alley 6Cd
Blacklands 31Bb
Blacklands La. 31Aa 31Ab 31Bb
Blackman St. 25Ac
Blackmans Mews 11Dd 11Dc
Blackmoor St. 13Dc
Blackwall 29Dc 30Ac 30Ab
Blackwall Causeway 30Ab 30Aa
Blackwall La. 30Cd 30Bd
Blackwall Reach 40Bb 40Ba 40Aa 39Ad
Blackwall Stairs 30Ab
Blackwell Hall 15Bb
Blakes Ct. 27Aa
Bland Ct. 13Cc 13Cb
Blandford Mews 11Da
Blandford St. 11Da
Blands Bldgs 5Ad
Bleeding Heart Yd. 14Ba 14Ca

Blenheim Mews 12Cb
Blenheim St. 12Bc
Blenheim St. 12Cb
Blewits Bldgs 14Bb
Blind Beggar 7Bb 7Cb
Blocks Ct. 6Bd
Bloody Bridge 31Ca
Bloomsbury Ct. 13Ca
Bloomsbury Market 13Ca
Bloomsbury Pl. 13Ca
Bloomsbury Sq. 13Ca
Blossom Inn 15Bb
Blossom St. 6Ad
Blue Anchor 36Db
Blue Anchor Alley 5Bd
Blue Anchor Ct. 25Aa
Blue Anchor Ct. 23Ad
Blue Anchor La. 26Cd 26Dd 36Da 36Db
Blue Anchor Rd. 36Bb 36Cb 36Db 37Ab 37Aa
Blue Anchor Yd. 15Bb
Blue Anchor Yd. 16Cd
Blue Anchor Yd. 22Dc
Blue Ball Ct. 25Ac
Blue Boar Inn 16Bc
Blue Boar Yd. 13Da
Blue Boar Yd. 23Bc
Blue Coat Bldgs 14Db
Blue Coat School 22Dd
Blue Cross St. 13Ad
Blue Gate Fields 17Bd
Blue Hart Ct. 15Cb
Blue Lion 3Dd
Blunderbuss Ct. 6Ab
Boar and Castle Yd. 13Ab
Boar Inn 16Bc
Boarded Entry 27Ba
Boars Head Ct. 14Da
Boars Head Ct. 25Ca
Boars Head Yd. 16Bb
Boddys Bridge 24Ba
Bolingbroke Row* 35Ad
Bolsover St. 12Cb
Bolt Ct. 14Bb
Bolt in Ton Ct. 14Bc
Bolton Row 22Ba
Bolton St. 22Ba
Bond Ct. 15Bc
Bond St. 24Dd 24Cd
Bond St., New 12Cd 12Bd 12Bc 12Bb
Bond St., Old 12Cd
Bonds Ct. 22Dd
Bonds Pl. 7Aa
Bonner St. 7Db
Bonners Hall 7Da
Boolingbrook Row 35Ad
Boot, The 3Cb
Booth Ct. 16Ca
Booth St. 5Dc
Booth St. 16Ba 16Ca
Borough Clink 25Da 25Db
Borough High St. 25Bc 25Bb 25Ba 25Ca
Borough Market 25Ba 25Bb
Borough Water Works 25Ca
Bosiers Ct. 13Ab
Bosket St. 27Aa
Boss Ct. 14Dc
Boswell Ct. 3Cd
Boswell Ct. 14Ac
Boswell Ct., New 14Ac 14Ab
Boswell Ct., Old 14Ac
Botanic Garden 31Bd
Botolph Alley 15Cd 15Dd
Botolph La.* 15Cd
Botolph Wharf 15Cd
Bottle Hay Yd. 4Cc
Bottolph La. 15Cd
Bough Ct. 6Ad
Boverie St. 14Bc
Bow 9Cb 9Cc
Bow Brewhouse 9Db
Bow Bridge 9Db
Bow Churchyard 15Ac
Bow Common 18Da
Bow Creek 30Da
Bow La. 15Ac
Bow La. 19Dd 19Dc 19Db 19Cb 19Da
Bow La. 29Da
Bow St. 13Cb
Bow St. 13Cc
Bow Yd. 13Bb
Bowling Alley 4Cd
Bowling Alley 15Ba
Bowling Green 1Bd
Bowling Green 25Bc
Bowling Green 34Ad
Bowling Green Bldgs 1Bd
Bowling Green La. 12Aa
Bowling Green La. 4Bc
Bowling Green Pl. 34Ad
Bowling Green Row 5Db
Bowling Inn Alley 14Ba
Bowling St. 23Bd
Box Farm 31Ac
Boyds Walk 32Ab
Boyle St. 12Cc
Brabant Ct. 15Cd
Brackley St. 5Ad
Bradshaw Rents 4Bd
Branches Bldgs 5Cc 5Dc
Brandon St. 35Da
Brandons Row 24Dd
Braynes Row 4Bc
Braziers Bldgs 14Cb
Bread St. 15Ac
Bread Street Hill 15Ad 15Ac
Breams Bldgs 14Ab 14Bb
Breezers St. 16Dd
Brewer St. 12Dd 12Dc
Brewer St. 13Bb
Brewer St. 22Bd
Brewers Ct. 13Bd
Brewers Green 22Dd
Brewers Hall 15Bb
Brewers Quay 26Aa
Brewers Row 22Dd
Brewery Ct. 25Db
Brewhouse Ct. 15Da
Brewhouse La. 15Bd
Brewhouse La. 27Ab
Brewhouse Turning 25Db
Brewhouse Yd. 14Ca
Brewhouse Yd. 14Cb
Brewhouse Yd. 27Ac
Brian St. 6Ad
Brice Hill La. 15Bd
Brick Ct. 14Ac 14Bc
Brick La. 5Ac
Brick La. 16Cb 16Ba 6Bd 6Bc
Brick St. 22Aa
Brick St. 24Dd
Brickells Bldgs 24Dd
Bricklayers Arms 35Ca
Bride La. 14Cc
Bride St. 25Db
Brides Ct. 14Cc
Brides Pass. 14Cc
Bridewell 22Dd
Bridewell Hospital 14Cc
Bridewell Prison, New 4Cc
Bridewell Prison, Old 4Cc
Bridewell Walk 4Cc
Bridge Ct. 23Bc
Bridge Pl. 4Cb
Bridge Pl. 26Cd
Bridge Pl. 38Bd
Bridge Rd. 23Dc
Bridge Row 32Ab
Bridge St. 23Bc
Bridge St., Little 14Cc
Bridge St., New 14Cc
Bridge St., New 33Cd
Bridge Yd. 25Ca
Bridgewater Gdns 5Ad
Bridgewater Sq. 5Ad
Bridle La. 12Dc
Brighton Pl. 34Da
Brill Pl. 3Ba
Brill Row 3Ba
Brill Ter. 3Ba
Bristow St. 14Cc
Britannia 18Cd
Britannia Ct. 5Ad
Britannia Gdns 5Da
Britannia Row 23Dc
Britannia St. 3Db
Britans Ct. 16Dd
British Museum 13Ba
British Wine Manufactory 14Bb
Brits Bldgs 5Da
Britten Ct. 14Bc
Broad Arrow Ct. 15Ba
Broad Bridge 17Cd
Broad Ct. 13Cc
Broad Pl. 6Ac 6Ab
Broad St. 12Dc
Broad St. 13Bb 13Cb
Broad St. 15Cb 15Db
Broad St. 18Ad
Broad St. 26Ab

For Key Map see p. 1

Broad St. **27Aa**
Broad St. **33Cb 33Db**
Broad St., New **15Cb 15Db**
Broad Street Bldgs **15Da**
Broad Street Pl. **15Db**
Broad Wall **24Cb 24Ba**
Broad Way **14Cc**
Broad Way **22Dd 23Ac**
Broad Way **25Cb**
Broad Yd. **4Cd**
Broad Yd. **5Ad**
Broad Yd. **25Ac**
Brocks Wharf **15Ad**
Broken Wharf **15Ad**
Broker Row **15Cb 15Db 15Da**
Brokers Alley **13Cb**
Bromley Bridge **10Ac**
Bromley Hall **19Db**
Bromley Hall Callico Houses **19Db 20Ab**
Bromley Hall Field **19Db**
Brompton Cres. **21Ad**
Brompton Grove **21Ad**
Brompton Row **21Ad 21Ac 21Bc**
Brook Pl. **4Ab 4Ac**
Brook St. **2Cc**
Brook St. **12Ac 12Bc**
Brook St. **14Ba**
Brook St. **17Dd**
Brook St. **18Ad**
Brook St., Little **2Cc**
Brook St., Little **12Bc**
Brook St., Upper **11Cc 11Dc**
Brookes **22Ca**
Brooks Ct. **24Ac**
Brooks Market **14Ba**
Brooks Mews **12Ac 12Bc**
Brooks Mews **34Ac**
Brooks Pl. **2Cc**
Brooks Pl. **34Ac**
Brooks St. **34Ba**
Brooks Wharf **26Ab**
Brooksby St., Lower **2Cb**
Brooksby St., Upper **2Ca**
Brothers Row **33Ca**
Brown and Co. Wharf **14Ac**
Brown Ct. **11Dc**
Brown St. **11Bb 11Ba**
Brown St. **12Dc 12Ac**
Brownes Bldgs **15Dc**
Brownlow Mews **4Ad**
Brownlow St. **13Cb**
Brownlow St. **14Aa**
Browns Bldgs **13Dc**
Browns Bldgs **16Bd**
Browns Bldgs **25Cb**
Browns Ct. **11Aa**
Browns La. **16Ba**
Browns Quay **26Cb**
Brunswick Mews **3Cc**
Brunswick Mews **11Cb**
Brunswick Pl. **3Cd**
Brunswick Pl. **5Cb**
Brunswick Sq. **3Cc**
Brunswick St. **6Ca**
Brunswick St. **24Ca**
Brunswick St., Little **24Ca**
Brush Ct. **26Ba**
Bruton Mews, South **12Bd**
Bruton Pl. **12Bd 12Bc**
Bruton St. **12Bd**
Bruton St., Little **12Bd 12Bc**
Bryanstone Sq. **11Ba 11Bb 11Ca 11Cb**
Bryanstone St. **11Cb**
Bryanstone St., Upper **11Bc 11Cc 11Cb**
Brydges St. **13Cc 13Dc**
Buckbridge St. **13Bb**
Buckingham Ct. **23Ba**
Buckingham Gate **22Cc**
Buckingham House **22Bc**
Buckingham Pl. **35Cb 35Db**
Buckingham Row **22Dd**
Buckingham St. **2Cd**
Buckingham St. **13Cd**
Buckle St., Little **16Cc**
Bucklersbury **15Bc**
Bucknels Ct. **25Bd**
Budge Row **15Bc**
Bugden Hill **11Ad**
Bugsbys Marsh **30Bc 30Cb 30Cc**
Bull Alley **33Cb**
Bull and Gate Yd. **13Db**
Bull and Mouth St. **15Ab**
Bull Bridge **25Db**
Bull Ct. **14Db**
Bull Ct. **16Ab**
Bull Head Ct. **14Db**
Bull Head Ct. **25Db**
Bull Inn **15Ab**
Bull Inn **15Dc**
Bull Inn **15Db**
Bull Inn **16Bc**
Bull La. **18Ab**
Bull Shed Bldgs **9Dc 9Dd**
Bull Stairs **14Bd**
Bull Stake Ct. **16Cb**
Bull Wharf La. **15Ad**
Bull Yd. **4Bd**
Bull Yd. **5Ad**
Bullards Pl. **7Db**
Bullen Ct. **13Cd**
Bulls Head **25Ad**
Bulls Head Ct. **14Ca**
Bulls Head Ct. **23Ad**
Bulls Yd. **18Ac 18Ad**
Bully Rag Row **7Cb**
Bulstrode Mews **12Aa**
Bulstrode St. **12Aa**
Bunhill Fields Burying Ground **5Cc 5Bd 5Cd**
Bunhill Row **5Bd 5Bc**
Burleigh St. **13Cc 13Cd**
Burlington Gdns **12Cd**
Burlington Ho. **12Cd**
Burlington Mews **12Cc**
Burlington St., New **12Cc**
Burlington St., Old **12Cd 12Cc**
Burr St. **26Ca**
Burr St., Little **26Ca**
Burrows Bldgs **24Cb**
Burton Cres. **3Bb**
Burton St. **3Bc**
Bury Ct. **15Db**
Bury Pl. **13Ca**
Bury St. **13Ca**
Bury St. **16Ac 16Ab**
Bury St. **22Ca**
Busby Ct. **6Cc**
Busby St. **6Cc**
Bush La. **15Bd**
Bush La., Little **15Bd**
Bushels Rents **26Cb**
Butcher Hall La. **14Db**
Butcher Row **18Ad**
Butcher Row **26Ba 26Ca**
Butlers Alley **15Ba**
Butlers Ct. **15Ba**
Buttons Entry **18Ac**
Buxton Pl. **24Ad**

Cable St. **16Cd 16Dd**
Cadogan Pl. **21Cd**
Cadogan Pl., Little **21Cd**
Cadogan Pl., Upper **21Cd**
Cadogan Sq. **21Cd**
Cadogan Ter. **31Ca**
Cains Pl. **16Dd 16Dc**
Calanders Gdns **27Ad 27Bd**
Calender Yd. **15Da**
Calico Bldgs **26Cd**
Calmel Bldgs **11Db**
Calthorpe Pl. **31Bd**
Calverts Brewery **15Bd**
Camberwell Toll Gate **35Ad**
Cambridge Pl. **6Ca**
Cambridge St. **12Dc**
Cambridge St., Great **6Ca**
Cambridge St., Little **6Ba 6Ca**
Cambridge Terr. **1Cc**
Camden Ct. **15Ba**
Camden St. **35Ac 35Ab**
Camdens Garden **7Bc**
Camdens Pl. **7Ac**
Cammomile St. **15Db**
Campion La. **15Bd**
Can Yd. **16Cd**
Canal Iron Works **28Dc**
Cane Pl. **24Dc**
Cannon Brewery **21Cb**
Cannon Pl. **17Ba**
Cannon Row **23Bc 23Bb**
Cannon St. **15Bc 15Bd 15Cd**
Cannon St. **17Ad**
Cannon St. **24Dc**
Canon Alley **14Dc**
Canterbury Bldgs **24Ad**
Canterbury Ct. **14Dc**
Canterbury Pl. **34Aa 24Ad**
Canterbury Pl. **34Dc**
Canterbury Pl., Little **34Aa**
Canterbury Row **34Cc 34Cb**
Canterbury Sq. **25Cb**
Canterbury Walk **24Ad**
Canton Pl. **19Ad**
Cape of Good Hope **37Cb**
Capel Ct. **15Cc**
Car Sq. **15Ba**
Carburton St. **2Bd**
Cardigan Pl. **34Ac**
Cardigan St. **34Ac**
Carey St. **14Ab**

Carlisle Chapel 34Bb
Carlisle La. 24Ad 24Ac
Carlisle Pl. 23Dd 24Ad
Carlisle School 24Ad
Carlisle Sq. 24Ac
Carlisle St. 12Db 13Ab
Carlton House 23Aa
Carlton House Gdns 22Da 23Aa
Carlton Pl. 23Aa
Carmarthen Sq. 2Dc 3Ac
Carmarthen St. 2Dd
Carnaby Market 12Cc
Carnaby St. 12Cc
Caroline Ct. 14Ca
Caroline Mews 13Aa 13Ba
Caroline Pl. 3Dc
Caroline St. 13Aa
Carpenter St. 12Ad
Carpenter St. 33Ba
Carpenters Bldgs 15Cb
Carpenters Hall 15Cb
Carpenters Rents 16Ac
Carrier St. 13Bb
Carrington Mews 22Aa
Carrington Pl. 22Ab 22Aa
Carrington St. 22Aa
Carrols Ct. 26Ac
Carron Warehouse 14Cd 14Cc
Carter La. 25Ca
Carter La., Great 14Dc
Carter La., Little 14Dc
Carter St. 6Bd 6Cd
Carteret St. 23Ac
Carters Ct. 16Ab
Carthusian St. 14Da 15Aa
Cartwright Sq. 16Bd 16Cd
Cartwright St. 16Cd 16Bd
Cary La. 15Ab
Caslon's Factory 14Cc
Castle and Falcon Inn 15Ab
Castle Ct. 6Ab
Castle Ct. 6Bc
Castle Ct. 12Db
Castle Ct. 13Cd
Castle Ct. 14Aa
Castle Ct. 15Ba
Castle Ct. 15Bb
Castle Ct. 15Bc
Castle Ct. 15Cc
Castle Ct. 16Bb
Castle Ct. 25Aa
Castle Inn 15Ab
Castle La. 15Ad
Castle La. 16Bb
Castle La. 22Cd
Castle La. 25Aa
Castle Mews 12Db
Castle Pl. 16Bb
Castle Pl. 34Ca
Castle St. 4Cd
Castle St. 5Cd 5Dd
Castle St. 6Bc
Castle St. 6Bc 6Bb
Castle St. 12Dd
Castle St. 13Bb
Castle St. 13Bc 13Cc 13Cb
Castle St. 13Bc 13Bd
Castle St. 14Bb 14Ba
Castle St. 14Cb
Castle St. 14Cd 14Cc
Castle St. 15Ab 15Aa
Castle St. 16Ab
Castle St. 25Ab 25Bb
Castle St. 25Cd
Castle St., Great 12Bb 12Cb
Castle St., Little 12Cb 12Db
Castle St., Old 16Bb
Castle Yd. 22Dc 22Dd
Cateaton St. 15Bb
Catherine Ct. 16Ad
Catherine St. 6Cb 6Ca
Catherine St. 13Dc
Catherine St. 17Ac
Catherine St. 18Bb
Catherine St. 22Cc
Catherine St., Little 13Dc
Catherine Wheel Alley 16Ab
Catherine Wheel Ct. 16Bb
Catherine Wheel Inn 25Ab 25Bb
Catherine Wheel Yd. 22Cb
Cato St. 11Aa 11Ba
Cats Head Ct. 23Ad
Cats Hole 26Ba
Cavendish Sq. 12Bb
Cavendish St. 12Bb
Cavendish St., New 12Ba
Cecil Ct. 13Bd
Cecil St. 13Cd
Cevy Ct. 12Ba
Chalton Ct. 3Bb
Chalton St. 3Bb
Chambers St. 16Bd 16Cd
Champion Alley 33Ba
Champions Ct. 16Bd
Chancellor Ct. 6Ac
Chancery La. 14Bc 14Bb 14Ab
Chandler St. 12Ac
Chandlers Hall 15Bd
Chandlers Rents 14Dc
Chandos St. 12Bb 12Ba
Chandos St. 13Bd
Change Ct. 13Cc 13Dc 13Dd
Chapel Ct. 12Ab 12Bb
Chapel Ct. 12Cc
Chapel Ct. 13Bc
Chapel Ct. 15Aa
Chapel Ct. 25Bb
Chapel Mews 12Ba
Chapel Path 3Ba
Chapel Row 21Ad 21Ac
Chapel Royal 22Cb
Chapel St. 2Dd
Chapel St. 3Dd
Chapel St. 4Bc
Chapel St. 5Dd
Chapel St. 11Aa
Chapel St. 11Dd
Chapel St. 15Ba
Chapel St. 16Aa
Chapel St. 17Ac
Chapel St. 22Ac
Chapel St. 22Dd
Chapel St., East 22Aa
Chapel St., Great 12Db
Chapel St., Little 12Db
Chapel St., West 22Aa
Chapman Pl. 17Ad 17Ac
Chapman St. 17Ad
Chapman St., Lower 17Ac
Chapmans Bldgs 25Bb, 25Bc
Chapter House Ct. 14Dc
Chapter St. 32Db 33Ab
Charing Cross 23Ba
Charles Ct. 13Cd 23Ca
Charles Ct. 22Da
Charles Ct. 27Aa
Charles Pl. 4Bc
Charles Pl. 5Cb
Charles Sq. 5Dc 5Db
Charles St. 2Cc
Charles St. 3Aa
Charles St. 4Cb 4Db
Charles St. 4Db
Charles St. 5Ad
Charles St. 5Cb 5Db
Charles St. 5Dc
Charles St. 7Ac
Charles St. 7Cd 7Cc
Charles St. 9Db
Charles St. 11Ca
Charles St. 11Da
Charles St. 12Ad
Charles St. 12Ca 12Da
Charles St. 13Ab
Charles St. 13Cc
Charles St. 13Cc 13Cb
Charles St. 14Ba 14Ca
Charles St. 16Da
Charles St. 16Db
Charles St. 17Bd 17Bc
Charles St. 22Aa 12Bd
Charles St. 22Da 23Aa
Charles St. 23Bb
Charles St. 24Ac
Charles St. 24Bc 24Bd
Charles St. 24Cb
Charles St. 26Ac
Charles St. 27Aa
Charles St. 31Ca
Charles St. 35Ba
Charles St. 35Bd
Charlott Ct. 15Aa
Charlotte Bldgs 14Aa 14Ba
Charlotte Chapel 12Da
Charlotte Ct. 16Db
Charlotte Mews 2Dd
Charlotte Mews 13Bb
Charlotte Pl. 24Bc
Charlotte Pl. 24Dc
Charlotte Pl. 36Bb
Charlotte Row 15Bc
Charlotte Row 25Cc

For Key Map see p. 1

Charlotte Row **27Db**
Charlotte Row **35Ad**
Charlotte Row, Little **25Cc**
Charlotte St. **2Bd**
Charlotte St. **3Da**
Charlotte St. **5Dc**
Charlotte St. **6Bc**
Charlotte St. **6Cc** **6Dc**
Charlotte St. **12Da** **2Bd**
Charlotte St. **13Bb** **13Ba**
Charlotte St. **16Db**
Charlotte St. **21Bc**
Charlotte St. **22Bc** **22Cc**
Charlotte St. **24Cb** **24Db**
Charlotte St., Great **24Cb**
Charlotte St., Little **12Da**
Charlotte St., Little **22Bd** **22Bc**
Charlottes Row **1Bd**
Charlton St. **2Cd**
Charlton St., Upper **2Cd**
Charterhouse **4Dd**
Charterhouse La. **14Da**
Charterhouse Sq. **4Dd** **14Da**
Charterhouse St. **14Da**
Chatham Gdns **5Cb** **5Ca** **5Ba**
Chatham Pl. **14Cc**
Cheapside **15Ab** **15Ac** **15Bc**
Cheapside, Little **5Ad**
Cheesemans Ct. **6Cd**
Chelsea Bridge **32Ab**
Chelsea Common **31Ab**
Chelsea Common Field **31Ab** **31Ac**
Chelsea Hospital **31Cc** **31Cd** **31Dc** **31Dd**
Chelsea Market **31Cb**
Chelsea Reach **31Cd** **31Dd** **32Ad**
Chelsea Waterworks **32Ad**
Chelsea Waterworks and Pimlico Wharf, Cuts to Supply **32Ab** **32Bb** **32Ba**
Cheltons Ct. **13Bd**
Chenie Mews, Upper **2Dd**
Chenies St. **3Ad**
Chequer Alley **5Bd**
Chequer Alley **25Ca**
Chequer Yd. **15Bd**
Chequer Yd. **16Bc**
Cherrington Row **7Ab**
Cherry Garden Stairs **26Dc**
Cherry Garden St. **27Ac** **27Ad**
Cherry Tree **4Bc** **4Cc**
Cherry Tree Alley **5Bd**
Cherry Tree Ct. **5Ad**
Cherry Tree Ct. **15Aa**
Chester Pl. **7Cb**
Chester Pl. **34Ac** **34Ab**
Chester St. **22Ac**
Chester Ter. **2Ba**
Chesterfield House **22Aa**
Chesterfield St. **12Aa**
Chesterfield St. **22Aa**
Chesters Quay **26Aa**
Cheyne Walk **31Aa** **31Bd**
Chichester Rents **14Ab**
Chick La. **14Ca**
Chicksand St. **16Ca**
Chigwell St. **17Ad**
Childs Ct. **23Ac**
Childs Pl. **14Ac** **14Bc**
China Ct. **34Aa**
China Ter. **34Aa** **24Ad**
Chinia Hall **37Ca**
Chinia Hall Pl. **37Ca**
Chiswell St. **15Ba** **15Ca**
Choppens Ct. **27Ab**
Christ Church, Bennet St. **24Ca**
Christ Church, Newgate St. **14Db**
Christ Church, Spitalfields **16Ba**
Christ Church Workhouse **24Cb**
Christlan St. **16Dd** **16Dc**
Christopher Ct. **26Ba**
Christopher Row **35Bc**
Christopher St. **4Bd**
Christopher St. **5Cd**
Christopher St. **6Bc**
Christophers Alley **15Ca** **15Da**
Christophers Ct. **16Cc**
Christophers Inn **25Db**
Christs Hospital **14Db**
Church Alley **14Dc**
Church Alley **15Bc**
Church Alley **15Bb**
Church Ct. **13Bd**
Church Ct. **15Cd**
Church Ct. **16Ac**
Church Ct. **22Dd**
Church Entry **14Cc** **14Dc**
Church La. **13Bb**
Church La. **13Bd**
Church La. **16Cb** **16Cc**
Church La. **16Cd** **16Cc**
Church La. **18Cd**
Church Pass. **12Dd**
Church Pass. **13Bc** **13Bb**
Church Pl. **16Cb**
Church Pl. **34Db**
Church Rd. **17Bd** **17Bc**
Church Row **5Ac**
Church Row **6Cd** **6Cc**
Church Row **16Ac**
Church Row **18Ab**
Church Row **18Cd**
Church Row **26Ac**
Church Row **34Cb**
Church Stairs **27Bc**
Church St. **6Ac** **6Bc** **6Cc**
Church St. **13Ab** **13Bb**
Church St. **13Ac**
Church St. **16Ac** **16Bc**
Church St. **16Ba**
Church St. **16Ca** **16Da**
Church St., or Stepney Causeway **17Dd** **17Dc**
Church St. **23Bd**
Church St. **24Ca**
Church St. **25Ba**
Church St. **25Bc**
Church St. **26Ac**
Church St. **27Ab**
Church St. **27Bc**
Church St. **33Ca** **33Da**
Church Way **3Aa**
Church Yard Alley **15Cd**
Church Yard Row **34Cb**
Churchyard Ct. **14Cb**
Cinnamon St. **27Bb**
Circus **16Ad**
Circus St. **1Bd**
City Arms **5Aa**
City Chambers **15Cc** **15Dc**
City Chambers, Old **15Dc**
City Chapel **15Ba**
City Coffee House **15Bc**
City Gdns **4Da**
City Rd. **4Ca** **4Da** **5Ab** **5Bb** **5Cb** **5Cc** **5Cd**
City Road Brewery **5Cc**
City Ter. **5Bb**
Clarance Pl. **6Bb**
Clare Ct. **13Dc**
Clare Market **13Db** **13Dc**
Clare St. **7Ba**
Clare St. **13Dc**
Clarence House **31Dd** **31Dc**
Clarence Market **2Cb**
Clarence Pass. **3Ba** **3Bb**
Clarence Pl. **3Da** **4Aa**
Clarence Pl.* **6Bb**
Clarence Pl. **24Dd**
Clarence St. **2Ba**
Clarence St. **27Cc**
Clarence St., Upper **27Cc** **27Dc** **27Dd**
Clarendon Pl. **3Aa**
Clarendon Sq. **3Aa**
Clarges St. **22Ba**
Clark St. **4Dc**
Clarks Bldgs **14Cb**
Clarks Ct. **4Bd**
Clarks Orchard **27Bc**
Clay Hall Gdns **9Ca**
Clay St. **11Ca**
Clayton Pl. **34Bc** **34Cc**
Clayton St. **34Ad**
Cleaveland Mews **2Cd**
Cleaveland St. **2Cd**
Cleaver St. **34Ac** **34Bc**
Clements Ct. **15Ab**
Clements Inn **14Ac**
Clements Inn Pass. **13Dc**
Clements La. **13Dc** **14Ac**
Clerkenwell Close **4Cd** **4Cc**
Clerkenwell Green **4Cd**
Clerkenwell Workhouse **4Bc**
Cleveland Ct. **22Ca**
Cleveland Mews* **2Cd**
Cleveland Row **22Cb**
Cleveland St.* **2Cd**
Cleveland Yd. **22Da**
Clifford St. **12Cd**
Cliffords Inn **14Bb** **14Bc**
Cliffords Inn Gdns **14Bb**
Cliffords Row **31Db** **32Ab**
Clifton St. **2Ca**
Clink St. **25Ba**
Clipstone St. **2Cd**
Cloak La. **15Bc** **15Bd**
Cloth Fair **14Da**
Clothworkers Hall **15Dd**
Cloysters, The **14Db**
Club Row **6Bd** **6Bc**
Coades Row **23Dc**
Coak's Bldgs **16Ab**

Coal Exchange **15Dd**
Coal Wharf **23Dc**
Cobhams Head **4Bc**
Cobbs Yd. **16Ab**
Cock, The **13Ad**
Cock Alley **6Ac**
Cock Alley **6Ad**
Cock Alley **15Ba**
Cock Alley **26Ba**
Cock and Crown Ct. **15Aa**
Cock and Hoop Yd. **16Ab**
Cock Ct. **4Cd**
Cock Ct. **12Dc**
Cock Ct. **14Ca**
Cock Ct. **14Cc**
Cock Ct. **15Ab**
Cock Ct. **15Bb**
Cock Ct. **16Ac**
Cock Hill **6Bd**
Cock Hill **16Ab**
Cock Hill **17Dd**
Cock La. **6Ac**
Cock La. **14Cb** **14Db**
Cock Pit **23Ac**
Cock Pit Alley **13Cc** **13Cb**
Cock Pit Yd. **3Dd**
Cock Yd. **23Ac**
Cockspur St. **23Aa** **23Ba**
Coffee House Alley **15Ad**
Coffee House Walk **5Da**
Colchester St. **16Ad**
Colchester St. **16Bc** **16Cc** **16Cb**
Cold Bath **4Bc**
Cold Bath Sq. **4Bc**
Cole Harbour **15Bd**
Cole Harbour Stairs **15Bd**
Cole Harbour St. **6Cb** **6Ca**
Cole Stairs **27Da**
Colebrook Pl. **5Da**
Colebrook Sq. **6Aa**
Coleman Ct. **25Aa**
Coleman St. **15Bb**
Coleman St. **27Ba**
Coleman St., Lower **5Bd** **5Bc**
Coleman St. Bldgs **15Cb**
Colemans Ct. **25Ab**
Colemans Pl. **5Bb**
Colemans Yd. **25Dc** **25Dd**

Coles Bldgs **4Da**
Coles Pl. **25Bd**
Collate St. **24Bc**
Colledge St. **25Db**
College Hill **15Bd** **15Bc**
College Mews **23Bd**
College of Physicians **14Db**
College St. **23Bd**
College St. **23Db**
College St.* **25Db**
College St., Little **23Bd**
College Yd. **25Bb**
Collet Pl. **18Ac**
Collier St. **3Da**
Collier St. **4Aa**
Colliers Ct. **5Ad**
Colliers Rents **25Bc**
Collingwood St. **5Bb** **5Cb**
Collingwood St. **6Bc**
Collingwood St. **17Ba** **7Bd**
Collins Ct. **27Ba**
Collins Pl. **29Da**
Collitch Pl. **34Db**
Colonnade, The **3Cd**
Colyers Ct. **25Db**
Commerce Row **24Cb**
Commercial Dock no. 1 **38Aa** **38Ba**
Commercial Dock no. 2 **38Aa** **38Ab**
Commercial Dock no. 3 **38Aa** **38Ba**
Commercial Dock no. 4 **28Bc** **28Bd**
Commercial Dock no. 5 **28Bb** **28Bc**
Commercial Pl. **17Cc**
Commercial Rd. **17Ac** **17Bc** **17Cc** **17Dc** **18Ac** **18Bc** **18Cd** **18Dd** **29Aa**
Common Pleas Office **14Bc**
Compton Pass. **4Dc**
Compton St. **3Cc**
Compton St. **4Cc** **4Dc**
Compton St. **13Ac**
Compton St., Little **13Ac**
Compton St., New **13Ac** **13Bc** **13Bb**
Conduit Ct. **13Bc**
Conduit St. **12Bc** **12Cc**
Connaught Pl. **11Bc**
Constitution Brewery **16Ab**
Constitution Hill **22Ab**
Constitution Row **3Dd**

Convict Transport, Wet Dock **38Bb** **38Cb** **38Cc** **38Bc**
Conway Ct. **11Da**
Conway St. **2Cd**
Conway St., Upper **2Cc**
Cookes Wharf **27Da**
Cooks Almshouses **17Cd**
Cooks Ct. **5Dd**
Cooks Ct. **14Ab**
Cooper Ct. **16Cd**
Cooper St. **23Ad**
Coopers Almshouses **17Dd**
Coopers Ct. **4Bd**
Coopers Ct. **5Ac**
Coopers Ct. **5Bd**
Coopers Ct. **26Ba**
Coopers Gdns **6Bb**
Coopers Hall **15Bb**
Coopers Row **16Ad**
Copenhagen Pl. **18Cc**
Coplands Yd. **33Aa**
Copper Wharf **14Cd** **14Cc**
Coppice Row **4Bc** **4Bd**
Copthall Ct. **15Cb**
Coram St., Great **3Cc**
Corbets Ct. **15Cc**
Corbets La. **37Ac** **37Bc** **37Bb** **37Cc**
Corbetts Ct. **16Ba**
Cordwainers Hall **15Ac**
Cork Cutters Alley **23Ac**
Cork St. **12Cd**
Cork St. Mews **12Cd**
Corn Exchange **15Dd**
Cornbury Pl. **35Db**
Cornhill **15Cc**
Cornhill Work House **7Cb**
Cornwall Pl. **2Bc** **2Bb**
Cornwell St. **17Ad**
Cornwell St., Lower **17Bd**
Cornycap Alley **25Aa**
Corporation Ct. **4Cc**
Corporation Row **4Cc**
Cottage Row **29Ca**
Cottage St. **29Ca**
Cotton St. **29Da**
Cottons Wharf **25Ca**
Counter **14Db**
Counter St. **25Bb**

County Goal **25Ad**
County Row **25Db**
County Ter. **35Aa**
County Terrace St. **35Aa**
Court of Request **13Bd**
Court of Requests **16Cb**
Court St. **17Aa**
Cousin La. **15Bd**
Covent Garden **13Cc**
Covent Garden Theatre **13Cc**
Covent Garden Workhouse **2Cd**
Coventry Ct. **13Ad**
Coventry Pl. **36Ab**
Coventry St. **7Bc**
Coventry St. **13Ad**
Cow Ct. **27Bc** **27Cc**
Cow Cross St. **14Ca**
Cow La. **14Ca**
Cow La. **17Bd**
Cow La. **18Ab**
Cow La. **28Bc** **28Cc**
Cow Yd. **1Cd**
Cow Yd. **4Ad**
Cow Yd. **4Ca**
Cow Yd. **11Bb**
Cow Yd. **17Ba**
Cow Yd. **17Ca**
Cow Yd. **25Dd**
Cowheel Alley **5Ad**
Cowley St. **23Bd**
Cox Ct. **15Aa**
Cox's Ct. **14Db**
Cox's Quay **15Cd**
Cox's Sq. **16Ab**
Crabtree Row **6Bb**
Cradle Ct. **15Aa**
Craigs Ct. **23Ba**
Cranbourn Alley **13Bd**
Cranburn St. **13Ad** **13Bd** **13Bc**
Crane Ct. **14Bc** **14Bb**
Crane Ct. **14Dc**
Craven Bldgs **5Cb**
Craven Bldgs **13Dc**
Craven Ct. **23Ba**
Craven St. **5Cb**
Craven St. **23Ba** **23Ca**
Craven Yd. **13Dc**
Crawford St. **11Ba** **11Ca**

For Key Map see p. 1

Crawfords Pass. 4Bc 4Bd
Creechurch La. 16Ac
Creed La. 14Dc
Crescent 15Aa
Crescent 16Ad
Crescent Pl. 6Bb
Crescent Pl. 14Cc
Crescent Pl. 24Cd
Crescent St. 2Dc
Crimscott St. 35Da 36Aa
Cripplegate Bldgs 15Ba
Crispin St. 16Aa
Croan Ct. 16Bb
Crooked Billet Ct. 15Da
Crooked Billet Yd. 6Ab
Crooked La. 15Cd
Crookets Alley 33Ca
Crosby Bldgs 6Ac
Crosby Row 25Bc
Crosby Row 35Ac
Crosby's Sq. 15Dc
Cross Alley 14Cb
Cross Alley 27Ab
Cross Ct. 12Cc
Cross Ct. 13Cc
Cross Gun Ct. 16Cd
Cross Keys 24Ca
Cross Keys Inn 15Cc
Cross Keys Sq. 15Ab
Cross Keys Yd. 25Cb 25Db
Cross La. 13Bc 13Cc
Cross La. 13Cb
Cross La. 15Bd
Cross La. 15Dd
Cross La. 32Bc 32Cc
Cross Row 17Da
Cross St. 4Bd
Cross St. 4Dd
Cross St. 5Cb
Cross St. 5Da
Cross St. 5Dc
Cross St. 6Bc
Cross St. 7Bc
Cross St. 7Db
Cross St. 12Cc
Cross St. 15Ca
Cross St. 16Dc
Cross St. 17Bd 17Bc
Cross St. 21Bc
Cross St. 24Cb 24Ca
Cross St. 26Ac 26Ab
Cross St. 26Dc
Cross St. 34Da
Cross St. 35Ac
Cross St. 35Da
Crown, The 4Cd
Crown Alley 6Ac
Crown Alley Yd. 25Bd
Crown and Anchor 14Ac
Crown and Scepter Ct. 22Ca
Crown Brewery 17Ba
Crown Ct. 4Ad
Crown Ct. 4Bd
Crown Ct. 5Ad
Crown Ct. 5Ad
Crown Ct. 6Ad 6Ac
Crown Ct. 6Bd
Crown Ct. 6Cc
Crown Ct. 8Bd
Crown Ct. 12Db
Crown Ct. 12Dc
Crown Ct. 13Cb 13Bb
Crown Ct. 13Cc
Crown Ct. 14Ac
Crown Ct. 14Ca
Crown Ct. 14Cc 14Bc
Crown Ct. 14Db
Crown Ct. 15Ac
Crown Ct. 15Ba
Crown Ct. 15Bb
Crown Ct. 15Cb
Crown Ct. 15Da
Crown Ct. 16Ac
Crown Ct. 16Cd
Crown Ct. 17Cd
Crown Ct. 23Bb
Crown Ct. 23Da 24Aa
Crown Ct. 25Bb
Crown Ct. 26Ab
Crown Ct. 27Bb
Crown Mews 12Cc
Crown Office 14Bc
Crown Office Row 14Bc
Crown Pl. 16Bd
Crown Pl. 34Db
Crown Row 8Ad
Crown Row 34Db 34Da
Crown St. 5Dc 5Db
Crown St. 13Ac 13Ab
Crown St. 15Ca 15Da
Crown St. 23Bb
Crown Yd. 25Bd
Croydon St. 11Ba
Crucifix La. 25Dc
Crutched Friars 16Ad
Cuckolds Ct. 25Aa
Cuckolds Point 28Cb
Culloden Ter. 1Cc
Cullum St. 15Dc
Cumberland Gdns 33Bd 33Bc
Cumberland Market 2Cb
Cumberland Mews 11Bb 11Cc
Cumberland Mews, North 11Bb
Cumberland Pl. 1Bd
Cumberland Pl. 35Db
Cumberland Pl., Great 11Cb
Cumberland Row 3Ca
Cumberland Row 34Ac
Cumberland Sq. 1Ab
Cumberland St. 1Bd
Cumberland St. 6Ad
Cumberland St. 6Ca
Cumberland St. 12Da
Cumberland St. 24Ca
Cumberland St. 31Aa
Cumberland St. Great 11Cc 11Cb
Cumberland Street North, Great 11Cb
Cumberland Ter. 1Ba
Cumming St. 4Aa
Cupers Bridge 24Aa
Cupids Ct. 5Ad
Curriers Ct. 15Ba
Cursitor St. 14Ab 14Bb
Curtain Rd. 5Dd 6Ac
Curtis's Row 24Bb
Curzon St. 22Aa 22Ba
Cushion Ct. 14Ca
Cushion Ct. 15Cb 15Cc
Custom House 15Dd 25Da
Custom House Ct. 15Dd
Custom House Quay 25Da
Custom House Stairs 25Da
Cut Throat La. 8Dc
Cut Throat La. 23Dd
Cutler St. 16Ab
Cutlers Hall 15Bc 15Bd

Dacre St. 23Ac
Dagger Ct. 15Ba
Daggets Ct. 15Da
Dalby Ter. 4Ca
Danish Church 16Dd
Darby St. 16Cd
Dark House La. 15Ad
Dark House La. 15Cd
Darling Row 17Ba
Dartmouth Row 23Ac
Dartmouth St. 23Ac
Darts Alley 16Cb
Davey and Sawyers Wharf 14Bd
Daveys Rents 25Cb
David Street 1Cd
Davies Mews 12Ac
Davies St. 12Ad 12Ac
Davis's Wharf 26Ab
Deacons Gdns 33Db
Deadmans Place Burying Ground 25Aa
Deal St. 16Ca
Deal Yd. 6Ac
Deal Yd. 18Cc 18Cd
Deals Ct. 16Bb
Dean St. 6Cc
Dean St. 12Db 13Ab 13Ac
Dean St. 13Da
Dean St. 14Bb
Dean St. 15Ca
Dean St. 17Cd 17Dd
Dean St. 21Da 22Aa
Dean St. 23Ad 23Ac
Dean St. 24Dc
Dean St. 25Cb
Dean St. 26Ca
Deans Bldgs 35Bb 35Cb
Deans Ct. 6Ab
Deans Ct. 14Cb
Deans Ct. 14Dc
Deans Ct. 15Ab
Deans Mews 6Ac
Deans Pl. 24Bd
Deans Row 34Dc 34Db
Deans Yard, Great, Westminster 23Bc
Deans Yard, Little, Westminster 23Bc
Deers Place 3Ba
Delahay St. 23Ac
Delap Ct. 22Dc
Denmark Ct. 5Ad
Denmark Ct. 13Ab 13Bb
Denmark Ct. 13Cd 13Cc
Denmark St. 13Ab 13Bb
Denmark St. 17Ad

Dentons Buildings 3Ba
Denzell St. 13Dc
Deptford and Greenwich Rd. 28Dc 28Dd 38Da 38Db 39Ab 39Ac
Deptford Lower Rd. 27Bd 38Ac 38Bd
Deptford Rd. 38Ab 38Aa 28Bd 28Cd
Derby Ct. 12Dd
Derby St. 22Aa
Derby St. 23Bb
Devonshire Bldgs 5Dd
Devonshire House 22Ba
Devonshire Mews 2Ad
Devonshire Mews, East 2Bd
Devonshire Mews, North 2Ad
Devonshire Mews, West 2Ad
Devonshire Pl. 2Ad
Devonshire Pl. 18Bb
Devonshire Pl. 33Dd 33Dc
Devonshire Place Mews 2Ad
Devonshire Row 2Bd
Devonshire Sq. 16Ab
Devonshire St. 2Ad
Devonshire St. 7Cd
Devonshire St. 13Da 13Ca 3Cd
Devonshire St. 15Db 16Ab
Devonshire St. 34Ac
Devreux Ct. 14Ac
Diamond Ct. 14Ca
Diana Pl. 2Cc
Dice Quay 15Dd
Digby Row 7Cb
Digby St. 7Cc
Dinow Row 7Cc
Diot St. 13Bb
Dirty La. 13Cd
Distaff La. 15Ac
Distaff La., Little 15Ac
Ditchmans Gdns 6Ab 6Ac
Dobneys Ct. 4Ba
Dobneys Pl. 4Ba
Doby Ct. 15Aa
Dock St. 16Cd
Dock St. 17Bc
Doctors Commons 14Dc
Dods Pl. 27Cc
Dog and Bear Yd. 25Bb
Dog and Bear Yd. 25Dc 25Db
Dog and Duck Stairs 38Ca
Dog Row, The 17Ba 7Bd 7Bc
Dolphin Ct. 5Ac
Dolphin Ct. 14Cc
Dolphin Ct. 16Aa
Dorans Row 17 Bc
Dorants Hotel 22Ca
Dorchester House 21Da
Dorrington St. 4Ad
Dorrington St. 14Ba
Dorset Ct. 14Cc
Dorset Mews 11Da
Dorset Mews West 11Ca
Dorset Sq. 1Bd
Dorset St. 11Ca
Dorset St. 14Cc
Dorset St. 16Aa 16Ba
Dorset Wharf 14Cc
Doughty Mews 3Dd
Doughty St. 3Dd
Dove Ct. 14Ba
Dove Ct. 15Ab
Dove Ct. 15Ac
Dove Ct. 15Cc
Dove Ct. 17Ba
Dove Ct. 25Ab
Dove St. 29Ba
Dover Pl. 35Ba
Dover Pl. 35Db 35Dc
Dover St. 22Ca 12Cd 12Bd
Dover St. 24Cc
Dover St., Great 25Bc 25Bd 35Ca
Dowdings Cooperage 27Ca
Dowgate Dock 15Bd
Dowgate Hill 15Bd 15Bc
Dowgate Wharf 15Bd
Down St. 22Ab 22Aa
Downing St. 23Bb
Downson Pl. 16Cb 16Ca
Doyle St. 31Ca
Drake St. 13Da
Drapers Almshouses 6Ab
Drapers Almshouses 9Bc
Drapers Almshouses 17Ba
Drapers Almshouses 34Da
Drapers Bldgs 15Cb
Drapers Gdns 15Cb
Drapers Hall 15Cb
Drapers Pl. 5Bc
Drum Ct. 16Cb
Drummond St. 2Db 3Ab
Drury La. 13Dc 13Cc 13Cb
Drury Lane Theatre 13Cc 13Dc
Duchess Mews* 12Ba
Duchess St.* 12Ba
Duck La. 12Dc
Duck La. 23Ad
Ducking Pond Mews 22Aa
Ducking Pond Row 17Aa
Ducks Foot La. 15Bd
Dudman's Ct. 38Bb
Dudman's Yd. 38Bb 38Cb
Dufours Pl. 12Dc
Duke of Yorks Chapel 23Ac
Duke Shore 28Ca
Duke St. 5Dd
Duke St. 6Bc 6Cc
Duke St. 11Db
Duke St. 12Ac 12Ab 11Db
Duke St. 12Ba
Duke St. 13Bb 13Ba
Duke St. 13Cd
Duke St. 13Db
Duke St. 14Da
Duke St. 16Aa
Duke St. 16Ac
Duke St. 17Bd 17Bc
Duke St. 22Da 22Ca 12Cd
Duke St. 23Ab 23Ac
Duke St. 24Bc 24Cc 24Cd
Duke St. 24Db
Duke St. 25Ac 25Ab
Duke St. Chapel 23Ac
Dukes Ct. 6Ab
Dukes Ct. 13Bc
Dukes Ct. 13Bd
Dukes Ct. 13Cc
Dukes Ct. 22Cd
Dukes Ct. 23Ac
Dukes Ct. 24Db
Dukes Head Ct. 15Ba
Duke's Head Ct. 25Cb
Dukes Head Pass. 14Db
Dukes Pl. 16Ac
Dukes Pl., Little 16Ac
Dukes Row 3Bb
Dukes Row 22Bd
Dukes St. 16Ac
Dulwich Almshouses 5Bc
Duncan Pl. 4Ca
Duncan St. 16Bc
Duncan Ter. 4Ca
Duncomb Ct. 6Ac
Dunk St. 16Ca
Dunnings Alley 15Da 16Aa
Dunstan Pl. 17Dd
Dunster Ct. 15Dd
Durham House 31Bc
Durham Pl. 24Ad 24Bd
Durham Pl. 31Bc
Durham Yd. 14Ca
Durweston Mews 11Ca 1Cd
Dutch Church 15Cb
Dutch Church Burial Ground 16Bc
Dutchess Mews 12Ba
Dutchess St. 12Ba
Dutton St. 3Cb
Dye House 6Bc 6Cc
Dyers Almshouses 4Db 4Da
Dyers Bldgs 14Bb
Dyers Ct. 15Bb
Dyers Ct. 16Cb
Dyers Hall 15Bd
Dyers Hall Wharf 15Bd
Dyers Pl. 3Ca
Dyers Row 9Dc

Eagle Ct. 4Cd 4Dd
Eagle Ct. 13Da
Eagle Ct. 13Dc
Eagle Pl. 7Cd
Eagle St. 12Dd
Eagle St. 13Da
Earl St. 14Cc 14Dc
Earl St. 24Cd
Earl St. 26Ab 26Ac
Earl St., Great 13Bc
Earl St., Little 13Bc
Earls Ct. 13Bc
Easleys Mews 12Ab
East:
With the exceptions below, names preceded by 'East' will be found under the second element, e.g. Harding St., East

For Key Map see p. 1

East Country Dock 38Bb
East Greenwich 40Da
East India Almshouses 19Cd
East India Dock Masters House 30Ca
East India Dock Rd. 18Dd 19Ad 19Bd 19Cd 19Dd
East India Docks 20Ad 20Bd 30Aa 30Ba
East India Docks, Engineers House 20Cd
East India Volunteers Drill Ground 5Ba 5Ca
East India Warehouses 16Ab 16Bc 16Ac 16Ad
East India Warehouses 25Ca
East La. 26Cd 26Cc
East La. 29Da
East La. 35Dc 35Db
East La. 40Ad
East Lane Stairs 26Cc
East London Water Works 9Ca
East Mews 34Ab
East Pl. 34Ab 34Aa
East Row 5Cb
East St. 1Dd
East St. 3Dd
East St. 8Ab
East St. 11Da 1Dd
East St. 16Ba
East St. 34Ab
East St. 34Ca
East St. 35Ac
Eastcheap, Great 15Cd
Eastcheap, Little 15Cd 15Dd
Eaton La., North 22Bd
Eaton St. 22Bd
Eaton St., Upper 22Bd
Ebden Ct. 24Cc
Ebenezer Pl. 24Cd
Ebenezer Pl. 34Bb
Ebenezer Sq. 16Ab
Ebury Pl. 32Aa
Eccleston St. 32Aa
Eden St. 2Cc
Edgware Rd. 11Bc 11Bb 11Ab 11Aa
Edingtons Wharf 14Cc
Edith Gdns 6Cb
Edna Pl. 20Ad
Eele Pl. 16Ca
Edward Ct. 12Ba
Edward Ct. 13Ad
Edward St. 2Ba
Edward St. 2Cb
Edward St. 6Cd 6Cc
Edward St 12Bb 12Ba
Edward St. 12Dc
Edward St. 18Ab 18Aa
Edward St. 18Bc 18Bb
Edward St. 24Ca
Edwards Mews 11Db
Edwards St. 11Db 12Ab
Eight Bells Yd. 13Ab
Eight Houses 38Bd
Elbow La. 15Bd
Elbow La., 17Bd
Elbow La., Little 15Bd
Elder St. 6Ad
Eldon Bldgs 4Ab
Elephant and Castle 34Da
Elephant La. 27Bc
Elephant Stairs 27Bc
Elizabeth Ct. 5Bc
Elizabeth Ct. 6Bd
Elizabeth Lodge 34Ab
Elizabeth Pl. 23Ad
Elizabeth Pl. 34Ab 34Ac
Elizabeth St. 6Da 6Db
Elizabeth St. 16Dd 16Dc
Elizabeth St. 21Bd
Ellies Row 6Dc
Elliot and Co's Brewery 22Cd
Elliots Row 34Ca
Elliotts Ct. 14Cb
Ellis Sq. 34Dc
Ellis St. 31Ca
Elm Ct. 4Ad
Elm Ct. 14Bc
Elm Ct. 34Db
Elm Row 17Cd 17Dd
Elm St. 4Ad
Elsworth Pl. 5Ad
Ely Ct. 14Ba
Ely Pl. 7Cc
Ely Pl. 14Ba
Ely Pl. 24Cd
Ely Place Mews 14Ba
Emanuel Hospital 22Dd
Engine St. 22Ba
Enoch Ct. 16Bd
Epping Pl. 17Ba
Ernest St. 2Bb
Essex Alley 16Bb
Essex Ct. 14Ac
Essex Ct. 16Bb
Essex Pl. 28Aa
Essex Pl. 33Db
Essex St. 6Aa
Essex St. 7Cc
Essex St. 14Ac
Essex St. 16Bb
Essex St. 16Db
Essex St., Little 14Ac
Essex Wharf 14Ac
Etham Pl. 35Ca
Eton Ct. 5Ac
Europa 27Bc 27Bd
Europe Pl. 5Ac
Euston Cres. 3Ab
Euston Grove 3Ab
Euston Pl. 2Dc
Euston Sq. 3Ab
Euston St. 2Db
Evangelist Ct. 14Cc
Evans Ct. 15Bb
Evelyn Pond 38Ad 37Dd
Everard Pl. 16Cd 16Cc
Everett St. 3Cc
Evesham Bldgs 3Aa
Evesham Bldgs, Upper 3Aa
Ewers St. 24Db
Ewings Bldgs 8Bd 8Cd
Exchange Alley 15Cc
Exchange Ct., New 13Cd
Exchequer Office 14Bc
Excise Office 15Db
Excise Office 17Ad
Exeter Change 13Dd
Exeter Ct. 13Dc
Exeter Pl. 21Bc
Exeter Pl. 22Bd
Exeter St. 13Cc 13Dc
Exeter St. 21Bc
Exeter St., Little 21Bc
Eyre Place 4Bd
Eyre St. 4Bd

Fair Cloth Ct. 33Ca
Fair St. 26Ab 26Ac
Fairfield 9Bb 9Bc
Falcon Coal Wharf 24Da
Falcon Ct. 14Cb
Falcon Ct. 25Ab 25Ac
Falcon Ct. 25Bb
Falcon Ct. 25Bc
Falcon Ct., Little 25Ac
Falcon Pl. 4Bd
Falcon Sq. 15Ab
Falcon St. 15Ab
Falconbridge Ct. 13Ab
Falconer Ct. 13Ab
Falkners Ct. 14Ca
Fan Ct. 5Ad
Fan St. 5Ad
Farm Mews 12Ad
Farm St. 12Ad
Farmer Row 18Cc
Farmer St. 27Ba 17Bd
Farmers Rents 13Ab
Farrers Rents 15Da
Farthing Alley 26Ca
Farthing Alley 26Cc
Farthing Fields 27Ba
Farthing St. 6Bd
Fashion St. 16Ba
Feamoor Rents 26Ac
Feather Ct. 13Dc
Feathers Ct. 13Db 13Da
Feathers Ct. 14Ba
Featherstone Bldgs 13Da
Featherstone Bldgs 18Cc
Featherstone Ct. 5Bc 5Cc
Featherstone St. 5Bc 5Cc
Felix St. 7Ba
Felix St. 23Dc
Fell St. 15Aa
Fellmongers 25Dd
Fen Ct. 15Dc
Fenchurch Bldgs 16Ac
Fenchurch St. 15Cc 15Dc 16Cc
Fendall St. 26Ad
Fenton St. 17Ac
Fenwick Ct. 14Aa
Fergusons Rents 25Cc
Ferry St. 33Ca
Fetter La. 14Bb
Field Ct. 14Aa
Field La. 14Ca
Field Pl. 34Dd
Field Row 3Da
Field St. 3Da
Fieldgate St. 16Db

Fifteenfoot La. **3Da**
Figtree Ct. **14Bc**
Figtree Ct. **15Aa**
Filbert Ct. **13Da**
Fillibet Ct. **15Ab**
Finch La. **15Cc**
Finch St. **16Cb** **16Ca**
Finches Bldgs **24Db**
Finch's Ct. **29Ca**
Finmore Ct. **16Cd**
Finsbury Ct. **5Cd**
Finsbury Market **5Dd**
Finsbury Pl. **15Ca**
Finsbury Sq. **5Cd** **15Ca**
Finsbury St. **15Ca**
Finsbury Ter. **5Cc**
Fire Ball Ct. **16Ab**
Fish St. **15Ac**
Fish Street Hill **15Cd**
Fish Street Hill, Old **15Ad** **15Ac**
Fisher St. **13Da**
Fishers Alley **14Cc**
Fishers Alley **16Ab**
Fishmonger Alley **25Bb**
Fishmongers Almshouses **34Da**
Fishmongers Hall **15Cd**
Fishmongers Pass. **15Dc**
Fitzroy Market **2Cc**
Fitzroy Row **2Cc**
Fitzroy Sq. **2Cd**
Fitzroy St. **2Cd**
Five Bells Bridge **9Cb**
Five Constable Row **17Ba**
Five Fields Row **31Db** **32Aa**
Five Foot La. **15Ad** **15Ac**
Five Garden Row **26Ac**
Five Inkhorn Ct. **16Cc** **16Cb**
Five Pipes, The **26Ab**
Fivefields Chapel La. **31Da**
Fives Ct. **16Bc**
Fleet La. **14Cb**
Fleet Market **14Cb**
Fleet Prison **14Cb**
Fleet River **4Ab** **4Ac**
Fleet Row **4Bd**
Fleet St. **6Cd**
Fleet St. **14Bc** **14Cc**
Fleet Street Hill **6Cd**
Flemings Church Yard **26Ba**
Fleur Delis St. **6Ad**
Flint St. **24Cc** **24Dc**
Flint St. **35Cc** **35Cb**
Flour Wharf **26Bb**
Flower and Dean St. **16Ba**
Flower de Lis Ct. **4Ad**
Flower de Lis Ct. **14Bb**
Flower de Lis Ct. **14Cc**
Flower de Lis St.* **6Ad**
Flower de Luce Ct. **4Cd**
Fludyer St. **23Bb**
Flying Horse Ct. **15Ab**
Flying Horse Ct. **15Ba**
Flying Horse Yd. **15Da**
Flying Horse Yd. **16Ca**
Foley Pl. **12Ba** **12Ca**
Folks Bldgs **15Dd**
Foot Guards Knightsbridge Barracks **21Cc**
Fore St. **15Ba** **15Bb**
Fore St. **28Ba** **28Ca** **28Da**
Fore St. **33Cb** **33Ca**
Fort Pl. **34Ba**
Fort Pl. **36Ba**
Fort St. **16Aa**
Foster La. **15Ab**
Foster St. **15Da**
Fosters Bldgs **5Bd**
Fosters Bldgs **6Ac**
Foubert Pass., Major **12Cc**
Foul La. **25Ba** **25Bb**
Foundling Hospital **3Cc**
Foundry Row **5Db**
Fountain Ct. **13Cd** **13Dd**
Fountain Ct. **14Ac** **14Bc**
Fountain Ct. **15Ac**
Fountain Ct. **16Ac** **16Bc**
Fountain Ct. **26Ac** **26Bc**
Fountain Garden **34Aa**
Fountain Pl. **5Bb** **5Cb**
Fountain Stairs **26Dc**
Four Mills, The **20Aa**
Four Swans Inn **15Db**
Fox Alley **33Cb**
Fox and Goose Yd. **27Ba**
Fox and Knot Ct. **14Ca**
Fox Ct. **4Bd**
Fox Ct. **14Aa** **14Ba**
Fox Ct. **16Ab**
Fox Ct. **22Ca**
Fox Ordinary Ct. **15Cc**
Fox Under The Hill Stairs **13Cd**
Fox's Bldgs **25Bc**
Fox's La. **27Ca** **17Cd**
Frances Ct. **13Cd**
Frances Ct. **33Cb**
Francis St. **2Dd** **3Ad**
Francis St. **12Dd**
Francis St. **34Db** **34Dc**
Franklins Row **31Cc**
Frazers Ct. **24Ca**
Frederick Pl. **2Cb**
Frederick Pl. **34Cb** **34Db**
Frederick St. **2Bc**
Frederick St. **2Cb**
Fredericks Pl. **15Bc**
Free Ct. **33Cb**
Freemans Ct. **15Cc**
Freemans La. **26Ab**
Freemasons Hall **13Db** **13Cb**
Freemasons School **24Bc** **24Bd**
Freeschool St. **26Ab** **26Ac**
French Alley **5Ad**
French Alley **5Bc**
French Alley **6Ac**
French Church **13Ac**
French Church **15Cc**
French Church **15Cd**
French Church **16Ba**
French Hospital **5Bc**
French Row **5Bb**
French Yd. **4Bc**
Fresh Wharf **15Cd**
Friendly Pl. **5Cd** **5Dd**
Friendly Pl. **24Ab**
Friendly Pl. **35Db**
Friday St. **15Ac**
Friday St., Little **15Ac**
Frith St. **13Ac** **13Ab**
Frogwell Ct. **14Da**
Frosty Ct. **16Cb**
Fry and Steel **15Ba**
Fryars Ct. **16Ad**
Fryer St. **26Db**
Fryers Ct. **16Cd**
Fryers St. **14Dc**
Frying Pan Alley **4Cd**
Frying Pan Alley **16Aa**
Frying Pan Alley **25Ba**
Frying Pan Alley **25Cb**
Frying Pan Alley **33Cb**
Frys Alley **27Ca**
Fuller St. **6Cd** **6Cc**
Fullers Almshouses **6Ab**
Fullers Almshouses **7Cd**
Fullwoods Rents **14Aa**
Fulmers Row **22Dd**
Furnivals Inn **14Ba**
Furnivals Inn Ct. **14Ba**

Gainsford St. **26Ab** **26Bb** **26Bc**
Galley Quay **25Da**
Gap, The **37Db**
Garden Ct. **14Ac**
Garden Ct. **14Ba**
Garden Ct. **15Aa**
Garden Ct. **16Ab** **16Bb**
Garden Ct. **23Dc**
Garden Pl. **24Ab**
Garden Pl. **34Ca**
Garden Row **4Da**
Garden Row **24Cd**
Garden Row **31Cb** **31Cc**
Garden Row **34Db**
Garden St. **17Db**
Garden St., Great **16Cb**
Garden Walk **5Dc**
Gardeners La. **23Bb** **23Bc**
Gardners La. **22Dd** **22Dc**
Garlick Hill **15Ad** **15Ac**
Garmouth Row **35Ab** **35Aa**
Gascoigne Pl. **6Bb**
Gate St. **13Db**
Gatwards Bldgs **5Cd**
Gays Bldgs **7Bd**
Gaywood St. **24Cd**
Gee St. **4Dc** **5Ac**
Genuine Beer Brewery **5Ad** **5Bd**
George, The **13Ad**
George Alley **14Cb**
George Alley **15Bd**
George Alley **15Cc**
George and Blue Boar Inn **13Db** **13Da**
George Ct. **4Bd**

For Key Map see p. 1

George Ct. **4Cd**
George Ct. **12Dd**
George Ct. **13Cd**
George Ct. **13Ad**
George Ct. **14Dc**
George Ct. **15Ac 15Ad**
George Ct. **16Ab**
George Ct. **23Ad**
George Ct. **26Bb**
George Inn **14Da**
George Inn **15Bb**
George Inn **25Bb**
George La. **15Cd**
George Pass. **24Dd**
George Pl. **31Bd**
George Row **35Cb**
George Stairs **26Bb**
George Stairs **38Cb**
George St. **2Dc**
George St. **3Db**
George St. **6Ad**
George St. **6Cc 6Cb**
George St. **6Cd**
George St. **7Bb 7Ba**
George St. **11Cb 11Da**
George St. **11Dc**
George St. **12Bc**
George St. **12Ca**
George St. **13Cd**
George St. **15Ab**
George St. **15Bc**
George St. **16Ac**
George St. **16Ad**
George St. **16Bb**
George St. **16Ca**
George St. **17Da 18Aa**
George St. **17Db**
George St. **18Ac**
George St. **18Bc 18Bb**
George St. **22Cd 22Cc**
George St. **22Da**
George St. **23Bc**
George St. **24Cb 24Db**
George St. **24Dc**
George St. **26Ad 26Bd**
George St. **31Cb 31Db**
George St. **33Cc**
George St. **35Ac 35Bc**
George St. **38Bb**
George St., Great **23Bc**
George St., Little **7Bb**
George St., Little **16Ac**
George St., Little **31Cb**
George St., Lower **31Cb**
George St., Upper **31Ca**
George St., West **11Bb 11Cb**
George Yd. **3Bd**
George Yd. **4Ca**
George Yd. **5Ac**
George Yd. **5Ad**
George Yd. **11Dc 12Ac**
George Yd. **12Ac 11Dc**
George Yd. **13Ab**
George Yd. **13Ac**
George Yd. **13Cc**
George Yd. **13Dc**
George Yd. **14Ba**
George Yd. **14Ca**
George Yd. **14Cb**
George Yd. **15Ac 15Bc**
George Yd. **15Cc**
George Yd. **16Cb**
George Yd. **16Cb 16Bb**
George Yd. **25Ab 25Bb 25Bc**
George Yd. **25Ca**
George Yd. **33Ca**
George Yd., Little **25Ab**
George Yd., Old **25Bd**
Georges Ct. **25Bc**
Georges Mall **24Bd**
Georges Row **5Ab 5Bb**
Georges Row **26Cd 26Cc**
Georges Row **24Cb**
Georges Sq. **5Db**
German Chapel **13Dd**
German Church **16Cc**
Gerrard St. **13Ac**
Gibbons Rents **25Db**
Gibralter Pl. **34Ca**
Gibralter Row **34Ca**
Gibralter Walk **6Cc 6Cb**
Gibsons Ct. **26Bb 26Bc**
Gilbert St. **13Ba 13Ca**
Gilberts Bldgs **24Bd**
Gilberts Bldgs **33Cc**
Gilhams Ct. **27Ac**
Gilhams Fields **5Dd**
Gill St. **18Dd**
Giltspur St. **14Db**
Gin Alley **18Ad**
Girdlers Hall **15Bb**
Glanville Mews **12Da**
Glass Ct. **4Bd**
Glasshouse Alley **14Bc**
Glasshouse Ct. **33Cc**
Glasshouse St. **12Cd 12Dd**
Glasshouse St. **33Cc**
Glasshouse Yd. **5Ad**
Glasshouse Yd. **14Cc**
Glasshouse Yd. **16Bd**
Glasshouse Yd. **24Db**
Glean Alley **25Cb**
Globe Ct. **25Aa**
Globe Ct. **26Db**
Globe Ct. **34Ab**
Globe La. **7Dd 7Dc 7Cc**
Globe Pl. **7Cb**
Globe Stairs **28Aa**
Globe Stairs Alley **28Aa**
Globe St. **7Cc 7Cb**
Globe Walk **25Aa**
Gloucester Bldgs **35Ab**
Gloucester Ct. **5Bd**
Gloucester Ct. **22Ca**
Gloucester House **11Dd**
Gloucester Mews **11Ca**
Gloucester Mews West **11Ca**
Gloucester Pl. **1Bd 1Cd**
Gloucester Pl. **11Ca 1Bd**
Gloucester Pl. **35Ab**
Gloucester Pl. **35Cd**
Gloucester Row **5Da**
Gloucester Row **6Ad**
Gloucester St. **5Da**
Gloucester St. **11Cb**
Gloucester St. **13Ca**
Gloucester St. **16Db**
Gloucester St. **24Bc**
Gloucester St. **33Cb**
Gloucester St., Little **11Ca**
Gloucester St., Upper **1Cd**
Gloucester Ter. **5Da**
Gloucester Ter. **16Db**
Glovers Hall **15Ba**
Goat St. **26Ab 26Ac**
Goat Yd. **5Ad**
Goat Yd. **25Ac**
Godfrey's Row **23Dc**
Godliman St. **14Dc**
Gold Sq. **16Ad**
Gold St. **17Db 17Da**
Gold St. **27Ba**
Golden Ct. **5Ad**
Golden Cross Inn **23Ba**
Golden Fleece Ct. **16Ac**
Golden La. **5Ad 5Ac**
Golden Leg Ct. **15Bc**
Golden Lion Yd. **14Aa**
Golden Lion Yd. **24Da**
Golden Mine Ct. **15Ab**
Golden Pl. **13Cc 13Cb**
Golden Sq. **12Dc**
Goldens Pl. **34Bb**
Golds Hill **17Dd**
Goldsmith St.* **14Bb**
Goldsmith St. **15Ab**
Goldsmiths Almshouses **6Da**
Goldsmiths Ct. **14Bb**
Goldsmiths Pl. **6Da**
Goldsworthy Ter. **37Ca**
Golsmith St. **14Bb**
Goodge St. **12Da**
Goodmans Gdns **6Bb**
Goodmans Still **16Cc**
Goodmans Yd. **16Bd**
Goodwins Ct. **13Bd**
Goswell Ct. **4Db**
Goswell St. **5Ad 4Dd 4Dc**
Goswell Ter. **4Db**
Gough House **31Bd**
Gough Sq. **14Bb**
Goulds Ct. **23Dc**
Goulston Sq. **16Bb**
Goulston St. **16Bc 16Bb**
Goulston St., New **16Bb**
Goveys Pl. **8Bd**
Gower Mews **13Aa**
Gower Mews, Upper **3Ad**
Gower St. **2Dc**
Gower St. **13Aa 3Ad**
Gower St., North **2Dc**
Gower St., Upper **3Ad**
Gowers Walk **16Cc**
Gracechurch St. **15Cd 15Cc 15Dc**
Gracers Alley **16Cd**
Grafton Ct. **11Da**
Grafton Mews **2Cd**
Grafton St. **2Cd**
Grafton St. **12Bd**
Grafton St. **13Bc 13Ac**

Grafton St., East 2Dc
Granby Bldgs 33Cb 33Db
Granby St. 2Ca
Granby St. 6Cc
Granbys Row 6Cc
Granbys Row 6Dc
Grand Junction Wharf 14Bc
Grand Surrey Canal 38Aa 38Ab 38Bc 38Bd 38Ad
Grand Surrey Inner Dock 28Ac 28Ad 38Aa
Grand Surrey Outer Dock 27Db 27Dc 28Ab 28Ac
Grange, The 36Aa 36Ba
Grange Ct. 13Bd
Grange Ct. 14Ab
Grange Rd. 25Dd 35Da 36Aa 36Ba 36Ca
Grange Road, The 36Ac 36Ab 36Bb
Grange Walk 25Dd
Grantham Pl. 22Ab
Gravel La. 16Ac 16Ab
Gravel La. 24Db 24Da
Gravel Lane, New 27Bb 27Ba 17Bd
Gravel La., Old 27Ab 27Aa 17Ad
Gravel Walk 5Bd
Gray Coat St. 32Da
Gray St. 11Db 12Ab
Grays Bldgs 11Db
Grays Inn Gdns 14Aa 4Ad
Grays Inn La. 3Ca 3Da 3Db 3Dc 4Ac 4Ad 14Aa
Grays Inn La., Little 4Ad
Grays Inn Pass. 13Da
Grays Inn Pl. 14Aa
Grays Inn Sq. 14Aa
Grays Walk 34Ab 33Da 33Db
Great
With the exceptions below names preceded by ‘Great’ will be found under the second element, e.g. Portland St., Great
Great Garden 26Ba
Great Gun 23Ba
Great St. Helens 15Dc
Great St. Helens Church 15Db
Great Yd. 25Db 25Dc
Greek St. 13Ac 13Ab
Green Arbor Ct. 14Dc
Green Bank 25Db
Green Bank 27Ab
Green Church Yard 26Ba
Green Coat Pl. 22Dd
Green Coat School 22Dd
Green Ct. 15Bb
Green Ct. 24Ca 24Da
Green Dragon Alley 18Bd
Green Dragon Alley 27Bb 27Ba
Green Dragon Ct. 14Ca
Green Dragon Ct. 16Cb
Green Dragon Ct. 25Ba
Green Dragon Inn 15Db
Green Dragon Yd. 13Cb
Green Dragon Yd. 14Db
Green Gate Gdns 6Bb
Green Harbour Ct. 5Ad
Green Harbour Ct. 14Cb
Green Harbour Ct. 15Ba
Green House Row 24Cd
Green Lettice La. 15Bd 15Cd
Green Man 36Ac
Green Park 22Ba 22Ca 22Ab 22Bb 22Cb
Green Pl. 7Db
Green St. 3Dd
Green St. 7Cb 7Db
Green St. 11Cc 11Dc
Green St. 13Ad 13Bd
Green St. 24Ca
Green St., Upper 24Dc
Green Walk 24Cb 24Ca
Green Walk 24Cc 24Dc
Green Walk 26Cc
Green Yd. 15Ba
Green Yd. 16Cd
Greenfield St. 16Db
Greenhills Rents 14Ca 14Da
Greenland Pl. 3Cb
Greens Ct. 12Dc
Greens Row 31Bc
Greenwood Ct. 26Ca
Gregory Pl. 25Cb
Gregs Alley 16Bb
Gresse St. 13Ab 13Aa
Grevell St. 3Aa
Greville St. 14Ba
Grey Coat Pl. 22Dd
Grey Coat School 22Dd
Grey Coat St.* 32Da
Grey Eagle St. 6Bd
Grey St. 11Db 12Ab
Greyhound 14Ca
Greyhound Ct. 14Ac
Greyhound Ct. 26Ba
Greyhound La. 17Aa
Griffin Inn 25Bc
Griffin St. 27Ca
Griffins Wharf 25Da
Griffiths Rents 25Db
Griggs Ct. 16Bd
Grocers Ct. 6Ac
Grocers Hall 15Bc
Grocers Hall Ct. 15Bc
Grog Ct. 18Cd
Grosvenor Market 12Ac
Grosvenor Mews 12Bc 12Bd
Grovesnor Mews, Upper 21Dc
Grosvenor Pl. 22Ac 21Dc 21Db
Grosvenor Pl., Lower 22Bd
Grosvenor Row 31Db
Grosvenor Sq. 11Dc 11Dd 12Ac 12Ad
Grosvenor St. 12Ac 12Bc
Grosvenor St. 33Ba
Grosvenor St., Little 12Bd 12Bc
Grosvenor St., Upper 11Dd
Ground St., Upper 24Ba 24Ca
Grove House 21Cc
Grove Pl. 1Ac
Grove Pl. 7Ba
Grove Pl. 17Ba
Grove Pl. 38Cd
Grove Rd. 8Bb 8Bc 8Cc
Grove St. 1Ac
Grove St. 16Dc
Grove St. 38Bb 38Bc
Grub St. 15Ba
Grub St. 33Ba
Grubs Yd. 25Aa
Guildhall 15Bb
Guildhall, Middlesex 23Bc
Guildford Mews 3Cd
Guilford Pl. 3Dd
Guilford St. 3Dd
Guilford St., Great 25Ab 25Aa 24Da
Guilford St., Little 3Cb
Guilford St., Little 25Ab
Guilford St., Upper 3Cd
Gun Alley 15Ba 15Ca
Gun Alley 25Dc
Gun Alley 27Ab
Gun Alley, Upper 27Ab
Gun and Shot Wharf 25Da
Gun Ct. 4Dd
Gun Ct. 16Cd
Gun Dock 27Ab
Gun Gdns 24Cd
Gun House Alley 33Cc
Gun La. 18Dd
Gun Sq. 16Ac
Gun St. 16Aa
Gun St. 24Cc 24Dc
Gunhouse Stairs 33Cc
Gunners House 23Ba
Gunpowder Alley 14Bb 14Cb
Gutter La. 15Ab
Guys Hospital 25Cb
Guys Hospital Garden 25Bb
Guys Mad House 25Bb
Gwyns Buildings 4Ca
Gynns Pl. 1Ac

Haberdashers Almshouses 5Db
Haberdashers Ct. 14Cb
Haberdashers Pl. 5Db
Haberdashers Sq. 15Ba
Haberdashers St. 5Cb 5Db
Haberdashers Walk 5Db
Hackney Rd. 6Ab 6Bb 6Ba 6Ca 6Da
Hackney Road Cres. 6Bb
Hadlow St. 3Bb
Hagley Pl. 35Aa
Haglins Gateway 25Cb
Hale Street 29Ba
Half Moon Alley 15Ba
Half Moon Alley 16Bc
Half Moon Ct. 4Bd
Half Moon Ct. 26Cb
Half Moon Inn 25Bb 25Bc
Half Moon St. 15Da
Half Moon St. 22Ba
Half Nicols St. 6Ac 6Bc
Half Paved Ct. 14Cc
Half Penny Hatch 33Ab 33Bb

For Key Map see p. 1

Halfpenny Hatch 24Bb
Halfpenny Hatch 35Aa
Halfway House 37Db
Halifax St. 16Ca 16Da
Halls Ct. 26Ba
Hallsey Pl. 9Cc
Halsey Ct. 25Ac
Ham Yd. 12Dd
Hamden Pl. 7Db
Hamden St. 3Aa
Hamet St. 16Ad 16Bd
Hamilton Row 3Da
Hamilton St. 22Ab
Hammer Alley 25Cb
Hammer and Crown Ct. 18Ad
Hampshire Hog Yd. 13Bb
Hampstead Rd. 2Cb
Hampton St. 34Db
Hanbury Pl. 29Aa
Hand Alley 15Da
Hand and Pen Ct. 16Ac
Hand Ct. 5Ad
Hand Ct. 13Cd
Hand Ct. 14Aa
Hand Ct. 15Bd
Hand Ct. 16Ac
Handcocks Yd. 14Cc
Hanging Field 4Aa
Hangmans Gains 26Ba
Hanover Ct. 15Ba
Hanover Ct. 16Cb
Hanover Sq. 12Bc 12Bb
Hanover Stairs 27Cb
Hanover St. 12Bc 12Cc
Hanover St. 13Cc
Hanover St. 27Cb 27Cc
Hanover St. 34Db
Hans Pl. 21Bd
Hans Row 7Ac
Hans St. 21Bd 21Cd
Hans Town Brewery 31Cb
Hanway St. 13Ab
Harcourt 11Ba
Harcourt Bldgs 14Bc
Harding St., East 14Bb
Harding St., West 14Bb
Hare, The 7Ba
Hare Alley 6Ac
Hare Ct. 6Cd
Hare Ct. 14Bc
Hare Ct. 15Aa
Hare Marsh 6Cd 6Cc
Hare Row 7Ba
Hare St. 6Aa
Hare St. 6Cd
Hare Walk 6Aa
Harebrain St. 16Cd
Hares La. 6Dc 6Db
Harewood Pl. 12Bb
Harford and Co. Brewery 28Ca
Harford La. 34Dc 35Ac
Harford Pl. 13Dc
Harley Mews 12Bb 12Ba
Harley Mews, North 12Aa
Harley St. 12Ba 12Aa
Harley St., Upper 2Ad
Harlow Pl. 17Ba
Harp Alley 14Cb
Harp Ct. 15Ba
Harp La. 15Dd
Harpur St. 13Da
Harpurs Walk 33Ca
Harrards Alley 16Cd
Harrells Row 27Ab
Harrison St. 3Cb
Harris's Ct. 17Ad
Harris's Ct. 17Dd
Harrow Alley 16Ab
Harrow Alley 16Bc
Harrow Ct. 14Dc
Harrow Dunghill 25Ac
Harrow St. 25Ac
Hart St. 11Dc 12Ac
Hart St. 13Bb 13Cb 13Ca
Hart St. 13Bc 13Cc
Hart St. 15Aa 15Ba
Hartleys Wharf 26Ab
Hartshorn Ct. 5Ad
Hartshorn Ct. 16Ac
Harvey Bldgs 13Cd
Hat and Tun Yd. 4Bd
Hatchcliffs Bldgs 40Dd
Hatfield Pl. 24Ca
Hatfield Pl. 24Cd
Hatfield St. 5Ad
Hatfield St. 24Ba
Hatton Chapel 4Bd
Hatton Garden 14Ba 4Bd
Hatton Wall 4Bd
Haughton St. 13Dc
Haunch of Venison Yd. 12Bc
Hawes Almshouses 29Da
Hawkes Wharf 14Bc
Hawkins Ct. 16Cd
Hawksbury Pl. 35Bb
Hawley Pl. 27Dc
Hay Hill 12Bd
Hay Market 13Ad 23Aa
Haydon Sq. 16Bc
Haydon Yd. 16Bc
Haymarket* 13Ad 23Aa
Hays Ct. 13Ac
Hays Mews 22Aa 12Ad
Hays Wharf 25Ca 25Da
Hazle Wood Ct. 5Bd
Heath Pl. 7Ba
Heath St. 17Dc
Heddon Ct. 12Cc
Heddon St. 12Cd 12Cc
Hedges Ct. 24Cc
Helmet Ct. 13Dc
Helmet Ct. 14Dc
Helmet Ct. 15Bb
Helmet Ct. 15Db
Helmet Ct. 15Dc
Helmet Ct. 26Ba
Helmet Row 5Ac
Hemlock Ct. 14Ab
Hemmings Row 13Bd
Hen and Chicks 35Cc
Henrietta St. 3Cc
Henrietta St. 6Cb 6Ca
Henrietta St. 12Ab 12Bb 12Cb
Henrietta St. 13Cd
Henry Pl. 35Cc
Henry Row 22Cd
Henry St. 2Cc
Henry St. 4Aa
Henry St. 4Ad
Henry St. 5Bc
Heralds Office 14Dc
Herberts Pass. 13Cd
Hercules Bldgs 24Ad
Hercules Hall 24Ad
Hereford St. 11Cc
Hermes St. 4Aa
Hermitage 9Ca 9Cb
Hermitage Stairs 26Cb
Hermitage St., Gt. 26Cb 26Db
Hermitage St., Little 26Cb
Herns Ct. 16Cd
Herring Ct. 18Ac
Hertford Pl. 7Dd
Hertford Row 3Da
Hertford St. 3Ba
Hertford St. 2Dd
Hertford St. 22Aa
Hewets Ct. 13Bd
Hickmans Folley 26Bc 26Cc
Hickmans Rents 26Ac
High Bridge 40Ad
High Holborn 13Cb 13Da 14Aa
High Park 35Cc
High Row 21Bc 21Bb
High St., Islington 4Ca
High St., Lambeth 33Cb 33Ca 33Da
High St., Marylebone 12Aa 11Da 1Dd 2Ad
High St., Newington 34Cb 34Db
High St., St. Giles' 13Ab 13Bb
High St., or, Upper Shadwell 17Bd 17Cd
High St., Whitechapel 16Ca
High Timber St. 15Ad
Highlers La. 24Bb 24Bc 24Cc 24Dc
Hill Ct. 6Ad
Hill St. 5Cd
Hill St. 22Aa 12Ad
Hilliards Ct. 27Bb
Hills Bldgs 32Ab
Hind Ct. 14Bb
Hind Alley 24Da
Hinde Mews 12Ab
Hinde St. 12Ab
Hinds Ct. 15Ab
Hoare and Co. 14Cc
Hobson Pl. 16Ca
Hobsons Bldgs 26Ac
Hog La. 5Dd 6Ad
Hog Yard, The 16Cd
Holborn 14Ba
Holborn Ct. 14Aa
Hole in Wall Pass. 14Ba
Holland St. 24Ca
Hollen St. 12Db
Holles St. 12Bb
Holliday Yd. 14Dc
Hollis St. 13Dc
Holliwell Row 5Dd
Hollow, The 5Ac
Holloway St., Great 16Cb 16Db
Holloway St., Little 16Db

Holyfield Row 34Ac 34Ab
Holywell La. 6Ad
Holywell St. 13Dc 14Ac
Homer Pl. 11Aa
Homer Row 11Aa
Homer St. 11Aa 11Ba
Honduras Iron Wharf 24Da
Honduras Wharf 24Da
Honey Lane Market 15Ac 15Bc
Honey Suckle Ct. 15Ba
Hoods Iron Wharf 14Cc 14Cd
Hoole Place 3Ba
Hooper St. 4Dd
Hoopers Ct. 16Ca
Hoopers Ct. 21Bc
Hoopers Sq. 16Cc
Hope St. 6Bd
Hope St. 16Cb
Hope Town 6Cc
Hopkins St. 12Dc
Hoptons Almshouses 24Ca 24Da
Horatios Pl. 35Bd
Horn Alley 4Ad
Horn Brewery 24Bb
Horn Ct. 6Ab
Horney La. 26Ad 26Bd
Horns 34Ad 34Bd
Horse and Dolphin Yd. 13Ac
Horse and Grome 13Da
Horse and Groom Yd. 34Cb
Horse Ferry Rd. 18Bd
Horse Ferry Rd. 22Dd 23Ad 33Aa 33Ba
Horse Guards 23Bb
Horse Row 25Bb 25Bc
Horsemonger La. 25Ad
Horseshoe Alley 5Ac
Horseshoe Alley 15Ca 15Da
Horseshoe Alley 16Ab 16Bb
Horseshoe Alley 25Aa
Horseshoe Alley Stairs 25Aa
Horseshoe Brewery 13Ab 13Bb
Horseshoe Ct. 14Ac
Horseshoe Ct. 14Cc
Horseshoe St. 16Bb
Horsley St. 35Ad
Horsleydown New Stairs 26Bb
Horsleydown Old Stairs 26Ab
Horslydown La. 26Ab
Hosier La. 14Ca
Houndsditch 15Db 16Ab 16Ac
Howard St. 14Ac
Howards Green 4Da
Howards Pl. 7Ba
Howland Mews 2Dd
Howland Mews West 2Cd
Howland St., Little 2Cd 2Dd
Hoxton 6Ab 6Aa
Hoxton Market Pl. 5Dc 5Db
Hoxton Sq. 5Db
Hoziers Mill 27Ac
Hudson St. 34Db
Hudsons Wharf 14Cd 14Cc
Huggin La. 15Ab
Hugging La. 15Ad 15Ac
Hugh Middleton's Head, Sir 4Cb
Hughes's Ct. 24Dd
Huish Ct. 14Cc
Hulls Pl. 5Ab
Hulls St. 5Ab
Humbers St. 16Dc
Hungerford Market 23Ba 23Ca
Hungerford Stairs 23Ca
Hungerford St. 13Bd 23Ba 23Ca
Hunt Ct. 26Ab
Hunt St. 6Cd
Hunter St. 3Cc
Huntingdon St. 6Aa
Hunton St. 3Cc
Hunts Bldgs 38Db
Hunts Ct. 6Cd
Hunts Ct. 13Bd
Hunts Ct. 17Cd
Hupts Ct. 13Bd
Husband St. 12Dc
Hyde Park 11 21
Hyde Park Corner 21Bb 21Bc
Hyde Park Turnpike 21Db
Hyde St. 13Cb
Hylords Ct. 16Ad

Idol La. 15Dd
India House 15Dc
Inmans Bldgs 34Da
Inn Holders Hall 15Bd
Inn St., New 6Ac
Innage La. 16Ac
Inner Temple 14Bc
Inner Temple La. 14Bc
Inverness Street 1Bb
Ireland Row 17Ca
Ireland Yd. 14Dc
Iron Bridge 20Cd
Iron Gate Stairs 26Ba
Iron Gate Wharf 26Ba
Ironmonger La. 15Bc 15Bb
Ironmonger Row 5Bc 5Ac
Ironmongers Almshouses 6Aa 6Ba
Ironmongers Company Land 5Bc
Ironmongers Hall 15Dc
Isaacs Pl. 3Bb
Island Row 18Cd
Isle of Dogs 29 30
Islington 3Ab 3Ca
Islington Rd. 4Cc 4Cb 4Ca
Ivey Bridge 13Cd
Ivy La. 5Da
Ivy La. 14Db
Ivy St. 13Bb

Jacksons Ct. 14Dc
Jacob St. 26Bc 26Cc
Jacobs Ct. 14Ca
Jacobs Mews 11Da
Jacobs Well 15Aa
Jamaica House 27Ad
Jamaica Pl. 18Dd
Jamaica Pl. 24Cc
Jamaica Row 26Dd
James Ct. 5Cc
James, James and Co.'s British Wine Manufactory 15Ca
James Pl. 27Ba
James Rents 6Ab
James Row 24Dc
James St. 1Ad
James St. 3Bb
James St. 5Cc
James St. 5Dc
James St. 6Cd 6Cc
James St. 7Cc
James St. 12Ac 12Ab
James St. 13Ad
James St. 13Cc
James St. 13Cd
James St. 16Dc 17Ac
James St. 18Aa
James St. 18Bc 18Bb
James St. 22Cc
James St. 24Ac
James St. 24Cc
James St. 29Ac
James St. 35Ac
James St., Great 3Dd
James St., Little 3Dd 4Ad
James St., Lower 12Dd 12Dc
James St., Upper 12Dc
James's Pl. 6Da
James's Pl. 26Dd
Jane Pl. 35Ca 35Da
Jane Shore Alley 6Ac
Jane St. 6Ca
Jane St. 17Ac
Jeffreys Bldgs 23Ac
Jeffries Sq. 15Dc
Jenkins Ct. 28Ca
Jermyn Ct. 12Dd
Jermyn St. 22Ca 22Da 12Dd
Jermyn St., Little 22Ca
Jerusalem Ct. 4Cd
Jerusalem Ct. 4Cd 4Dd
Jerusalem Ct. 15Cd
Jetsom St. 24Cc
Jewin Ct. 15Aa
Jewin St. 15Aa
Jewry St. 16Ac
Jews Burial Grounds 7Ad
Jews Burying Ground 7Dd
Jews Burying Ground 8Bd
Jews Ct. 12Ab
Jews Hospital and Burial Ground 8Ad
Jews Row 31Cc 31Cb 31Db
Jews Walk 7Bb
Jockeys Fields 14Aa
John Ct. 3Bb
John Ct. 15Ab
John Ct. 16Ca
John St. 1Bd
John St. 4Ad
John St. 5Dc
John St. 7Bd
John St. 7Db

For Key Map see p. 1

John St. 11Aa
John St. 12Cb
John St. 12Da 2Da
John St. 13Cd
John St. 16Ad
John St. 16Ba
John St. 16Ca
John St. 16Dd 17Ad
John St. 17Aa
John St. 17Ad
John St. 17Bc
John St. 17Cc
John St. 18Aa
John St. 18Bc
John St. 22Aa 12Ad
John St. 22Da
John St. 23Bd
John St. 24Ca
John St. 24Cb
John St. 25Ac
John St. 25Cb
John St. 26Ac 26Ab
John St. 26Cd 26Cc
John St. 34Aa
John St. 35Ca 35Da
John St. 35Cc 35Cb
John St., Lower 12Dd
John St., Upper 2Dd
John St., Upper 12Dc 12Cc
Johns Bldgs 23Ad
Johns Ct. 16Bc
Johns Ct. 26Ba
Johns Ct. 26Bc
Johns Mews 4Ad
Johns Pl. 5Ac 5Ab
Johns Row 5Ab
Johns Sq. 16Cc
Johnson St. 17Bd
Johnson St. 27Aa
Johnsons Bldgs 3Ca
Johnsons Bldgs 17Bd
Johnsons Bldgs 24Cd
Johnsons Ct. 14Bb
Johnsons Ct. 16Cc
Johnsons Ct. 23Ad
Johnsons Ct. 24Cd
Joiners Alley 15Bd
Joiners Hall Bldgs 15Bd
Joiners Pl. 24Bd
Joiners St. 25Cb 25Ca

Jones Ct. 7Dd
Joseph St. 3Cb
Jubilee Pl. 17Cc 17Bc
Jubilee Pl. 31Ac 31Ab
Judd Pl., East 3Ca
Judd Pl., West 3Bb
Judd St. 3Bb
Judge Fullers Almshouses 6Ab
Judge Fullers Almshouses 7Cd
Jurston St. 24Bc

Keat Ct. 16Bb
Keat St. 16Bb
Keens Row 35Ad 35Ac
Keeps Alley 5Ac
Kemps Ct. 12Dc
Kendalls Mews 11Da
Kennet Wharf 15Ad
Kennings Bldgs 27Cc
Kennington Common 34Bd
Kennington Cross 34Ac
Kennington Green 34Ad 34Ac
Kennington La. 33Cd 33Dc 34Ab 34Bc 34Bb 34Cb
Kennington Meeting 34Bc
Kennington Oval 33Dd 34Ad
Kennington Pl. 33Dc
Kennington Pl. 34Ac
Kennington Pl. 34Ad 34Bd
Kennington Pl., Upper 34Ad
Kennington Row 34Bd
Kent Pl. 35Da 35Db
Kent Road, The 35Ca 35Db 35Dc 36Ac 36Bd 36Cd
Kent St. 25Bc 25Bd 25Cd
Kent Street Rd. 35Ca
Kent Ter. 1Ba
Kentish Bldgs 25Bb
Kenton St. 3Cc
Keppel St. 3Bd
Keppel St. 25Ab
Keppel St. 27Aa
Kepple St., Little 3Ad
Key Ct. 14Ca
Keys Mews 12Aa
Kinder St. 17Ac
King and Queen Stairs 27Da
King Davids La. 17Bd
King Edward St. 14Cc
King Edward St. 16Da

King Edward St. 27Bb
King Edwards Stairs 27Bb
King Harry 8Ad
King Henry Ct. 27Ba
King Henry VII's Chapel 23Bc
King Henry Yd. 26Ca
King James's Stairs 27Ca
King John Ct. 6Ad 6Ac
King Johns Ct. 28Da
King Johns Palace 18Ab
King Sq. 6Bd
King Square Ct. 12Db
King Stairs 27Ac
King St. 4Dc
King St. 5Bc
King St. 5Dc 5Db
King St. 6Bb 6Cb
King St. 6Bd
King St. 11Ca
King St. 11Dd
King St. 12Cc 12Cb
King St. 13Ac
King St. 13Bc 13Bb
King St. 13Bc 13Cc
King St. 13Ca
King St. 13Cb
King St. 14Da
King St. 15Bc 15Bb
King St. 16Ac
King St. 16Bd
King St. 16Da
King St. 16Dc
King St. 22Da
King St. 23Bc 23Bb
King St. 24Dc
King St. 25Ac 25Ab
King St. 25Bb
King St. 26Db
King St. 27Ab 27Bb 27Ba
King St. 27Ac
King St. 31Db
King St. 33Da
King St. 35Ac
King St. 35Da
King St. 35Dc
King St., Little 22Ca
King St. Mews 11Cd 11Dd
King St. West 11Bb
Kings Arms and Hand Inn 25Dd
Kings Arms Ct. 11Cb

Kings Arms Gdns 17Cd 17Cc
Kings Arms Inn 15Dc
Kings Arms Row 8Aa
Kings Arms Stairs 23Db
Kings Arms Yd. 15Ba
Kings Arms Yd. 13Cb
Kings Arms Yd. 14Cb 14Ca
Kings Arms Yd. 15Bb 15Cb
Kings Arms Yd. 33Cc
Kings Bench 24Dc 25Ac
Kings Bench Office 14Bc
Kings Bench Row 24Dc
Kings Bench Ter. 24Dc
Kings Bench Walk 14Bc
Kings Bench Walk 24Cc 24Dc
Kings Ct. 24Dc
Kings Gate St. 13Da 13Ca
Kings Head 14Aa
Kings Head Ct. 5Bd
Kings Head Ct. 6Ad
Kings Head Ct. 9Cc
Kings Head Ct. 14Bb
Kings Head Ct. 15Ab
Kings Head Ct. 15Cd
Kings Head Ct. 15Da
Kings Head Ct. 16Ab
Kings Head Ct. 23Ac
Kings Head Ct. 23Bd
Kings Head Ct. 24Da
Kings Head Inn 25Bb
Kings Head Yd. 13Bb
Kings Head Yd. 13Db
Kings Head Yd. 24Ca
Kings Head Yd. 25Db
Kings Head Yd. 33Ca
Kings Mews 4Ad
Kings Mews 13Bc 23Ba
Kings Mill 27Cb
Kings Pl. 22Da
Kings Pl. 35Ac
Kings Private Road, The 21Bb 21Cb 21Db
Kings Rd. 4Ad
Kings Rd. 27Cc 27Cd
Kings Rd. 29Cb 29Ca
Kings Rd. 31Bc 31Bb 31Cb
Kings Rd. 31Ca 31Da 21Dd 22Ad
Kings Road Ter. 31Ac
Kings Row 4Aa
Kings Row 7Bd

Kings Row **21Bc**
Kings Row **22Bd**
Kings Row **26Bb**
Kings Row **27Cd** **27Cc**
Kings Row **35Ad**
Kingston Rd. **33Bd**
Kingstons Wharf **26Db**
Kirby St. **14Ba**
Kirkmans Pl. **13Aa**
Kirmand St. **2Cb**
Kittelby Ct. **16Cd**
Kittisford Pl. **6Ba**
Knight Rider Ct. **14Dc**
Knight Rider St., Great **14Dc**
Knight Rider St., Little **14Dc**
Knights Ct. **24Da**
Knights Ct. **27Ab**
Knightsbridge **21Cb** **21Db**
Knightsbridge Barracks **21Cc**

Labour in Vain Ct. **15Ac**
Labour in Vain St. **27Ca**
Lad La. **15Ab** **15Bb**
Lads Ct. **24Da**
Lady Lumley's Almshouses **5Bb**
Lady Owens Almshouses **4Ca**
Laizenby Ct. **13Bc**
Lamb Alley **15Da**
Lamb Alley **25Dc**
Lamb Ct. **15Da**
Lamb Ct. **16Ba**
Lamb Ct. **4Cd**
Lamb Green **25Dc**
Lamb Pass. **5Bd**
Lamb Row **7Ad**
Lamb St. **16Aa** **16Ba**
Lambeth Butts **33Db**
Lambeth Churchyard **33Ca** **33Da**
Lambeth Hill **15Ac**
Lambeth Marsh **23Dc** **24Ac**
Lambeth Mews **22Ba**
Lambeth Palace **33Ca** **33Da**
Lambeth Rectory House **33Da**
Lambeth Rd. **24Bd** **24Cd**
Lambeth Stairs **33Ca**
Lambeth St. **16Cc**
Lambeth Ter. **24Ad**
Lambeth Water Works **23Da**
Lambeth Workhouse **33Db**
Lambs Bldgs **5Bd**
Lambs Bldgs **14Bc**
Lambs Conduit Pass. **13Da**
Lambs Conduit St. **3Dd**
Lambs Pl. **35Db**
Lamp Yard **3Dd**
Lancaster Ct. **13Bd**
Lancaster St. **3Bb**
Langdale St. **16Dc**
Langley St. **13Bc**
Langleys Bldgs **35Cc**
Langthorn Ct. **15Cb**
Langs Ct. **13Ad**
Lansdown House **12Bd**
Lansdown Mews **3Dd**
Lansdown Pl. **3Cc**
Lant St., New **25Ac**
Lant St., Old **25Ac**
Lascells Ct. **13Bb**
Lascells Pl. **13Bb**
Laundry Yd. **23Ad**
Lavender La. **28Ba**
Lavender Pl. **28Ba**
Lawn, The **33Cd**
Lawrence La. **15Bc** **15Bb**
Lawrence Pountney La. **15Cd**
Laystall St. **4Ad** **4Bd**
Layton's Bldgs **25Bc**
Lea, River **20** **10**
Lea Cut **19**
Lead Yd. **16Cc**
Leadenhall Market **15Dc**
Leadenhall St. **15Dc** **16Ac**
Leading St. **17Cd**
Leather La. **14Ba** **4Bd**
Leathersellers Bldgs **15Cb**
Leblond's Bldgs **6Ac**
Lees Ct. **26Ba**
Lees Mews **11Dc**
Lees Row **24Cd**
Leg Alley **13Cc**
Leg Ct. **23Ad**
Leg of Mutton Gdns **6Ab**
Leicester Ct. **13Bd**
Leicester Pl. **13Ac** **13Ad**
Leicester Sq. **13Ad**
Leicester St. **12Cd**
Leicester St. **13Ad**
Leigh St. **3Bc**
Leigh St. **13Da**
Leman St. **16Cc**
Lemon Ct. **33Cb**
Lemon Ct., Great **33Cb**
Lemon Row **16Cd**
Lemon St. **24Db**
Leonard Ct. **5Dc**
Leonard Sq. **5Dc**
Leonard St. **5Cc** **5Dc**
Leopard Ct. **14Ba**
Lepards Ct. **28Aa**
Lestock Pl. **35Ac**
Leverington Pl. **5Db**
Lewingtons Bldgs **5Cc**
Lexwood Pl. **2Cc**
Life Guards Barracks **21Ab** **21Bb**
Life Guards Stables **11Ca**
Lilly St. **4Cd**
Lillyput La. **15Ab**
Lime St. **15Dc**
Lime Street Sq. **15Dc**
Lime Wharf **14Cc**
Lime Wharf **23Ba** **23Ca**
Limehouse **28Da** **28Db**
Limehouse Causeway **28Da**
Limehouse Churchyard **18Cd** **18Dd**
Limehouse Cut **18Cd** **18Dd** **18Dc** **19Ac**
Limehouse Dock **18Bd**
Limehouse Hole **28Da**
Limehouse Hole Stairs **28Ca**
Limekiln Ct. **28Da**
Limekiln Dock **28Ca** **28Da**
Limetree Ct. **23Da** **24Aa**
Lincolns Inn Fields **13Db** **14Ab**
Lincolns Inn Gdns **14Ab**
Lincolns Inn New Sq. **14Ab**
Lincolns Inn Old Bldgs **14Ab**
Lion St. **35Ab** **35Aa** **34Da**
Lion Wharf **25Aa**
Liquorpond St. **4Ad**
Lisbon St. **17Ba**
Lisle St. **13Ad** **13Ac**
Lisson Green **1Ad**
Lisson Grove House **1Bd**
Lisson Grove La. **1Bd**
Lisson Grove North **1Ac**
Lisson Grove Rd. **1Ac**
Lisson Grove South **1Ad**
Lisson Mews **11Aa**
Lisson Pl. **1Ad**
Lisson Row **1Ad**
Lisson St. **11Aa**
Litchfield St. **13Ac** **13Bc**
Little
With the exceptions below, names preceded by 'Little' will be found under the second element, e.g. Portland St., Little
Little Britain **14Db** **15Ab**
Little Ct. **13Bc**
Little St. Helens Church **15Db**
Little Turnstile **13Db**
Lloyds Ct. **13Ab** **13Bb**
Lloyd's Yd. **15Cb**
Lock Hospital **22Ac**
Lock Pl. **35Ac**
Locks Fields **35Bb**
Locks Row **35Ac**
Lockwood Ct. **4Cd**
Lomans Pond **24Db**
Lomans Pond St. **24Db**
Lombard St. **14Bc**
Lombard St. **15Cc**
Lombard St. **16Ca**
Lombard St., Great **25Ab**
Lombard St., Little **25Ab**
Lomber Ct. **13Bc**
Lomber St. **13Bc**
London Bridge **15Cd** **25Ca**
London Cavalry Riding House **5Bb**
London Coffee House **14Cc** **14Cb**
London Dock **26Da** **27Aa**
London Hospital **17Aa**
London House Yd. **14Dc**
London Light Horse Stables **4Ac**
London Light Horse Stables **5Dd**
London Light Horse Target Ground **4Ab**
London Mews **2Dd**
London Rd. **24Cd** **24Dd** **34Da**
London Spa **4Bc**
London St. **2Cd**
London St. **18Ad**
London St. **24Dd**
London St. **26Bc** **26Cc**
London St., New **16Ad** **16Ac** **15Dc**

For Key Map see p. 1

London Tavern **15Dc**
London Wall **15Ba 15Bb 15Cb 15Db**
London Workhouse **15Da**
Long Acre **13Bc 13Cc 13Cb**
Long Alley **15Da 5Dd**
Long Alley **16Dd**
Long Alley Sq. **15Da**
Long La. **14Da**
Long La. **25Bc 25Cc 25Cd 25Dd**
Long Walk **25Dd**
Long Yd. **3Dd**
Longs Bldgs **5Bd**
Longs Ct. **13Ad**
Longs Ct. **27Bc**
Lothbury **15Bb**
Love Ct. **4Cd**
Love Ct. **14Cb**
Love Ct. **16Bb**
Love La. **15Ab 15Bb**
Love La. **15Cd 15Dd**
Love La. **17Dd**
Love La. **24Da**
Love La. **27Ab**
Love La. **27Ac**
Love La., Little **15Ab**
Lovers Ct. **14Db**
Lowdells Pass. **24Bb**
Lower
With the exception below, names preceded by 'Lower' will be found under the second element, e.g. Thames St., Lower
Lower Turning **27Ca**
Lownds Ct. **12Cc**
Lucas Pl. **17Cc**
Lucas St. **3Cb**
Lucas St. **17Cc**
Lucas St. **27Ac 27Ad**
Ludgate, Old **15Da**
Ludgate Hill **14Cc**
Ludgate St. **14Cc 14Dc**
Luke St. **5Dc**
Lumley Ct. **13Cd**
Lumley's Almshouses, Lady **5Bb**
Luntley Pl. **16Cb 16Ca**
Luxfords Row **5Dd**
Lyceum **13Dc**
Lynn St. **24Cd**
Lyon St. **13Cb**
Lyons Inn **13Dc**
Lyons Quay **15Cd**
Mabledon Pl. **3Bb**
Macclesfield St. **13Ac**
Macords Rents **27Ab**
Maddox St. **12Cc**
Maddox St., Little **12Bc**
Magdalen Hospital **24Cc**
Magdalen St. **25Db**
Magpie Ct. **15Ab**
Maid La. **24Da 25Aa**
Maiden La. **3Ca**
Maiden La. **13Cd**
Maiden La. **15Ab**
Maiden La. **15Ad 15Bd**
Maidenhead Ct. **6Ad 6Bd**
Maidenhead Ct. **15Aa**
Maidenhead Ct. **15Ba**
Maidenhead Ct. **15Bc**
Maidenhead Ct. **26Ba**
Maidenhead Ct. **27Ab**
Maidenhead Ct. **27Ba**
Maidmann Row **8Bd**
Maidstone Bldgs **25Bb**
Maines's Pl. **26Dd**
Major Foubert Pass. **12Cc**
Maling Pl. **27Cc 27Dc**
Manchester Bldgs **23Bc**
Manchester House **11Db 11Da**
Manchester Mews **11Da**
Manchester Sq. **11Db**
Manchester St. **11Da**
Manor Bldgs **31Ac**
Manor House Farm **34Dc**
Manor Pl. **31Ac**
Manor Pl. **34Dc**
Manor Row **17Bd**
Manor Row **31Ac**
Manor Row **34Dc**
Manor Row **37Cb**
Manor St. **31Ad**
Manor Ter. **31Ac**
Manor Way **40Db**
Mansel St. **16Ad 16Ac**
Mansfield Pl. **24Cd**
Mansfield St. **12Ba**
Mansfield St. **24Cd**
Mansion House **15Bc**
Mansion House Row **34Bb 34Bc**
Mansion House St. **15Bc**
Maps Row **17Da**
Marble St. **25Cb**
Marchmont St. **3Cc**
Marden Ct. **24Ba**
Margaret Ct. **12Cb**
Margaret St. **12Bb 12Cb**
Margaret St. **23Bc**
Margaret St. **33Db**
Margarets St. **3Ab**
Maria Pl. **36Cb**
Marine Cres. **26Cd**
Maritime Almshouses **18Da**
Mark La. **15Dd 15Cd**
Mark St. **5Dc**
Market Hill **17Cd**
Market La. **23Aa 13Ad**
Market Row **12Cb**
Market Row **13Ad**
Market St. **12Cb**
Market St. **12Dd**
Market St. **13Ac**
Market St. **24Dd 24Cd**
Market St. **34Bb**
Market St., New **27Bb**
Markham Row **31Ac**
Marlborough Ct.* **12Cc**
Marlborough Gdns **31Ba**
Marlborough House **22Db**
Marlborough Pl. **34Ac**
Marlborough Pl. **34Db**
Marlborough Row **12Dc 12Cc**
Marlborough Sq. **23Ad**
Marlborough St., Great **12Cc 12Cb**
Marlborough St., Little **12Cc**
Marlborough Tavern **31Bb**
Marlbro Ct. **12Cc**
Marmaduke Ct. **17Ac**
Marmaduke St. **16Dc**
Marman St. **16Dc**
Marques Ct. **13Dc**
Marsh Pl. **24Ac**
Marshall St. **12Dc**
Marshall St. **24Cd**
Marshalsea **25Bb**
Marsham St. **33Ba 33Aa 23Ad**
Martha St. **17Bc**
Martin Ct., New **16Cd**
Martin St. **13Ad**
Martin St. **16Bb**
Martins Bldgs **5Bc**
Martins Bldgs **27Ba**
Martlet Ct. **13Cc**
Mary Ann St. **16Dc**
Mary Pl. **2Cb**
Mary St. **2Cc**
Mary St. **17Ad 17Ac**
Marygold Ct. **25Dd**
Marygold St. **26Dd 26Dc**
Marylebone **12Aa**
Marylebone La. **12Ab 12Aa**
Marylebone Mews **12Aa**
Marylebone Pass. **12Cb**
Marylebone St. **12Dd**
Marylebone St., Great **12Aa**
Marylebone St., Little **12Aa**
Marylebone St., Upper **12Ca 2Cd**
Marys Row **7Ab**
Mason St. **3Ba**
Mason St. **23Dc**
Mason St. **35Cb 35Ca**
Masons Arms Mews **12Cc 12Bc**
Masons Bldgs **5Cb**
Masons Ct. **6Ac**
Masons Ct. **16Cb**
Masons Yd. **12Ca**
Masons Yd. **13Cb**
Masons Yd. **22Da**
Masons Yd. **33Ba**
Masters in Chancery's Office **14Ab**
Matthew St. **5Dc**
Matthews Pl. **7Aa**
Maudlins Rents **26Ca**
Maxwell Ct. **15Ca**
May Bldgs **34Ad**
May Pole Alley **25Bb**
Mayfair Chapel **22Aa**
Maynard St. **13Ab**
Mayors Row **21Cb**
Mays Bldgs **13Bd**
Mays Bldgs **22Aa**
Mays Bldgs, Little **13Bd**
Mays Row **18Cd**
Maze, The **25Cb**
Maze Ct., Great **25Cb**
Maze Ct., Little **25Cb**
Maze Pond **25Cb**
Mead Pl. **24Bd**
Mead Row **24Ad 24Bd**
Mead St. **6Bc**
Meadow Row **34Da 35Aa**
Meads Ct. **12Cd**
Meards Ct. **13Ac**

Mecklenburgh Sq. 3Dc
Medway St. 33Aa
Meeting House Alley 27Ab
Meeting House Ct. 5Dd
Meeting House Ct. 14Cc
Meeting House Ct. 26Bb
Meeting House Walk 25Cc
Meeting House Yd. 26Bc
Meggs Almshouses 16Db
Melina Pl. 24Bd
Mellins Rents 14Cb
Meltor St. 25Cb
Mercer St. 13Bc
Mercers Almshouses 18Ab
Mercers Ct. 15Dd
Mercers Hall 15Bc
Mercers Row 17Bd
Merchant Taylors Almshouses 16Bd
Merchant Taylors Hall 15Cc
Merchant Taylors School 15Bd
Merchants Row 18Dc
Merlins Cave 4Bb
Merlins Pl. 4Bb
Mermaid Ct. 25Bb 25Bc
Mermaid Row 25Cc
Merrets Bldgs 15Da
Merton Ct. 16Dd
Mestaers Rents 27Da
Mestaers Yd. 27Da
Meux's Brewery 4Bd
Michaels Grove 21Ad
Michaels Pl. 21Ad
Middle Row 14Aa
Middle Row 21Bc
Middle Shadwell 17Cd
Middle St. 14Da
Middle Temple 14Ac 14Bc
Middle Temple La. 14Bc
Middle Turning 27Ca
Middlesex Bldgs 6Bb
Middlesex Ct. 13Cb
Middlesex Guildhall* 23Bc
Middlesex Hospital 12Da
Middlesex Pl. 1Ad
Middlesex Pl. 6Bb
Middlesex St. 3Ba
Middlesex St. 16Bb
Middletons Bldgs 12Ca
Middleton's Head, Sir Hugh 4Cb
Midford Pl. 2Dd
Midway Pl. 37Dc
Mile End Corner 17Ba
Mile End Green 17Aa 17Ba
Mile End Old Town 17Ba 17Ca 17Da 7Dd 8Ad 8Bd 8Cd 8Cc
Mile End Row 17Ca
Miles's La. 15Cd
Miles's Rents 25Cd
Milford La. 14Ac
Milford Lane Wharf 14Ac
Military Hospital 22Dc
Milk Alley 13Ac
Milk St. 15Ac 15Ab
Milk St. 35Ad
Milk Yd. 27Ba
Mill Bank Distillery 32Bd 32Bc
Mill Bank Row 33Ba
Mill Bank Stairs 33Bc
Mill Bank St.* 33Ba 23Bd
Mill Bank Wall 33Ac 33Bc 33Bb
Mill Hill Mews 12Ab
Mill La. 25Db 25Da
Mill Pl. 18Cd
Mill Pond Bridge 27Ad
Mill Pond Row 27Ad
Mill Pond St. 27Ad
Mill St. 12Cc
Mill St. 26Bc 26Cc
Mill Wall Stairs 28Dd
Mill Yd. 4Bd
Mill Yd. 16Cd 16Cc
Millbank St. 33Ba 23Bd
Millers Ct. 15Bb
Millman St. 3Dd
Millman St., New 3Dd
Mills Bldgs 21Bb
Mill's Ct. 5Dc
Mills Rents 35Ac
Mincing La. 15Dd
Minor Pl. 24Dc
Minories 16Ac 16Bd
Mint Sq. 25Ab
Mint St. 25Ac
Mr.
For names preceded by 'Mr.' see under the name
Mitcham St. 1Ad
Mitchell Ct. 5Ac
Mitchell St. 5Ac
Mitre Ct. 14Ba
Mitre Ct. 14Bc
Mitre Ct. 15Ab
Mitre Ct. 15Ac
Mitre Ct. 16Ac
Mitre Ct. 25Ac
Moffatt St. 5Bb 5Ba
Molton St., South 12Bc 12Ac
Molyneux St. 11Ba
Money Bag Alley 16Cd
Monks Bldgs 5Da
Monkwell St. 15Ab 15Aa
Monmouth Ct. 13Ad
Monmouth Ct. 13Bc
Monmouth Pl. 35Cc 35Dc
Monmouth St. 13Bc 13Bb
Monmouth St. 17Cd
Monster, The 32Bb
Monster Row 32Ac 32Ab 32Bb
Montague Close 25Ba
Montague Ct. 14Da
Montague Ct. 16Aa
Montague House 11Cb
Montague Mews 11Cb 11Ca
Montague Mews 13Ca 13Ba
Montague Mews North 11Ca
Montague Mews South 11Cb
Montague Pl. 11Ca
Montague Sq. 11Ca 11Cb
Montague St. 11Cb
Montague St. 13Ca 13Ba
Montague St. 16Ab
Montague St. 16Ba 16Ca
Montague St., Old 16Cb
Montague St., Upper 11Ca
Montfort Pl. 34Ad
Montpelier Tea Gardens 34Dd 35Ad
Monument Yd. 15Cd
Moon Rakers Alley 24Dc
Moor Alley 6Ad
Moor Fields, Little 15Ca
Moor La. 15Ba
Moor Pl. 24Ad
Moor Pl. 34Aa 34Ba
Moor Pl., Little 34Ba
Moor Sq. 15Ba
Moor St. 11Bb 11Ba
Moor St. 13Ac 13Bc
Moorfields, Little* 15Ca
Moorfields, Little 15Cb
Moors Ct. 16Bb
Moors Gdns 5Dd
Moors Yd. 13Bd
Moors Yd. 16Ba
Moreland and Co., Bricklayers 5Ac
Morgans La. 25Db 25Da
Morgans Row 16Dc
Morgans Wharf 27Da
Morley's Floor Cloth Manufactory 21Cc
Morman and Smith, Sawmaker 5Ac
Mornington Pl. 2Ca
Morris Ct. 26Bb
Morrison St. 27Dc
Morris's Walk 25Aa
Mortimer Market 2Dd
Mortimer St. 12Ca
Morton St. 24Dd
Moss's Alley 24Da
Motley Ct. 5Dd
Motley St. 5Dc
Mouldmakers Row 15Ab
Mount, The 20Ac
Mount, The 25Bc
Mount Ct. 16Ab
Mount Ct. 35Ad
Mount Gdns 24Ad 24Ac
Mount Pl. 6Bc
Mount Pl. 35Ad
Mount Pleasant 4Ad
Mount Pleasant 5Cb
Mount Pleasant 19Ac
Mount Row 5Cb
Mount Row 12Ad
Mount Row 17Aa
Mount Row 24Ac
Mount Row 35Ca
Mount St. 6Bc
Mount St. 11Dd 12Ad
Mount St. 17Aa
Mount St. 17Ab
Mount St. 24Ac
Mount St. 35Ad
Muds Ct. 17Dd

For Key Map see p. 1

Muggridge Bldgs **25Ab**
Mulberry Ct. **15Da**
Mulberry Ct. **25Ab**
Mulberry Ct. **25Cd**
Mulberry St. **16Db** **16Cb**
Mulbery Gdns **16Da**
Mumford Ct. **15Bb**
Muscovy Ct. **16Ad**
Music House Ct. **17Cd**
Mutton La. **4Cd**
Mutton La. **17Ca**
Myrtle St. **5Da**

Nags Head **6Da**
Nags Head Ct. **5Ad**
Nags Head Ct. **13Dc**
Nags Head Ct. **15Cc** **15Cd**
Nags Head Inn **25Bb**
Nags Head Yd. **6Da**
Naked Boy Alley **33Cb**
Naked Boy Ct. **14Cc** **14Cb**
Narrow St. **18Ad** **18Bd**
Narrow Wall **23Db** **23Da** **24Aa** **24Ba**
Nassau St. **13Ac**
Naval Row **30Aa**
Neales Pass. **13Bc**
Neales Yd. **13Bc** **13Bb**
Neat Boys Ct. **16Ba**
Neat House Gdns **32**
Neat House Row **32Bc** **32Bb**
Neckenger, The **26Bd**
Nelson Pl. **5Bb**
Nelson Pl. **35Bb**
Nelson Sq. **24Cb**
Nelson St. **3Ab**
Nelson St. **5Bb**
Nelson St. **6Bc**
Nelson St. **6Ca**
Nelson St. **16Bc**
Nelson St. **17Ab**
Nelson Ter. **4Da**
Nelsons Ct. **35Bb**
Nelsons Head **36Bd**
Nelsons Pl. **29Da**
Nelsons Pl. **35Db**
Neptune Ct. **27Bd**
Neptune Ct. **35Bb**
Neptune Pl. **24Bb** **24Ba**
Neptune Pl. **35Bb**
Neptune St. **16Dd**
Neptune St. **27Bc** **27Bd**
Nesbeth Rents **28Da**
Nevills Ct. **14Bb**
New
With the exceptions below, names preceded by 'New' will be found under the second element, e.g. Tothill St., New
New Alley **28Ca**
New Bldgs **15Cb**
New Bldgs **26Ca**
New Ct. **4Cc**
New Ct. **4Dc**
New Ct. **5Ad**
New Ct. **5Dd**
New Ct. **6Ad**
New Ct. **6Ad** **6Ac**
New Ct. **6Bc**
New Ct. **6Bd**
New Ct. **14Ac**
New Ct. **14Ac** **14Ab**
New Ct. **14Bb**
New Ct. **14Ca** **14Da**
New Ct. **14Cb**
New Ct. **15Aa** **15Ba**
New Ct. **15Ac**
New Ct. **15Bc**
New Ct. **15Da**
New Ct. **16Aa**
New Ct. **16Ab**
New Ct. **16Ab** **16Aa**
New Ct. **16Ac**
New Ct. **16Ad**
New Ct. **16Ba**
New Ct. **16Bb**
New Ct. **16Db**
New Ct. **22Dd** **22Dc**
New Ct. **23Ad**
New Ct. **25Aa**
New Ct. **25Bc**
New Ct. **34Cb**
New Crane Dock **27Bb** **27Ba**
New Crane Stairs **27Bb**
New Cut **18Cd**
New Cut **24Bb**
New Grove Cottage **8Dc**
New Inn **13Dc**
New Inn **14Cb**
New Inn Stables **23Dc**
New Inn Pass. **13Dc**
New Inn Yd. **6Ac**
New La. **26Bc** **26Bb**
New Penitentiary, The **33Ab** **33Bb** **33Ba** **33Aa**
New Ranelagh **32Cd**
New Rents **15Ab**
New River Head **4Bb**
New River Office and Yard **14Cc**
New Rd. **16Dd**
New Rd. **17Ac** **17Ab** **16Db**
New Rd. **31Ca** **31Cd** **31Bd** **31Bc**
New Road Nursery **3Ca**
New Sq. **16Ac**
New Sq. **23Ad**
New St. **1Cd**
New St. **5Bb**
New St. **5Bc**
New St. **6Bb** **6Ba**
New St. **12Dc**
New St. **13Bb**
New St. **13Bd**
New St. **14Da**
New St. **14Dc**
New St. **16Ab**
New St. **16Db**
New St. **17Ab**
New St. **21Bc**
New St. **23Ba**
New St. **24Cc**
New St. **25Ab**
New St. **25Cb**
New St. **26Ac**
New St. **26Ba**
New St. **27Bd**
New St. **27Ca**
New St. **27Cc**
New St. **33Cc**
New St. **33Dc**
New St. **34Bc** **34Cc**
New St. **35Ab** **35Aa**
New St. **35Bc**
New St., Great **14Bb**
New St., Little **14Bb** **14Cb**
New St., Little **24Dc**
New St., Middle **14Bb**
New Street Hill **14Cb**
New Street Sq. **14Bb**
New Ter. **5Cc**
New Walk **26Bc**
New Way **23Ad** **23Ac**
New Way **25Cb**
Newby Pl. **29Da**
Newcastle Ct. **14Ac**
Newcastle Ct. **15Bd**
Newcastle Pl. **4Cd** **4Cc**
Newcastle Pl. **17Ba**
Newcastle St. **4Cc**
Newcastle St. **13Dc**
Newcastle St. **16Bb**
Newgate **14Db**
Newgate Market **14Db**
Newgate St. **14Db** **15Bb**
Newhams Rents **16Db**
Newington **34Cb** **34Da**
Newington Causway **24Dd**
Newington Pl. **34Bd** **34Bc** **34Cc**
Newington Rd. **34Da** **24Dd** **25Ad**
Newman Mews **12Db**
Newman St. **12Db** **12Da**
Newman St., Upper **12Da**
Newmans Row **25Dd**
Newnham St. **11Aa** **11Ba**
Newnhams Pl. **16Aa**
Newport Ct. **13Ac** **13Bc**
Newport Market **13Bc**
Newport St. **13Bc**
Newport St., Little **13Ac** **13Bc**
Newports Yd. **5Bc**
Newton St. **13Cb**
Newton Ter. **34Ad**
Nicholas La. **15Cd** **15Cc**
Nicholsons Timber Yd. **14Bd**
Nicols Ct. **16Cd**
Nicols Row **6Bc**
Nicols Sq. **15Aa**
Nicols St., Half **6Ac** **6Bc**
Nicols St., New **6Ac** **6Bc**
Nicols St., Old **6Ac** **6Bc**
Nightingale Ct. **26Ca**
Nightingale La. **18Cd**
Nightingale La. **26Ca**
Nile Pl. **34Da**
Nile St. **5Cb**
Nine Elms, Hamlet of **33Ad**
Noahs Ark Alley **18Bd**
Noahs Ark Ct. **23Dc**
Noble St. **4Dc** **5Ac**
Noble St. **15Ab**
Noble St. **29Ba**
Noel St. **12Db**
Noel St. **35Ca**

Norfolk College 40Bd
Norfolk House 22Da
Norfolk Pl. 6Ac
Norfolk Pl. 7Dd
Norfolk Pl. 26Dd 26Dc
Norfolk Pl. 34Ca 34Da
Norfolk Row 33Da
Norfolk St. 11Cc
Norfolk St. 14Ac
Norfolk St. 17Ab
Norfolk St. 24Db 25Ab
Normans Bldgs 5Ac
Normans Ct. 16Dd
Normans St. 5Ac
Norris St. 13Ad
North
With the exceptions below, names preceded by 'North' will be found under the second element, e.g. Seymour Pl., North
North East Alley 16Dd
North Green 5Dd
North Mews 2Dd
North Mews 4Ad
North Pl. 4Ad
North Pl. 5Bc
North Pl. 7Cb
North Pl., Upper 4Ac
North Row 11Cc 11Dc
North Row 35Ac
North Row Mews 11Dc
North St. 2Dd
North St. 3Da
North St. 5Cc
North St. 7Ad
North St. 7Db
North St. 11Da
North St. 15Ca
North St. 16Ba
North St. 17Aa
North St. 19Bd 19Bc
North St. 21Bc
North St. 23Bd
North St. 29Ba 19Bd
North St. 35Bc 35Bb
North St., New 13Da
North St., Old 13Da
Northampton Arms 4Db
Northampton Bldgs 4Cc
Northampton Ct. 4Cc
Northampton Field 4Bb
Northampton Pl. 4Cc
Northampton Pl. 6Da
Northampton Pl. 35Dc
Northampton Row 4Bc
Northampton Sq. 4Db
Northampton St. 4Cc
Northampton St. 35Bb
Northampton St. 35Dc
Northampton St., Little 4Cc
Northampton Ter. 5Ab
Northams Buildings 3Ba
Northumberland Ct. 4Dc
Northumberland Ct. 14Aa
Northumberland Ct. 23Ba
Northumberland Gdns. 23Ba
Northumberland Mews 1Dd
Northumberland St. 1Dd
Northumberland St. 23Ba
Norton Falgate 6Ad
Norton St. 2Cd
Norton St. 8Ab
Norwell Pl. 6Cc 6Dc
Norwich Ct. 14Bb
Norwich Ct. 26Ba
Nottingham Ct. 13Bc 13Bb
Nottingham Mews 1Dd
Nottingham Pl. 1Dd
Nottingham Pl. 16Db
Nottingham Pl. 35Bc
Nottingham St. 1Dd
Nursery Pl. 24Bd
Nursery Row 35Bb
Nutkins Corner 26Cc

Oakley St. 24Ac 24Bc
Oakleys Row 6Cc
Oakly Ct. 6Cd
Oat La. 15Ab
Oatmeal Yd. 25Dc
Obelisk, The 24Cd
Ocean St. 18Ab 18Aa
Off Alley 13Cd
Ogle Ct. 12Ca
Ogle St. 12Ca
Old
With the exceptions below, names preceded by 'Old' will be found under the second element, e.g. Swan La., Old
Old Artillery Ground 16Aa
Old Bailey 14Dc 14Db
Old Barge House Brewery 24Ba
Old Change 15Ac
Old Dock 30Ab
Old Jewry 15Bc 15Bb
Old Square 18Ab
Old St. 5Ad 5Ac 5Bc 5Cc
Old Street Rd. 5Cc 5Dc 6Ab
Old Street Sq. 5Bc
Oil Wharf 26Cb
Olivers Bldgs. 9Cc
One Swan Yd. 15Da
Onslow St. 4Bd
Opera House 23Aa
Orange Coffee House 31Db
Orange Ct. 13Cc 13Dc
Orange Ct. 16Db
Orange Pl. 37Ca
Orange Row 34Cb
Orange St. 12Cc
Orange St. 13Ad 13Bd
Orange St. 13Ca 13Da
Orange St. 24Db
Orchard, The 18Ad
Orchard, The 27Ca
Orchard House 30Da
Orchard St. 5Ac 5Ab
Orchard St. 11Dc 11Db
Orchard St. 23Ad
Ord St. 28Dc
Orions Bldgs 25Ab
Ormond Mews 3Cd 3Dd
Ormond Pl. 3Dd
Ormond St., Great 3Cd
Ormond St., Little 3Cd
Ormond St., New 3Dd
Ormond Yd. 22Da
Orphans Working School 4Db
Osborn Pl. 16Ca
Osborn St. 16Cb
Osnaburg St. 2Bc
Osnoburg Row 22Ad
Ossulston St. 3Aa
Owens Almshouses, Lady 4Ca
Owen Ct. 4Ca
Owens Pl. 4Ca
Owens Row 4Ca
Oxendon St. 13Ad
Oxford Arms 14Db
Oxford Bldgs 12Ac 12Ab
Oxford Chapel 12Ab 12Bb
Oxford Ct. 12Bb
Oxford Ct. 15Bc
Oxford Market 12Cb
Oxford Pl. 24Cc
Oxford Row 35Db
Oxford St. 12Ab 12Bb 12Cb 12Db 13Ab
Oxford St. 17Ab
Oxley Ct. 26Bc 26Cc

Packstones Alley 27Cc
Paddington Canal Wharf 11Aa
Paddington Street 1Dd
Pageant, The 28Ba
Pages Walk 35Da
Pagets Ct. 17Bd
Pagets Pl. 17Bd
Painters Rents 18Ad
Palace Row 2Dc
Palace St. 22Cd
Palace Yard, New 23Bc
Palace Yard, Old 23Bd 23Bc
Palace Yard Stairs 23Cc
Palatine Pl. 16Db
Palgrave Ct. 14Ac
Pall Mall 22Da 23Aa
Pall Mall Ct. 22Da
Palmers Rents 25Cc
Palmers Village 22Dd
Pancras St. 2Dd
Pancrass La. 15Bc
Pancrass Pl. 3Ba
Pantheon 12Cb 12Db
Panton Sq. 13Ad
Panton St. 13Ad
Paper Bldgs 14Bc
Paradise Ct. 3Da
Paradise Ct. 7Bb
Paradise Pl. 5Cc
Paradise Pl. 11Da
Paradise Pl. 29Ba
Paradise Row 3Ba

For Key Map see p. 1

Paradise Row **7Bb**
Paradise Row **24Db**
Paradise Row **27Aa**
Paradise Row **27Ad** **27Bd**
Paradise Row **31Bd**
Paradise Row **33Da**
Paradise St. **3Da**
Paradise St. **5Cc** **5Dc** **5Cd** **5Dd**
Paradise St. **11Da**
Paradise St. **27Ac** **27Bc** **27Bd**
Paradise Walk **31Bd**
Paragon **35Ba** **35Ca**
Paragon Pl. **35Ba**
Paragon Row **35Ab** **35Bb**
Paris Pl. **11Aa**
Parish St. **25Dc** **25Db**
Park La. **1Cc**
Park La. **22Ab** **22Aa** **21Da** **11Dd** **11Cd** **11Cc**
Park Pl. **1Cc**
Park Pl. **21Bb**
Park Pl. **22Ca**
Park Pl. **34Ac**
Park Pl. **35Cb** **35Cc**
Park Prospect **23Ac**
Park Row **21Bb**
Park Row **28Da**
Park Row **34Ac**
Park St. **1Cc**
Park St. **11Dd** **11Dc**
Park St. **23Ac**
Park St. **25Ba** **25Bb**
Park St. **28Da**
Park St. **34Ac**
Park St., Little **1Cd**
Park St., Little **33Dc** **33Db**
Parker La. **13Cb** **13Db**
Parker Row **26Bd** **26Bc**
Parkers Bldgs **36Ba**
Parliament St. **7Bc**
Parliament St. **23Bc** **23Bb**
Parrott Alley **5Bd**
Pars Bldgs **11Dc**
Parsonage Walk **34Ca** **34Da**
Parsonage Yd. **6Ac**
Parsons Ct. **14Cc**
Parsons Stairs **26Cb**
Parsons St. **16Cd** **16Dd**
Partridge Ct. **16Ab**
Pasfields Rents **27Ac**
Pater Noster Pl., Little **16Aa**
Paternoster Row **14Dc** **14Db** **15Ab**
Paternoster Row **16Aa** **16Ba**
Patience St. **6Bd**
Patriot Sq. **7Ba** **7Bb**
Patriot St. **16Dc**
Patterson Gdns **16Cc** **16Dc**
Patys Ct. **6Ad**
Paul Sq. **5Dd**
Paul St. **5Dd** **5Dc**
Pauls Alley **14Dc**
Pauls Alley **15Aa**
Pauls Chain **14Dc**
Pauls Ct. **15Ab**
Pauls Wharf **14Cd**
Paved Alley **22Da** **22Ca**
Pavilion, The **3Cc**
Peacock Brewery **15Aa** **15Ba**
Peacock Ct. **7Bb**
Peacock St. **34Cb** **34Db**
Peal Alley **17Cd**
Pear Tree Alley **27Bb**
Pear Tree St. **24Bb**
Pearl Row **24Cc**
Pearl St. **27Ba**
Pearl St., Great **6Bd**
Pearl St., Little **6Bd**
Pearsons Wharf **26Bc**
Peartree Alley* **27Bb**
Peartree Ct. **4Bc** **4Bd** **4Cc**
Peartree Ct. **6Ac**
Peartree Row **24Bb**
Peartree St. **4Dc** **5Ac**
Peartree St.* **24Bb**
Pedlars Acre **23Dc**
Peerless Pool **5Bc**
Peerless Row **5Bc** **5Cb**
Pelham St. **16Ba** **16Ca**
Pelican Stairs **27Ca**
Pell Pl. **16Dd**
Pell St. **16Dd**
Pembertons Row **14Bb**
Penitentiary, New **33Ab** **33Bb** **33Ba** **33Aa**
Pennington St. **26Da** **27Aa**
Penny Fields **29Aa**
Pennywinch Ct. **18Ad**
Pennywinch St. **18Ac** **18Ad**
Penton Grove **4Bb**
Penton Pl. **4Aa**
Penton Pl. **34Cc** **34Dc**
Penton Row **35Ac**
Penton St. **4Ba**
Penton St. **34Dc**
Pentonville Chapel **4Aa**
Pepper Alley **25Ca**
Pepper Alley Stairs **25Ca**
Pepper St. **24Db**
Perceval St. **4Dc**
Percy St. **12Da** **13Aa**
Perkins Rents **4Db**
Perkins Rents **23Ad**
Perrys Pl. **12Db**
Perrys Rents **6Bb**
Pershore Pl. **3Ca**
Pesthouse Row **5Bc**
Peter St. **6Bc**
Peter St. **12Dc**
Peter St. **13Bb**
Peter St. **14Ca**
Peter St. **15Da**
Peter St. **25Ab**
Peter St., Great **22Dd** **23Ad**
Peter St., Little **23Ad** **23Bd**
Peter St., New **23Ad**
Peterborough Ct. **14Cc** **14Cb**
Peters Ct. **13Bd**
Peters Ct. **16Bd**
Petticoat La. **16Ab**
Petticoat Sq. **16Ab**
Pettys Ct. **13Ab**
Philanthropic Society **24Cd**
Philip La. **15Bb**
Philip St. **16Dd** **16Dc**
Philip St. **17Bd**
Philips Bldgs. **3Ba**
Phillips Ct. **5Ad**
Phillips Row **2Dc**
Phills Bldgs **16Ab**
Philpot La. **15Cd** **15Dd**
Phipps Ct. **5Dd**
Phipps St. **5Dd** **5Dc**
Phoebe St. **28Da**
Phoenix Alley **13Cc**
Phoenix Brewery **25Db**
Phoenix Ct. **14Ca**
Phoenix Ct. **14Db**
Phoenix Fire Engine **23Ba**
Phoenix Row **24Cc**
Phoenix St. **3Aa**
Phoenix St. **6Bd**
Phoenix St. **13Ac** **13Bc** **13Bb**
Phoenix St. **13Bb**
Phoenix St. **35Bc**
Phoenix Wharf **27Ab**
Phoenix Wharf **33Cb**
Phoenix Yd. **12Bb**
Physicians, College of **14Db**
Piccadilly **21Db** **22Ab** **22Bb** **22Ba** **22Ca** **12Cd** **12Dd**
Pickle Herring Stairs **26Ab**
Pickle Herring Stairs **25Da**
Pig Alley **6Bd**
Pigs Quay **14Cc**
Pilgrim St. **14Cc** **14Dc**
Pillory La. **26Ba** **26Ca**
Pimlico Gdns **5Db**
Pimlico Wharf **22Bd**
Pimlico Wharf, Cuts to Supply **32Ab** **32Bb** **32Ba**
Pindar St. **3Cb**
Pinks Row **5Bb**
Pinner Ct. **14Aa**
Pinners Ct. **15Cb**
Pipemakers Alley **18Bd**
Pipemakers Alley **25Cb**
Pitchers Ct. **15Cb**
Pitfield St. **5Dc** **5Db**
Pitmans Bldgs **5Ab**
Pitmans Pl. **26Cd**
Pitt St. **7Cb**
Pitt St. **12Da**
Pitt St. **24Cb**
Pitt St. **34Ca**
Pitt St. **35Cb** **35Ca**
Pitts Head Mews **22Aa**
Pitts Pl. **35Ca**
Place Row **2Dc**
Plaistow Levels **20Ba** **20Ca** **20Da**
Playground for the Westminster Scholars **32Db** **32Da**
Play House Yd. **5Ad** **5Bd**
Playhouse Yd. **14Cc**
Pleasant Ct. **24Ba**
Pleasant Pl. **3Da**
Pleasant Pl. **6Dc** **6Db**
Pleasant Pl. **7Db**
Pleasant Pl. **24Da**
Pleasant Pl. **34Ca**
Pleasant Pl. **34Cb**

Pleasant Retreat 24Bc 24Cc
Pleasant Row 1Dd
Pleasant Row 3Da
Pleasant Row 6Aa
Pleasant Row 6Ac
Pleasant Row 7Ad
Pleasant Row 16Ca 16Da
Pleasant Row 18Cd
Pleasant Row 34Bb
Pleasant Row 35Ac
Pleasant Row 35Bc
Pleasant Row 38Bd
Plough, The 8Cc
Plough Ct. 14Bb
Plough St. 16Cc
Plough Tavern 30Ab
Plow Alley 26Db
Plow Ct. 14Aa 14Ba
Plow Yd. 6Ad
Plow Yd. 25Dc
Plumb Pudding Row 6Ac
Plumbers Row 16Db
Plumbers St. 5Cb
Plumbtree Ct. 14Cb
Plumbtree St. 13Bb
Poets Corner, Westminster Abbey 23Bc
Pointers Bldgs 6Ac 6Ab
Poitiers St. 35Ca
Poland St. 12Dc 12Db
Pollard St. 6Db
Pollen St. 12Cc
Polygon 3Aa
Pomona Pl. 1Ad
Pond Field 2Da
Pond Yd. 25Aa
Pontipool Row 24Cc
Pont St. 21Cd
Pools Bldgs 4Ad
Popes Head Alley 15Cc
Popes Head Ct. 6Bd
Popes Hill 17Cd
Poplar 29
Poplar Pl. 34Ad
Poplar Row 34Da
Poplar Row 35Cb
Poppings Ct. 14Cb
Porridge Pot Alley 5Ac
Portaville Pass. 13Ac
Porter St. 13Bc
Porters Quay 15Dd
Portland Mews 12Dc
Portland Pl. 12Ba 2Bd
Portland Pl. 35Bd
Portland Rd. 2Bd
Portland St. 12Db
Portland St. 35Bd
Portland St., Great 12Ca
Portland St., Little 12Cb
Portman Foot Barracks 11Db
Portman Mews, North 11Cb 11Db
Portman Mews, South 11Db
Portman Sq. 11Cb 11Db
Portman St. 11Cc 11Cb
Portpool La. 4Ad 4Bd
Portsmouth St. 13Db
Portugal Row 13Db
Portugal St. 11Dd
Portugal St. 13Db 14Ab
Post Office 15Cc
Postern Row 16Ad
Potters Fields 26Ab
Potters Fields 33Da
Potters Row 7Ba
Poultry 15Bc
Poultry Compter 15Bc
Powis Pl. 3Cd
Pownall Ter. 34Ab
Pratt St. 33Da
Prerogative Office 14Dc
Prescott St., Great 16Bd 16Cd
Prescott St., Little 16Bd
Prices Alley 12Dc
Prices Bldgs 25Bc
Prices Ct. 24Da
Prices Pl. 24Da
Prices St. 24Ca 24Da
Prickley Rd. 28Bd
Priest Alley 17Ad
Primrose Alley 25Ba
Primrose Hill 14Cc
Primrose St. 15Da 16Aa
Prince of Wales Circus 1Db
Princes Ct. 4Cd
Princes Ct. 6Bb
Princes Ct. 8Bd
Princes Ct. 13Ad
Princes Ct. 13Cb
Princes Ct. 15Bb
Princes Ct. 22Cc
Princes Ct. 23Ac
Princes Ct. 27Ab
Princes Ct. 33Cb
Princes Pl. 16Da
Princes Pl. 16Dd
Princes Pl. 22Bd
Princes Pl. 34Ac 34Ab
Princes Pl. 34Bc
Princes Rents 24Db
Princes Rd. 34Ac
Princes Sq. 16Dd
Princes Sq. 34Bc
Princes Stairs 27Bc
Princes St. 4Dc
Princes St. 5Dd
Princes St. 6Bc 6Cc
Princes St. 6Cc 6Cb
Princes St. 12Bb
Princes St. 12Bb 12Cb
Princes St. 13Ac 13Ad
Princes St. 13Da
Princes St. 13Db
Princes St. 13Dc
Princes St. 15Bc
Princes St. 16Ba
Princes St. 16Bd
Princes St. 16Da
Princes St. 16Dd
Princes St. 22Bd
Princes St. 23Ac
Princes St. 24Cd
Princes St. 24Db
Princes St. 26Db
Princes St. 27Aa
Princes St. 27Bc
Princes St. 33Cc 33Cb
Princes St. 35Ac
Princess Charlotte's Circus 1Db
Printer St. 14Bb
Printers Pl. 26Cd
Printers Sq. 14Cc
Printing House La. 14Cc
Printing St. 14Cc
Prior Pl. 35Cc
Privy Gardens 23Bb
Produce Ct. 27Ca
Prospect Pl. 17Ad
Prospect Pl. 17Da
Prospect Pl. 24Cd 34Ca
Prospect Pl. 27Ad
Prospect Pl., New 9Cd
Prospect Row 4Aa
Prospect Row 26Cd 26Bd
Prospect Row 34Db
Prospect Row 36Bb
Providence Bldgs 35Ba
Providence Chapel 4Ac
Providence Ct. 11Dc
Providence Ct. 23Ad
Providence Gdns 6Ab
Providence Island 38Aa
Providence Pl. 4Bd
Providence Pl. 35Cd
Providence Row 3Da
Providence Row 5Cd
Providence Row 24Dc
Providence St. 5Bb
Providence St. 35Bd
Providence St. 35Cc
Prugean Ct. 14Cb
Prussian Island 27Bb
Public Office 13Cc
Public Rd, The 21Bb 21Cb 21Db
Publicans Charity School 34Ac
Pudding La. 15Cd
Puddle Dock 14Cd 14Cc
Pulteney Ct. 12Dc
Pulteney St., Great 12Dd
Pulteney St., Little 12Dc
Pump Ct. 14Bc
Pump Ct. 15Ba
Pump Ct. 24Db
Pump Ct. 25Cc
Pundersons Pl. 7Bb
Pundersons Row 7Bc
Purim Pl. 17Ba
Pye Garden 24Da
Pye St., New 23Ad
Pye St., Old 23Ad

Quaker St. 6Bd
Quakers Burial Ground 16Da
Quakers Burial Ground 25Dd

For Key Map see p. 1

Quakers Burying Ground **5Bd**
Quakers Meeting and Burial Ground **17Dd**
Quakers Meeting and Burial Ground **25Ab**
Quakers Workhouse **4Ca** **4Cb**
Quality Ct. **14Ab**
Quebeck Mews **11Cb**
Quebeck St. **11Cc** **11Cb**
Quebeck St., Great **1Bd**
Quebeck St., New **11Cb**
Quebeck Street North **1Bd**
Queen Ann Street East **12Ca**
Queen Ann Street West **12Aa** **12Ba**
Queen Anne St. **17Aa**
Queen Anns Mews **12Ba**
Queen Hithe **15Ad**
Queen Hithe Stairs **15Ad**
Queen Sq. **3Cd**
Queen Sq. **15Ca**
Queen St. **4Dc**
Queen St. **5Db**
Queen St. **6Bd**
Queen St. **11Ab** **11Ba**
Queen St. **11Dc**
Queen St. **12Cb**
Queen St. **12Dd**
Queen St. **13Ac**
Queen St. **13Bb** **13Ba**
Queen St. **13Bc**
Queen St. **15Ad** **15Bd** **15Bc**
Queen St. **16Bd**
Queen St. **16Da**
Queen St. **18Ad** **18Bd**
Queen St. **21Bc** **21Bd**
Queen St. **22Aa**
Queen St. **25Ab**
Queen St. **27Ac**
Queen St. **27Bb**
Queen St. **29Ba**
Queen St. **31Db** **32Ab**
Queen St. **35Ab** **35Ac**
Queen St. **40Bd**
Queen St., Great **13Cb** **13Db**
Queen St., Great **23Ac**
Queen St., Little **11Bb**
Queen St., Little **13Db** **13Cb**
Queen St., Little **23Ac**
Queen St., Lower **28Cc** **28Cb**
Queenhithe* **15Ad**
Queenhithe Stairs* **15Ad**
Queens Arms Ct. **24Ca**
Queens Bldgs **21Bc**
Queens Bldgs, Upper **21Ac** **21Bc**
Queens Ct. **7Bd**
Queens Ct. **13Bc**
Queens Ct. **13Cb**
Queens Ct. **13Db**
Queens Ct. **18Ad**
Queens Ct. **22Bd**
Queens Ct. **24Dc**
Queens Ct. **25Ab**
Queens Ct. **25Bb**
Queens Ct. **33Db**
Queens Gdns **21Bc**
Queens Gdns **22Ac** **22Bc**
Queens Gdns **25Cc**
Queens Head Alley **27Ab**
Queens Head Ct. **12Dc**
Queens Head Ct. **14Aa**
Queens Head Inn **25Bb**
Queens Head Walk **6Aa**
Queens Mews, The **13Ad** **13Bd**
Queens Pl. **23Ad**
Queens Pl. **25Bb**
Queens Pl. **31Db**
Queens Pl. **33Dc**
Queens Pl. **34Bd**
Queens Row **4Aa**
Queens Row **6Aa**
Queens Row **7Bd**
Queens Row **21Bc**
Queens Row **22Bd**
Queens Row **27Bb**
Queens Row **34Bc** **34Bd**
Queens Row **35Bd** **35Ad**
Queens Sq. **15Aa**
Queens Sq. **22Dc** **23Ac**
Queens Square Pl. **22Dc**
Queens St. **25Bb**
Queens St. **26Ac** **26Ab**
Quickset Row **2Cc**

Racquet Ct. **14Cb**
Ragged Staff Ct. **13Cb**
Rahns Pl. **16Cc**
Raines Hospital **27Aa**
Ralphs Quay **15Dd**
Ram Alley **6Cd**
Ram Alley **28Aa**
Ram Ct. **14Bc**
Ram Inn **14Da**
Randall and Brent's Yd. **38Ba** **38Ca**
Randalls Lime Wharf **14Cc**
Randalls Rents **38Ba** **38Ca**
Ranelagh, New **32Cd**
Ranelagh Pl. **22Bd** **22Ad**
Ranelagh Rd., New **32Cd** **32Cc**
Ranelagh St. **22Ad** **22Bd**
Ranelagh Walk **31Db** **31Ab**
Ratcliff, Hamlet of **17Cd** **17Cc**
Ratcliff Ct. **5Ab**
Ratcliff Ct. **17Ad**
Ratcliff Cross **18Ad**
Ratcliff Highway **17Ad** **17Bd**
Ratcliff Sq. **18Ac**
Ratcliff Workhouse **18Ac**
Ratcliffe Layer **5Ac** **5Ab**
Ratcliffe Row **5Bb**
Rathbone Pl. **13Ab** **13Da**
Rathbone Pl., Upper **12Da**
Raven and Sun **26Ac**
Raven Row **17Ba**
Rawstorne St. **4Cb**
Ray Ct. **4Bd**
Ray St. **4Bd**
Red Bull Wharf **15Bd**
Red Bull Yd. **15Bd**
Red Cow La. **17Ca** **7Cd** **7Bd**
Red Cross Alley **25Cd**
Red Cross Bldgs **25Ab**
Red Cross Ct. **14Ca**
Red Cross Courts **25Ab** **25Bb**
Red Cross Sq. **15Aa**
Red Cross Sq. **15Dd**
Red Cross St. **15Aa**
Red Cross St. **25Ac** **25Ab** **25Bb**
Red Cross St. **26Ca**
Red Hart Inn **14Bb**
Red Lion Brewhouse **26Cb**
Red Lion Ct. **4Dd**
Red Lion Ct. **6Aa**
Red Lion Ct. **6Ab**
Red Lion Ct. **6Ad**
Red Lion Ct. **13Dc**
Red Lion Ct. **14Bb**
Red Lion Ct. **14Ca**
Red Lion Ct. **14Da**
Red Lion Ct. **14Db**
Red Lion Ct. **15Ab**
Red Lion Ct. **15Ac**
Red Lion Ct. **15Cb**
Red Lion Ct. **16Ba**
Red Lion Ct. **25Db**
Red Lion Ct. **26Ba**
Red Lion Ct. **27Ab**
Red Lion Inn **14Da** **15Aa**
Red Lion Market **5Bd**
Red Lion Pass. **3Bb**
Red Lion Pass. **13Da**
Red Lion Row **35Ad**
Red Lion Sq. **13Da**
Red Lion St. **4Cd**
Red Lion St. **13Da**
Red Lion St. **16Ba**
Red Lion St. **16Cc** **16Bc** **16Bb**
Red Lion St. **27Ab**
Red Lion Yd. **4Ad**
Red Lion Yd. **4Ad** **4Bd**
Red Lion Yd. **4Cd**
Red Lion Yd. **12Bb**
Red Lion Yd. **13Ca**
Red Lion Yd. **13Db**
Red Lion Yd. **16Bb**
Red Lion Yd. **25Bb**
Red Maid La. **26Cb** **26Db**
Red Rose Alley **15Ba**
Redford Ct. **38Ba**
Redmans Row **17Ca**
Reeves Mews **11Dd**
Regent Pl. **8Cd**
Regent St. **27Cc**
Regent St. **33Ab** **33Aa**
Regent St. **34Ab**
Regent's Canal **1Aa** **2Ca**
Regent's Circus **2Bc**
Reliance St. **6Ac**
Renon's Ct. **15Ca**
Rephidim St. **25Cd** **35Ca**
Reputation Row **6Aa**
Retreat, The **33Cd**
Rhodes Well **18Cb**
Rhodes Well Common **18Bb** **18Cb**
Rich St. **18Dd**
Richard St. **17Ac**
Richard St. **18Bb**
Richardson St. **25Cc**
Richmond Bldgs **13Ac**
Richmond Gdns **21Bc**
Richmond Mews **13Ac**
Richmond Pl. **35Bc**
Richmond Pl., Little **35Bc**

Richmond St. **5Bc**
Richmond St. **13Ac**
Rickards Ct. **14Cb**
Riding House La. **12Ba** **12Ca**
Riley St. **3Cb**
Ring, The **21Dc**
Robert St. **2Cb**
Robert St. **4Dd**
Robert St. **13Cd**
Robert St. **24Cb** **24Ca**
Roberts Bldgs **32Ab**
Roberts Ct. **29Ba**
Roberts Pl. **16Db**
Robin Hood Alley **15Ab**
Robin Hood Ct. **14Bb** **14Cb**
Robin Hood Ct. **25Db**
Robin Hood La. **30Aa**
Robin Hood Yd. **14Ba**
Robinsons La. **31Bd** **31Ad** **31Ac**
Robinsons Pl. **27Ba**
Rochester Row **22Dd** **32Ca** **32Da**
Rochester Row, New **32Ca** **32Da**
Rochester St. **25Ba**
Rockingham Ct. **34Da**
Rockingham Row **35Aa**
Rodney Bldgs **35Aa** **35Ba**
Rodney Pl. **35Aa**
Rodney St. **4Aa**
Rodney St. **25Ac**
Roe Buck Ct. **4Cd**
Roe Buck Ct. **15Ba**
Roebuck **33Ac** **33Bc**
Rogers St. **33Dc**
Rogers Timber Yd. **27Db**
Rolls Bldgs **14Bb**
Rolls Gdns **14Bb**
Romney St. **33Ba**
Romney Ter. **33Aa**
Rood La. **15Dd**
Rope Makers Fields **28Ca**
Rope Makers St. **15Ba** **15Ca**
Ropers Bldgs **16Ab**
Rose Alley **5Ad**
Rose Alley **13Da**
Rose Alley **16Ab**
Rose Alley **25Aa**
Rose Alley **26Ba**
Rose and Crown Alley **15Da**
Rose and Crown Ct. **4Ca**
Rose and Crown Ct. **14Cb**
Rose and Crown Ct. **15Ab**
Rose and Crown Ct. **15Da**
Rose and Crown Ct. **16Bb**
Rose and Crown Ct. **26Ba**
Rose and Crown Yd. **4Dd**
Rose Ct. **6Ac**
Rose Ct. **6Bc**
Rose Ct. **6Ad** **6Bd**
Rose Ct. **13Bc**
Rose Ct. **15Ba**
Rose Ct. **15Bc**
Rose Ct. **16Cd**
Rose Ct. **26Bd** **26Bc**
Rose Inn **14Ca** **14Da**
Rose La. **16Bb** **16Ba**
Rose La. **18Ad** **18Bd**
Rose Pl. **6Bc**
Rose St. **5Ac**
Rose St. **13Ab**
Rose St. **13Bc**
Rose St. **14Db**
Rose Yd. **6Ad**
Rosemary La. **16Bd** **16Cd**
Rosetta St. **18Bb**
Rosomons St. **4Cc** **4Bc**
Ross Alley **26Ab** **26Bb**
Ross Ct. **26Ab**
Rotherhithe Churchyard **27Bc**
Rotherhithe Stairs **27Ac**
Rotherhithe St. **27** **28**
Rotherhithe Wall **26Cc** **26Dc**
Rotherhithe Workhouse **27Bd**
Rothsay Ter. **2Ab**
Rotten Row **5Ad**
Round Ct. **15Ab**
Round Ct. **15Ba**
Round Ct., New **13Bd**
Round Ct., Old **13Cd**
Round House **9Dd**
Rowlands Row **17Ca**
Royal Adelphi Ter. **13Cd**
Royal Circus **24Cc**
Royal Ct. **26Ab**
Royal Dockyard **38Cd**
Royal Exchange **15Cc**
Royal Military Asylum **31Cb**
Royal Mint **16Bd**
Royal Oak **33Cd**
Royal Oak Ct. **25Bc**
Royal Oak Walk **5Db**
Royal Oak Yd. **25Dd**
Royal Row **23Dc** **23Dd** **24Ad**
Royalty Theatre **16Cd**
Roystone Pl. **4Cb**
Ruddicks Bldgs **15Da**
Rumbals Ct. **15Da**
Running Horse Yd. **24Ca**
Rupert St. **13Ac** **13Ad**
Rupert St. **16Cc**
Rural Pl. **7Dd**
Russell Ct. **13Dc**
Russell Ct. **16Cd**
Russell Ct. **17Ad**
Russell Ct. **22Cb**
Russell Mews **2Cd**
Russell Mews **22Cb**
Russell Pl. **2Dd**
Russell Pl. **13Cc**
Russell Pl. **35Ca**
Russell Sq. **3Bd**
Russell St. **13Cc**
Russell St. **25Cd**
Russell St. **26Ac**
Russell St. **38Ba** **28Bd**
Russell St., Great **13Ab** **13Ba** **13Ca**
Russell St., Little **13Ba** **13Ca**
Russell St., Little **13Cc**
Russell St., Upper **25Cd**
Russells Bldgs **26Ac**
Russells Bldgs **26Db**
Russia Lane **7Ba**
Rutland Pl. **4Dd**
Rutland Pl. **14Cd** **14Cc**
Rutland Sq. **2Ca**
Rutland St. **2Ca**
Rutland St. **17Ab**
Ryder St., Great **22Ca** **22Da**
Ryder St., Little **22Ca**
Ryders Ct. **13Ac**

Sackville St. **12Dd** **12Cd**
Sadlers Hall **15Ab**
Sadlers Wells **4Cb**
Sadlers Wells Field **4Ba**
Saffron Ct. **4Bd**
Saffron Hill, Great **14Ca** **4Bd**
Saffron Hill, Little **4Bd**
Saffron Pl. **4Bd** **4Cd**
Saffron St. **14Ca**
St. Agnes Cres. **5Dc**
St. Agnes Le Clair, near Hoxton **5Cc** **5Dc**
St. Agnes St. **5Dc**
St. Albans Church, Wood St. **15Ab**
St. Albans St. **23Aa** **13Ad**
St. Alphage Church, near Sion College, London Wall **15Bb**
St. Andrew Ct. **14Bb**
St. Andrew Holborn Church **14Cb**
St. Andrew Holborn Workhouse and Burial Ground **14Cb**
St. Andrew St., Great **13Bc** **13Bb**
St. Andrew St., Little **13Bc**
St. Andrew Undershaft Church, St. Mary Axe **15Dc**
St. Andrew Wardrobe Church, by Puddle Dock Hill **14Dc**
St. Andrews Hill **14Dc**
St. Andrews Wharf **14Cc**
St. Andrews Workhouse **4Ad**
St. Anns Church, near Aldersgate **15Ab**
St. Anns Church, Limehouse **18Cd** **18Dd**
St. Anns Church, Westminster, Dean St., Soho **13Ac**
St. Anns Ct., Great **23Ad**
St. Anns La. **15Ab**
St. Anns La., Little **23Ad**
St. Anns Row **18Dd**
St. Anns School **13Ab**
St. Anns St. **17Ac**
St. Anns St. **18Dd** **18Dc**
St. Anns St., Great **23Ad**
St. Anns Workhouse **13Ab**
St. Anthonys Church, Watling St. **15Bc**
St. Austins Church, Watling St. **15Ac**
St. Bartholomew and Bedlam Hospitals Lands **4Db**
St. Bartholomew, near The Royal Exchange **15Cc**
St. Bartholomew the Great Church **14Da**
St. Bartholomew the Less Church **14Da**
St. Bartholomews Hospital **14Da** **14Db**

For Key Map see p. 1

St. Bartholomews Hospital Burying Ground **4Dc**
St. Bartholomews Hospital Land **4Db**
St. Bennet Fink, Threadneedle St. **15Cc**
St. Bennets Church, Gracechurch St. **15Cc**
St. Bennets Church, Paul's Wharf **14Dc**
St. Botolph, Aldgate (mistakenly 'St. Ann' on map) **16Ac**
St. Botolph Church, Aldersgate **15Ab**
St. Botolph Church without Bishopsgate **15Db**
St. Brides Church, Fleet St. **14Cc**
St. Brides Wharf **14Cc**
St. Catherine Coleman Church, Fenchurch St. **16Ac**
St. Catherine Creechurch, Leadenhall St. **16Ac**
St. Catherines Ct. **26Ba**
St. Catherines Dock **26Ba**
St. Catherines Hermitage **26Cb**
St. Catherines La. **26Ba**
St. Catherines near the Tower Church **26Ba**
St. Catherines New Ct. **26Ba**
St. Catherines Sq. **26Ba**
St. Catherines Stairs **26Ba**
St. Clement Danes Burial Ground, Portugal St. **13Db**
St. Clement Danes Church, in the Strand **14Ac**
St. Clements Church, St. Clements La., near Great Eastcheap **15Cd**
St. Clements La. **15Cd** **15Cc**
St. Dionis Backchurch, Fenchurch St. **15Dc**
St. Dunstans Church, Stepney **18Ab**
St. Dunstans Ct. **14Bc** **14Bb**
St. Dunstans Hill **15Dd**
St. Dunstans in the East Church, St. Dunstans Hill **15Dd**
St. Dunstans in the West Church, Fleet St. **14Bc**
St. Dunstans Workhouse **15Dd**
St. Dunstans Workhouse **14Bb**
St. Edmund the King's Church, Lombard St. **15Cc**
St. Ermins Hill **22Dc**
St. Ethelburga's Church, Bishopsgate **15Db**
St. George the Martyr Burying Ground **3Cc**
St. George the Martyr Church, Queen Sq. **3Cd**
St. Georges Back Row **11Ac**
St. Georges Bloomsbury Burying Ground **3Cc**
St. Georges Burying Ground **12Ad**
St. Georges Burying Ground and Chapel **11Ab** **11Ac** **11Ad**
St. Georges Charity School **13Ba**
St. Georges Church, near Blackman St., Southwark **25Bc**
St. Georges Church, Botolph La. **15Cd**
St. Georges Church, Hanover Sq. **12Bc**
St. Georges Church, Hart St., Bloomsbury **13Ca** **13Ba**
St. Georges Ct. **16Dc**
St. Georges Crecent **24Cd**
St. Georges Hospital **21Db**
St. Georges in the East Church **17Ad**
St. Georges Market **12Ac**
St. Georges Market **24Dd**
St. Georges Pl. **24Cb**
St. Georges Pl. **32Ab**
St. Georges Rd. **24Bd** **24Cd**
St. Georges Row **24Bc**
St. Georges Row **32Ab**
St. Georges Row **11Ac** **11Bc**
St. Georges Row **5Ab**
St. Georges Sq. **24Bd**
St. Georges Ter. **16Dc**
St. Georges Workhouse **12Ad**
St. Georges Workhouse **27Aa**
St. Giles and St. Georges Charity Schools **13Ba**
St. Giles's Church in the Fields **13Bb**
St. Giles's Church, Cripplegate **15Aa**
St. Giles's Cripplegate Workhouse **15Ba**
St. Giles's Workhouse **13Bb** **13Bc**
St. Helens Church, Great **15Db**
St. Helens Church, Little **15Db**
St. Helens Gdns **37Cc**
St. Helens Pl. **15Db**
St. James Bldgs **4Cc**
St. James Market **12Dd** **13Ad**
St. James Pl. **2Cb**
St. James St. **4Cc**
St. James Walk **4Cc**
St. James's Chapel **2Db**
St. James's Burying Ground **2Db**
St. James's Church, Clerkenwell **4Cd**
St. James's Church, Dukes Pl. **16Ac**
St. James's Church, Garlick Hill **15Ad**
St. James's Church, Piccadilly **12Dd**
St. James's Infirmary **12Dc**
St. James's Palace **22Cb** **22Db**
St. James's Park **22** **23**
St. James's Pl. **22Ca**
St. James's School **12Cc**
St. James's Sq. **22Da**
St. James's St. **22Ca**
St. James's St., Little **22Ca**
St. John St. **6Cd**
St. John St. **14Da** **4Dd** **4Cc**
St. John the Evangelist's Church, near Millbank **23Bd** **33Ba**
St. Johns Chapel, Harford La. **34Dc**
St. Johns Church, Clerkenwell **4Cd**
St. Johns Church, Clerkenwell, Burial Ground **4Cd**
St. Johns Church near Horsleydown **26Ac**
St. Johns Church, Wapping **27Ab**
St. Johns Ct. **14Ca**
St. Johns Gate **4Cd**
St. Johns La. **4Dd** **4Cc**
St. Johns Sq. **4Cd**
St. Johns Workhouse **25Dc**
St. Katherine *see* St. Catherine
St. Lawrence Jewry Church **15Bb**
St. Leonards Church, Bromley **9Dc**
St. Leonards Shoreditch Church **6Aa** **6Ab**
St. Lukes Charity School **5Ac** **5Ad**
St. Lukes Church, Old St. **5Ac**
St. Lukes Hospital **5Bc** **5Dc**
St. Lukes Poor, Burial Ground **5Bc**
St. Lukes Workhouse **5Bb**
St. Magnus Church, near London Bridge **15Cd**
St. Margaret Pattens Church, Rood La. **15Dd**
St. Margarets Chapel **22Dd**
St. Margarets Church, Lothbury **15Cb**
St. Margarets Church, Westminster **23Bc**
St. Margarets Workhouse **23Ad** **23Ac**
St. Martin St. **24Cc** **24Dc**
St. Martins Almshouses **13Ac**
St. Martins Burial Ground **13Cc**
St. Martins Church, by Ludgate **14Dc**
St. Martins Ct. **13Bd**
St. Martins in the Fields Church **13Bd**
St. Martins La. **13Bc** **13Bd** **23Ba**
St. Martins La. **15Cd**
St. Martins La., Little **13Bc**
St. Martins Le Grand, Aldersgate **15Ab**
St. Martins National School **13Bd**
St. Martins Outwitch Church, Threadneedle St. **15Dc**
St. Martins Workhouse **13Bd**
St. Mary Aldermary Church, Bow La. **15Ac** **15Bc**
St. Mary at Hill Church **15Dd**
St. Mary Axe **15Dc** **15Db**
St. Mary Hill **15Dd**
St. Mary Le Bow Church, Cheapside **15Ac**
St. Mary Le Strand Burial Ground **13Dc**
St. Mary Le Strand Church **13Dc**
St. Mary Magdalen Church, Bermondsey **25Dd**
St. Mary Magdalen Church, Old Fish St. **15Ac**
St. Mary Somerset Church, Thames St. **15Ad**
St. Mary Stratford Le Bow Church **9Cb** **9Cc**
St. Mary St. **16Da**
St. Mary Woolnoth's Church **15Cc**
St. Marylebone **1Dd**
St. Marylebone and St. George's Burying Grounds **11Da**
St. Marylebone Church **1Dd**
St. Marylebone Workhouse **1Dd**
St. Marys Church, Abchurch La. **15Cc**
St. Marys Church, Aldermanbury **15Bb**
St. Marys Church, Lambeth **33Ca**
St. Marys Church, Newington **34Cb**
St. Marys Church, Whitechapel **16Cb**
St. Matthews Church, Bethnal Green **6Cc** **6Dc**
St. Matthews Church, Friday St. **15Ac**
St. Michael Bassishaw Church **15Bb**
St. Michael Royal's Church, College Hill **15Bd**
St. Michaels Alley **15Cc**
St. Michaels Church, Cornhill **15Cc**
St. Michaels Church, near Crooked Lane **15Cd**
St. Michaels Church, Queenhithe **15Ad**
St. Michaels Church, Wood St. **15Ab**
St. Mildreds Church, Bread St. **15Ac**
St. Mildreds Church, Poultry **15Bc**
St. Mildreds Ct. **15Bc**
St. Nicholas Cole Abbey Church **15Ac**
St. Nicholas Olive Church Yard **15Ac**
St. Olaves Church, Hart St. **16Ad**
St. Olaves Church, Old Jewry **15Bc**

St. Olaves Church, Tooley St. **25Ca**
St. Pauls Cathedral **14Dc** **15Ac**
St. Pauls Cathedral, Dean's House **14Dc**
St. Pauls Church, Covent Garden **13Cc**
St. Pauls Church, Upper Shadwell **17Cd**
St. Pauls Pl. **35Cd**
St. Peters Abbey, Westminster **23Bc**
St. Peters Alley **15Cc**
St. Peters Church, Cornhill **15Cc**
St. Peters Hill **14Dc**
St. Peters La. **14Da**
St. Peters-Le-Poor Church **15Cb**
St. Saviours Almshouses and Burial Ground **25Bb**
St. Saviours Church, Southwark **25Ba**
St. Saviours Dock **26Bc**
St. Saviours Dock **25Ba**
St. Saviours School and Burial Ground **25Ab** **25Bb**
St. Saviours Workhouse **24Db**
St. Sepulchres Church, near Newgate **14Cb** **14Db**
St. Sepulchres without Workhouse and Burying Ground **14Ca**
St. Sepulchres Workhouse **14Ca**
St. Shads Wells **3Da**
St. Stephens Church, Coleman St. **15Bb**
St. Stephens Church, Walbrook **15Bc**
St. Swithins Church, Cannon St. **15Bc** **15Bd**
St. Swithins La. **15Bc** **15Cc**
St. Thomas and Guys Hospital Burial Ground **25Cc**
St. Thomas Apostle **15Ac** **15Bc**
St. Thomas Apostle, Little **15Ac** **15Bc**
St. Thomas's Church, St. Thomas's St., Southwark **25Cb**
St. Thomas's Hospital **25Bb** **25Cb**
St. Thomas's Rents **25Cb**
St. Thomas's St. **17Aa** **16Da**
St. Vedast Church, Foster La. **15Ab**
St. Vincent Row **4Da**
Salisbury Ct. **14Cc**
Salisbury Cres. **35Bb**
Salisbury La. **26Cc**
Salisbury Mews **1Cd**
Salisbury Pl. **1Bd**
Salisbury Pl. **26Dd**
Salisbury Sq. **14Cc**
Salisbury St. **13Cd**
Salisbury St. **26Dd** **26Dc**
Salisbury St. **35Cb**
Salmon and Ball Ct. **5Bd**
Salmons La. **18Bc** **18Cc**
Salters Ct. **6Ab**
Salters Ct. **15Ac**
Salters Ct. **26Ac**
Salters Hall **15Bc**
Salters Hall Ct. **15Bc**
Salters Rents **6Ab**
Samuel St. **16Ca**
Samuel St. **18Bc** **18Bb**
Sand Wharf **14Cd** **14Cc**
Sand Yd. **4Cd**
Sanders Ct. **23Ad**
Sanders Gdns **6Ab**
Sandys Row **16Aa**
Sandys St. **16Aa** **16Ab**
Saracens Head **14Cb**
Saracens Head Inn **15Ac**
Saracens Head Inn **16Ac**
Sarahs Ct. **27Ba**
Satchwell Rents **6Cc**
Satchwell St. **6Cc**
Savage Gdns **16Ad**
Savana Pl. **6Aa**
Savells Bldgs **17Da**
Savile Pl. **33Da**
Saville Row **8Bd**
Saville Row **34Db**
Saville St. **12Cd** **12Cc**
Savoy **13Dd**
Savoy Alley **13Dd**
Savoy Chapel **13Dd**
School House La. **4Cc** **4Cd**
School House La. **17Dd**
Sclater St. **6Bd**
Sconcers Alley **27Ca**
Scotch Church **15Aa**
Scotch Ct. **13Cb**
Scotland Yd., Coal Wharf **23Ca**
Scotland Yd., Great **23Ba**
Scotland Yd., Little **23Ba**
Scotland Yd., Middle **23Ba**
Scotts Yd. **15Bd**
Scrub Sq. **24Ca**
Sea Water Baths **13Cd**
Seacoal La. **14Cb**
Secondarys Office **14Bc**
Seething La. **16Ad**
Selbys Mews **11Cb**
Sergeants Inn **14Bb** **14Bc**
Serle St. **14Ab**
Sermon La. **14Dc**
Serpentine River **21Aa** **21Ab** **21Ba** **21Bb**
Seven Houses **37Cb**
Seven Islands **27Ad**
Seven Star Alley **17Ad**
Seven Star Ct. **16Bd**
Seven Stars Alley **5Bd**
Seven Step Alley **27Bc**
Severn Pl. **7Bc**
Severn St. **16Dd**
Seward St. **4Dc** **5Ac**
Seymore Ct. **13Bd**
Seymore Pl. **3Bb**
Seymour Cres. **2Db** **3Ab**
Seymour House **31Ab**
Seymour Mews **11Db**
Seymour Pl. **3Ab**
Seymour Pl. **22Aa**
Seymour Pl. **11Bb** **11Ba**
Seymour Pl., North **3Ab**
Seymour Pl., South **3Ab**
Seymour St. **11Db**
Seymour St., Upper **11Cb**
Shacklewell St. **6Bc** **6Cc**
Shad Thames **26Ab** **26Bb** **26Bc**
Shadwell, Lower **27Ca** **17Dd**
Shadwell, Upper, or, High St. **17Bd** **17Cd**
Shadwell Church Yd. **17Cd**
Shadwell Dock **27Ca**
Shadwell Dock Stairs **27Ca**
Shadwell Market **17Cd**
Shadwell Water Works **27Ca**
Shadwell Workhouse **17Bd**
Shaftsbury Pl. **15Aa**
Shakspears Walk **27Ba** **17Bd**
Sharps Alley **14Ca**
Sheffield St. **13Db**
Shepherd and Shepherdess **5Bb**
Shepherd St. **12Bc** **12Bb**
Shepherds Alley **15Ad**
Shepherds Ct. **11Dc**
Shepherds Gdns **16Bc**
Shepherds Market **22Aa** **22Ba**
Shepherds Pl. **16Aa** **16Ba**
Shepherds Row **7Ac**
Shepherds Sq. **22Aa** **22Ba**
Shepherds St. **22Aa**
Shepherds Walk **5Bb** **5Ba**
Sheppards Ct. **14Bb**
Sherard Ct. **25Ca**
Sherborn La. **15Cc**
Sherrard St. **12Dd**
Ship Alley **16Dd**
Ship Alley **30Aa**
Ship Ct. **14Cb**
Ship Ct. **22Dc**
Ship Inn **25Ca**
Ship St. **27Bb** **27Ba**
Ship Yd. **14Ac**
Ship Yd. **15Aa**
Ship Yd. **25Db**
Shire La., Great **14Ac** **14Ab**
Shire La., Little **14Ac**
Shoe La. **14Cb**
Shoemakers Row **14Cc** **14Dc**
Shoreditch **6Ad** **6Ac**
Short St. **6Ad**
Short St. **15Ca**
Short St. **16Ab** **16Bb**
Shorter St. **16Dd**
Shorters Ct. **15Cc**
Shorts Bldgs **4Cc**
Shorts Gdns **13Bb** **13Cb**
Shoulder of Mutton Alley **18Bd** **18Cd**
Shouldham St. **11Ba**
Shovel Alley **26Ba**
Shovel Ct. **15Ab**
Shropshire Pl. **2Dd**
Sidmouth Pl. **3Db**
Sidmouth St. **3Cc**
Sidney Pl. **4Da**
Sidney Pl. **31Ac**
Sidney Pl. **33Dc**
Sidney St. **4Da**
Silk St. **15Ba**
Silver Lion Gdns **29Aa**
Silver St. **7Dd**
Silver St. **12Cc** **12Dc**
Silver St. **13Ca**

For Key Map see p. 1

Silver St. 14Bc
Silver St. 15Ab
Silver St. 16Ca
Silver St. 17Db 17Cb 17Ca 17Da
Silver St. 24Db
Silver St. 25Cb
Silver St. 27Ba
Silver St. 28Bb
Simons Bldgs 23Ad
Sion Chapel 16Cb
Sion College 15Bb 15Ba
Sion Gdns 15Bb
Sion Pl. 35Cc
Sion Sq. 16Cb
Sions Ct. 25Dd
Sir Hugh Middletons Head 4Cb
Sir William Warrens Sq. 27Bb
Sise La. 15Bc
Size Yd. 16Cb
Skin Market 4Cc 4Dc
Skin Market 15Dc
Skin Market 24Dc
Skinner St. 14Cb
Skinner St. 15Da
Skinners Almshouses 17Ba
Skinners Bldgs 38Cd
Skinners Company Cattle Field 4Cc
Skinners Hall 15Bd
Skinners Pl. 3Ba
Skinners Pl. 3Cb
Skinners St. 3Bb
Slades Bldgs 15Da
Slades Ct. 25Ab
Slate Yd. 25Aa
Slaters Ct. 16Cd
Sleeps Alley 4Cc
Sloane Pl. 21Bc
Sloane Sq. 31Ca 31Cb
Sloane St. 31Ca 21Cd 21Cc
Sloane St., Lower 31Cb
Sloane Ter. 31Ca
Smarts Bldgs 13Cb
Smarts Gdns 7Ac 7Bc
Smarts Quay 15Dd
Smith St. 4Dc
Smith St. 31Bc
Smith St., Great 23Ad
Smith St., Little 23Ad 23Bd
Smith St., Little 31Bc
Smith St., Upper 4Db
Smithfield, East 26Ba 26Ca
Smithfield, Lower east 26Bd 26Ca
Smithfield, West 14Da
Smithfield Barrs 14Da
Smiths Alley 28Ca
Smiths Bldgs 15Da
Smiths Bldgs 25Dd
Smiths Ct. 5Ad
Smiths Ct. 12Dc
Smiths Ct. 17Ac
Smiths Pl. 26Db
Smiths Pl. 34Ca
Smiths Rents 25Aa
Smiths Rents 25Dd
Smock Alley 16Aa
Sneads Ct. 22Ba
Snow Hill 14Cb
Snows Fields 25Cc 25Dc
Snows Rents 22Dc
Soap Yd. 25Bb
Socrates Pl. 6Ac
Soho Sq. 13Ab
Solls Row 2Cb
Somerford St. 7Ad
Somers Pl., East 3Bb
Somers Pl., West 3Bb
Somerset Bldgs 6Bb
Somerset Pl. 13Dc 13Dd
Somerset St. 11Db
Somerset St. 16Bc
Somerset St., Little 16Bc
Somerwood St. 16Dc
Sommers Town Coffee House 3Aa
South
With the exceptions below, names preceded by 'South' will be found under the second element, e.g. Seymour Pl., South
South Lambeth 33Cd
South London Waterworks 33Dd 34Ad
South Mews 11Da
South Pl. 34Bd
South Row 3Bb
South Sea Ct. 25Ab
South Sea House 15Dc
South Sea House, Old 15Cb
South St. 11Da
South St. 11Dd 12Ad
South St. 15Ca
South St. 16Ba
South St. 31Cb
South St. 34Ba 34Ca
South St. 35Bc
Southampton Bldgs 14Aa 14Ab
Southampton Ct. 2Dc
Southampton Ct. 3Cd
Southampton Ct. 14Aa
Southampton Cres. 3Ab
Southampton Mews 2Dc
Southampton Mews 3Cd
Southampton Pl. 2Dc
Southampton Row 11Aa
Southampton Row 3Cd
Southampton St. 3Da
Southampton St. 13Ca
Southampton St. 13Cc 13Cd
Souths Alms Houses 32Da
Spa Fields Chapel 4Bc
Spa Pl. 4Bc
Spa Tea Gdns 4Cb
Spanish Pl. 11Db 11Da
Spann Pl. 3Bb
Sparricks Row 25Cb
Sparrow Bldgs 26Ab
Sparrow Corner 16Bd
Sparrows Rents 4Ad
Speadens Gdns 29Ba
Spencer St. 4Cb
Spencer St. 17Bc
Spencers Row 4Db
Spicer St. 6Cd
Spillers Ct. 24Cc
Spital Sq. 16Aa
Spital St. 16Ca 6Cd
Spitalfields Churchyard 16Ba
Spitalfields Market 16Ba
Spitalfields Workhouse 16Da
Spotted Horse Ct. 6Ad
Sprauts Pl. 6Bb
Spread Eagle Ct. 14Aa 14Ba
Spread Eagle Ct. 15Cc
Spread Eagle Ct. 27Bc
Spread Eagle Ct. 28Da
Spread Eagle Inn 15Dc
Spread Eagle Yd. 23Ac
Spring Garden 23Ba
Spring Garden Ct. 7Dd
Spring Garden Mews 23Ba
Spring Garden Pl. 18Ab
Spring St. 11Ca
Spring St. 27Ca
Spring St., Little 27Ca
Spring St., Upper 1Cd
Spur Inn 25Bb
Stafford Pl. 22Bc 22Cc
Stafford Row 22Bc 22Cc
Stafford St. 12Cd
Staining La. 15Ab
Stamford St. 24Ca
Stamford St., Upper 24Ba
Standard 16Cb
Standard 21Db
Standard 25Ac
Standig Ct. 25Db
Stangages Bldgs 35Ca 35Da
Stangate 23Dd 23Dc
Stangate Pl. 23Dc
Stangate St. 23Dc
Stangate Wharf 23Dc
Stanhope St. 13Dc
Stanhope St. 21Da 22Aa
Stanhope St., Little 22Aa
Staple Ct. 25Dd
Staples Inn 14Ba 14Bb
Staples Inn Bldgs 14Aa
Staples Rents 27Ad
Stapleton Ct. 15Ba
Stapletons Wharf 14Bc
Star Alley 15Dc
Star and Garden Yd. 17Bd
Star Brewery 13Ab
Star Brewery 24Dc
Star Corner 25Dd
Star Ct. 13Cb
Star Ct. 15Ac
Star Ct. 15Ba
Star Ct. 25Ac
Star Ct. 26Ca
Star Yd. 14Ab
Star Yd., Old 17Ad
Starch Alley 5Ad
Starr St. 27Ca
Stationers Alley 14Dc
Stationers Hall 14Dc
Statuehall Ct. 16Cc
Stave Yd. 26Cc
Staverdon Row 34Da
Staye Yd. 26Db
Steel House La. 17Dc
Steel Yd. 15Ad
Steel Yd. 15Bd

Steel Yd. **16Ad**
Steers Pl. **15Aa**
Steldhurst St. **3Bb**
Stephen St. **13Aa**
Stepney Causeway, or, Church St. **17Dd** **17Dc**
Stepney Churchyard **18Ab**
Stepney Gap **17Cd**
Stepney Green **17Da** **17Db**
Stepney Meeting Almshouses **18Ac**
Stevens Bldgs **1Ad**
Stevens Mews **13Aa**
Steward St. **16Aa**
Stewards Bldgs **9Cc**
Stewards Ct. **4Dd**
Stewarts Rents **13Cc** **13Dc**
Still Alley **15Db**
Still Alley **16Ab**
Still Alley **17Bd**
Still House **20Aa**
Still Stairs **26Ab**
Stilwell Ct. **25Cb**
Stink Houses Bridge **19Bb**
Stock Exchange **15Cc**
Stock Weavers Almshouses **6Aa**
Stone Bldgs **14Ab**
Stone Cutter Yd. **25Bc**
Stone Cutters Bldgs **13Db**
Stone Cutters Ct. **13Bc**
Stone Stairs **17Dd**
Stone Stairs Ct. **17Dd**
Stone Wharf **23Bd**
Stone Wharf **32Ab**
Stone Yd. **4Bc**
Stone Yd. **14Bb**
Stone Yd. **25Ab**
Stone Yd. **31Cb**
Stonecutter St. **14Cb**
Stoney La. **16Ab**
Stoney La. **25Ba**
Stoney La. **25Db**
Store St., Great **13Aa**
Storeys Gate **23Ac**
Stracy St. **13Bc** **13Bb**
Strand **23Ba** **13Bd** **13Cd** **13Dd** **13Dc** **14Ac**
Strand La. **14Ad** **14Ac**
Stratford Pl. **12Ab**
Strathern Place **1Aa**
Stratton St. **22Ba**
Streatham St. **13Bb**
Stringers Row **27Bd**
Strutton Ground **22Dd** **23Ad**
Suffolk Ct. **25Ac**
Suffolk La. **15Bd**
Suffolk St. **12Ca**
Suffolk St. **17Ab**
Suffolk St., Great **13Ad** **23Aa**
Suffolk St., Great **24Dc** **25Ac**
Suffolk St., Little **13Ad**
Suffolk St., Little **24Dc**
Sugar Loaf Ct. **14Cc**
Sugar Loaf Ct. **15Ad**
Sugar Loaf Ct. **15Da**
Sugar Loaf Ct. **16Aa**
Sugar Loaf Ct. **16Bb**
Sugar Loaf Ct. **16Bd**
Sugar Loaf Ct. **25Db**
Sugar Loaf Lane **7Cb**
Summer St. **4Bd**
Sun Alley **5Ad** **5Bd**
Sun Alley **26Ba**
Sun Ct. **5Ad**
Sun Ct. **15Ba**
Sun Ct. **15Cb**
Sun Ct. **16Ac** **16Bc**
Sun Ct. **22Ba**
Sun Fire Office **15Cc**
Sun Pl. **34Ac**
Sun St. **15Da** **16Aa**
Sun St. **25Cc**
Sun St. **35Bc** **35Bb**
Sun Tavern Fields **17Cd**
Sun Yd. **4Ad**
Sun Yd. **26Ca**
Surrey Bldgs **35Db** **35Dc**
Surrey Canal **38Aa** **38Ab** **38Ad** **38Bc** **38Bd**
Surrey Inner Dock, Grand **28Ac** **28Ad** **38Aa**
Surrey Outer Dock, Grand **27Db** **27Dc** **28Ab** **28Ac**
Surrey Pl. **35Db** **35Dc** **36Ac**
Surrey Row **24Cb** **24Db**
Surrey Sq. **35Dc**
Surrey Stairs **14Ac**
Surrey St. **14Ac**
Surrey St. **24Ca**
Surrey St., Great **24Cc** **24Cb** **24Ca**
Susannas Row **5Dc**
Sussex Pl. **1Bb**
Sussex Pl. **36Bd** **36Cd**
Suters Bldgs **3Ba**
Sutton St. **13Ab**
Sutton St. **25Bb** **25Cb**
Sutton St., Great **4Dd**
Sutton St., Little **4Dc** **4Dd**
Suttons Ct. **15Db**
Swallow Gdns **16Bd**
Swallow St. **12Dd** **12Cd** **12Cc** **12Cb**
Swan **27Ad**
Swan Alley **14Da**
Swan Alley **26Ca**
Swan Alley, Great **15Bb**
Swan Alley, Little **15Cb**
Swan Ct. **6Bc**
Swan Ct. **16Bb**
Swan Ct. **16Cd**
Swan Ct. **23Da**
Swan Gdns **5Db**
Swan Inn **15Ab** **15Bb**
Swan La. **15Cd**
Swan La. **27Cc**
Swan La., Old **15Bd** **15Cd**
Swan Mead **35Da**
Swan Pl. **17Ba**
Swan Pl. **35Cb** **35Db**
Swan St. **6Bd** **6Bc**
Swan St. **16Bd**
Swan St. **25Ad** **25Ac**
Swan St. **35Db**
Swan Stairs, Old **15Bd**
Swan Walk **31Bd**
Swan Yd. **7Dd**
Swan Yd. **13Dc**
Swan Yd. **14Ca**
Swan Yd. **16Bc**
Swan Yd. **21Bc**
Swan Yd. **23Ac**
Swan Yd. **25Dc**
Swans Alley **27Ac**
Swedish Church **15Ac**
Swedish Church **16Dd**
Sweetapple Ct. **6Bb**
Sweetapple Ct. **15Da** **16Aa**
Sweetings Alley **15Cc**
Swifts Row **38Bd** **38Cd**
Swinton St. **3Db**
Symonds Inn **14Bb**
Symons St. **31Cb** **31Ca**

Tabernacle Pl. **5Cc** **5Dc**
Tabernacle Row **5Cc**
Tabernacle Walk **5Cd** **5Cc**
Tabernacle Walk, Lower **5Cc** **5Dc**
Talbot Inn **16Bc**
Talbot Inn **25Bb**
Talbott Ct. **15Cd**
Tanfield Ct. **14Bc**
Tar Yd. **18Bd**
Tarlings Ct. **24Bd**
Tash Ct. **4Ad**
Tash St. **14Aa** **14Ba**
Tattersalls Repository **21Dc** **21Db**
Tattle Alley **25Db**
Tatums Pl. **35Cc**
Tavistock Chapel **3Bc**
Tavistock Ct. **13Cc**
Tavistock Mews **13Aa**
Tavistock Pl. **3Bc**
Tavistock Row **13Cc**
Tavistock Sq. **3Bc**
Tavistock St. **13Aa**
Tavistock St. **13Cd** **13Cc**
Taylors Bldgs **13Bd**
Taylors Ct. **4Cb**
Taylors Ct. **15Ac** **15Bc**
Taylors Ct. **27Ba**
Taylors Pass. **12Cb**
Taylors Pass. **13Bd**
Temple Bar **14Ac**
Temple Church **14Bc**
Temple Gdns **14Bc**
Temple La. **14Bc**
Temple Pl. **24Cc**
Temple Stairs **14Bc**
Temple St. **14Bc**
Temple St. **34Ca**
Tench St. **27Ab**
Tennis Ct. **14Aa**
Tenter Alley **15Ba** **15Ca**
Tenter Row **5Bb**

For Key Map see p. 1

Tenterden St. **12Bc**
Terling St. **17Bc**
Terrace, The **4Ad**
Teviot St. **1Aa**
Tewksbury Ct. **16Bb**
Thames St. **25Aa**
Thames St. **38Ba** **28Bd**
Thames St., Little **26Ba**
Thames St., Lower **15Cd** **15Dd**
Thames St., Upper **14Dc** **15Ad** **15Bd** **15Cd**
Thanet Pl. **14Ac**
Thatched House Ct. **22Ca**
Thaves Inn **14Bb**
Thayre St. **12Ab** **12Aa**
Theobalds Road **13Da**
Thomas Bank Wharf **33Ac**
Thomas Pl. **26Bd** **26Cd**
Thomas St. **5Dc**
Thomas St. **6Cd** **6Cc**
Thomas St. **6Dc**
Thomas St. **7Bd**
Thomas St. **16Da**
Thomas St. **16Db**
Thomas St. **16Dd**
Thomas St. **18Aa**
Thomas St. **26Bc** **26Bb**
Thomas St. **34Da**
Thomas St. **35Bb**
Thomas St. **35Ca**
Thomas's Burying Ground **5Ad**
Thomas's Passage **7Ac**
Thomas's Pl. **2Cc**
Thomas's Pl. **35Cb** **35Ca**
Thomas's St. **25Bb** **25Cb**
Thorney St. **13Bb**
Thornhaugh St. **3Ad**
Thornhaugh St., Upper **2Dd**
Thorold Sq. **6Cc**
Thrawl St. **16Bb**
Threadneedle St. **15Cc** **15Dc**
Three Arrow Ct. **14Ab**
Three Colt Ct. **5Dd**
Three Colt Ct. **15Da**
Three Colt St. **18Cd** **18Dd**
Three Colt St. **28Da** **18Cd** **18Dd**
Three Colt Yd. **7Dd**
Three Colts Alley **27Bb**
Three Cow Ct. **6Cd**
Three Crane Ct. **22Cd**
Three Crane La. **15Bd**
Three Crane Stairs **15Ad**
Three Crane Yd. **25Bb**
Three Cranes Wharf **15Ad** **15Bd**
Three Crown Ct. **15Ad**
Three Cup Alley **6Ad**
Three Cup Alley **27Ca**
Three Cups Inn **5Ad**
Three Cups Yd. **13Da**
Three Fox Ct. **14Da**
Three Herring Ct. **15Aa**
Three King Ct. **16Bc** **16Cc**
Three Kings Yd. **12Ac**
Three Mariner Ct. **15Ba**
Three Nuns Inn **16Ac**
Three Oak La. **26Ac**
Three Pigeon Ct. **4Bd**
Three Ton Ct. **15Aa**
Three Ton Ct. **25Bc**
Three Tun Alley **16Ab** **16Bb**
Three Tun Pass. **14Db**
Three Tuns Tavern **25Bb**
Throgmorton St. **15Cb**
Thurlow Pl. **6Da**
Thurlow Pl. **7Cb**
Thurlow Pl. **35Cc**
Thurlow St. **24Cb**
Tilers Gateway **25Dc**
Tilney St. **21Da** **22Da**
Tilneys Ct. **5Bc**
Tindal's Burying Ground **5Cc** **5Bd** **5Cd**
Titchborne Ct. **13Da**
Titchborne St. **12Dd**
Titchfield St. **12Db**
Titchfield St., Great **12Cb** **12Ca**
Titchfield St., Little **12Ca**
Titchfield St., Upper **2Cd**
Tites Alley **18Bd**
Tittymouse Alley **27Ba**
Token House Yd. **15Cb**
Tomlins New Town **11Ab** **11Bb**
Toms Ct. **12Ac**
Tomsons Rent **15Da**
Tongue Yd., Little **16Db**
Tooks Ct. **14Bb**
Tooley St. **25Ca** **25Cb** **25Db**
Tooly Stairs **25Ca**
Tothill Ct. **23Ac**
Tothill St. **4Ad**
Tothill St. **23Ac**
Tothill St., New **23Ad** **23Ac**
Tottenham Ct. **2Dc**
Tottenham Ct. Rd. **13Ab** **13Aa** **12Da** **2Dd** **2Dc** **2Cc**
Tottenham Pl. **2Dc**
Tottenham Pl., Upper **2Dc**
Tottenham St. **12Da**
Tower **26Aa**
Tower Dock **26Aa**
Tower Hill **16Ad**
Tower Hill, Little **16Ad** **16Bd**
Tower Royal **15Bc**
Tower Stairs **26Aa**
Tower St. **13Bc**
Tower St. **24Bd** **24Bc**
Tower St., Great **15Dd**
Tower St., Little **15Dd**
Tower Wharf **26Aa**
Townsend Ct. **25Ab**
Townsend St. **35Cb**
Trafalgar Pl. **6Ca**
Trafalgar Pl. **34Ca**
Trafalgar Sq. **18Aa**
Trafalgar St. **5Cb**
Trafalgar St. **35Ad** **35Ac** **35Bc**
Traitors Bridge **26Aa**
Transport Office **23Bc**
Treasury **15Cc**
Treasury **23Bb**
Treasury Yd. **23Bb**
Trig La. **14Cd**
Trig Wharf **14Cd**
Trinity Almshouses **17Ba**
Trinity Buoy House **30Da**
Trinity Ct. **15Ab**
Trinity Ct. **15Ac**
Trinity House **16Ad**
Trinity La. **15Ac**
Trinity La., Little **15Ad** **15Ac**
Trinity Pl. **23Ba**
Trinity St. **28Bd** **28Cc**
Tripe Yd. **16Bb**
Trotterborn Alley **24Db**
Trump St. **15Bc**
Trundleys La. **37Dd** **37Dc**
Tuckers Row **29Ba**
Tudor St. **14Cc**
Tufton St. **33Ba** **23Bd**
Tufton St., Little **33Ba**
Tun Yd. **12Ac**
Tunbridge Pl. **3Bb**
Turk St. **6Bc** **6Bb**
Turks Head Ct. **5Ad**
Turks Head Yd. **4Cd**
Turks Row **31Cc** **31Cb**
Turn Again La. **14Cb**
Turner St. **17Ab**
Turners Ct. **13Bd**
Turners Sq. **5Da**
Turners Rents **24Db**
Turners St. **16Cd**
Turnmill St. **4Cd**
Turnstile, Great **14Aa**
Turnstile, Little **13Db**
Turnstile, New **13Db**
Turnwheel La. **15Bd** **15Bc**
Turpentine La. **3Bc**
Turville St. **6Bc**
Turville St., New **6Ac**
Tweezer Alley **14Ac**
Twig Folly **8Ab**
Twisters Alley **5Bd**
Two Brewers Ct. **5Ad**
Two Swan Yd. **15Db**
Tyburn Turnpike **11Cc**
Tyers St. **33Dc** **33Db**
Tylers Ct. **12Cc**
Tylers Ct. **12Dc**
Tylers St. **12Cc**
Type Ct. **15Ba**
Type St. **15Ba**
Tyrell St. **6Cc** **6Dc**
Tyson Ct. **15Ba**
Tyson Pl. **6Aa**
Tyssen St. **6Bc**
Tyssen St., New **6Cc**

Ulster Sq. **2Bb**
Ulster St. **2Ad**
Unanimous Row **16Ca**
Unicorn Ct. **25Bc**
Union Bridge Row **24Db**
Union Bldgs **4Bd**
Union Bldgs **6Ab** **6Bb**
Union Bldgs **6Ac**
Union Bldgs **35Aa**
Union Ct. **4Bd**
Union Ct. **14Ca**
Union Ct. **15Db**

Union Ct. 16Ba
Union Ct. 16Cd
Union Ct. 25Ac
Union Ct. 25Bc
Union Ct. 25Cb
Union Ct. 26Ac
Union Ct. 27Ba
Union Cres. 6Ab
Union Cres. 35Ca
Union Gdns 6Ab 6Bb
Union Hall 25Ab
Union Pl. 1Dd
Union Pl. 5Bb
Union Pl. 17Ca 17Da
Union Pl. 18Dd
Union Pl. 23Ad
Union Pl. 24Ca
Union Pl. 27Cc
Union Pl. 33Da
Union Pl. 34Db
Union Row 6Aa
Union Row 7Ac
Union Row 9Cb
Union Row 16Bd
Union Row 16Cb
Union Row 35Ab 35Aa
Union Stairs 26Db
Union St 3Aa
Union St. 5Cb 5Ca
Union St. 6Ab 6Bb
Union St. 12Bc
Union St. 12Ca
Union St. 14Cc
Union St. 16Aa
Union St. 16Cb
Union St. 17Bd
Union St. 19Dd
Union St. 22Aa 12Ad
Union St. 24Bc
Union St. 24Cc
Union St. 24Cd
Union St. 25Ab 25Bb
Union St. 34Aa 34Ab
Union St. 35Bc
Union Walk 6Ab
Union Yd. 25Db
United Public Brewery 25Aa
United Publicans Charity School 34Ac

Upper
With the exception below, names preceded by 'Upper' will be found under the second element, e.g. Thames St., Upper

Upper Turning 27Ca
Upton Pl. 25Cc

Vain St. 25Cb
Valentine Pl. 24Cc 24Cb
Valentine Row 24Cc
Vauxhall Almshouses 33Bd
Vauxhall Bridge 33Bc
Vauxhall Circle 33Dc 33Db
Vauxhall Gdns 33Cc 33Cd
Vauxhall Pl. 33Cd
Vauxhall Row 33Cd 33Cc
Vauxhall Sq. 33Cc
Vauxhall Stairs 33Bc
Vauxhall St. 33Dc
Vauxhall Turnpike 33Cd
Vauxhall Walk 33Cc 33Cb 33Db
Vere St. 12Ab
Vere St. 13Dc 13Db
Vernons Arms 3Da
Vernons Bldgs 3Ba
Verulam Bldgs 4Ad
Victory Pl. 35Ab
Victualling Office 38Bc 38Cc
Victualling Office Row 38Bc 38Bd 38Cd
Vigil Pl. 11Ba
Vigo La. 12Cd
Villa Row 35Cd
Villa St. 35Cd
Villers Ct. 22Ca
Villiers St. 13Cd 23Ca
Vinagar La. 17Cd 17Cc
Vinagar Yd. 4Dc 4Dd
Vincent Sq. 32Db 32Da
Vincent St. 6Ac 6Bc
Vincent St. 32Da 33Aa
Vine Ct. 5Ad
Vine Ct. 15Ba
Vine Ct. 16Db
Vine Ct. 23Db
Vine Ct. 25Ac
Vine Ct. 26Ca
Vine Inn 15Db
Vine Pl. 6Bd
Vine St. 4Ad 4Bd
Vine St. 4Bd
Vine St. 6Bd
Vine St. 12Dd
Vine St. 13Bb
Vine St. 13Bd
Vine St. 16Ac 16Ad
Vine St. 16Ba
Vine St. 18Bb
Vine St. 23Db 24Ab
Vine St. 33Ba
Vine St., Little 12Dd
Vine Yd. 5Ad
Vine Yd. 18Ad
Vine Yd. 25Db
Vinegar La.* 17Cd 17Cc
Vinegar Yd.* 4Dc 4Dd
Vinegar Yd. 13Bb
Vinegar Yd. 13Dc
Vinegar Yd. 24Dc
Vinegar Yd. 25Dc
Vinegar Yd. 33Bc
Vineyard Gdns 4Bc
Vineyard Gardens Walk 4Bc
Vineyard Walk 4Bc
Vintners Almshouses 17Ba
Vintners Hall 15Ad
Virginia St. 6Bb 6Cb

Wade Street 29Ba
Wades Pl. 8Bd
Wades Pl. 29Ba
Wagstaffs Bldgs 24Da
Wake Mason Yd. 33Ba
Wakefields Rents 5Cc
Walbrook Pl. 5Cb 5Ca
Walburge St. 17Ad 17Ac
Walcot Pl. 34Ab 34Aa
Walkers Ct. 12Dc
Wall, The 38Db 38Dc
Wallbrook 15Bc
Wallers Pl. 3Ba
Wallers Pl. 24Bd
Wallis's Ct. 25Ac
Wallis's Grove 6Bb
Wallis's Pl. 22Bd
Wallis's Yd. 6Ad
Walnut Tree Walk 34Aa
Walsingham Pl.* 24Ad
Walton Pl. 24Cc
Waltons Ct. 16Bd
Walworth 35Ad 35Ac 34Db
Walworth Common 35Cc 35Bd 35Cd 35Dc
Walworth Fields 35Ac 35Bc 35Ad 35Bd
Walworth Pl. 35Ad
Walworth Workhouse 35Ad
Wapping 26Cb 26Db
Wapping Chapel 27Ab
Wapping Dock Stairs 27Bb
Wapping Dock St. 27Bb
Wapping New Stairs 27Ab
Wapping Old Stairs 26Db
Wapping St. 27Ab 27Bb
Wapping Wall 27Ba 27Ca
Wardens Ct. 4Cd
Wardes Row 6Dc
Wardour Mews 12Dc 12Db
Wardour St. 12Dc 12Db
Wardrobe Pl. 14Dc
Wards Row 22Bd 22Bc
Warner St., Great 4Ad 4Bd
Warner St., Little 4Bd
Warnford Ct. 15Cb
Warren Mews 2Cd
Warrens, Sir William, Sq. 27Bb
Warwick Ct. 14Aa
Warwick La. 14Db
Warwick Pl. 14Aa
Warwick Pl. 22Bd
Warwick Row 22Bd
Warwick Row 24Cc
Warwick Sq. 14Db
Warwick St. 12Dd 12Dc
Warwick St. 23Aa
Water La. 14Bc
Water La. 14Cc
Water La. 15Dd
Water La. 26Cc
Water St. 14Ac
Water St. 14Cc
Waterhouse Field 4Bb 4Cb
Waterloo Bridge 13Dd
Watermans Stairs 14Bc
Waters Ct. 25Ba

For Key Map see p. 1

Watling St. **15Ac** **15Bc**
Watsons Bldgs **17Aa**
Watts Sq. **16Cd**
Weaver St. **6Cd**
Weavers Almshouses **6Dd**
Weavers Almshouses **6Ad**
Weavers Hall **15Bb**
Weavers La. **26Ab**
Webb Sq. **6Ad**
Webb St. **25Cb** **25Db**
Webb St. **35Da**
Webber Row **24Bc** **24Cc**
Webber St. **24Bd** **24Bc**
Webbers St. **24Bc** **24Cc**
Webbs Bldgs **6Cd**
Weelmore St. **29Da**
Welbeck Mews **12Ab**
Welbeck St. **12Ab** **12Aa**
Welbeck St., Little **12Ab**
Welch*Charity School **3Dc**
Welclose Pl. **16Dd**
Well Alley **25Cb**
Well Alley **28Ca**
Well Alley, Lower **27Ab**
Well Alley, Upper **27Ab**
Well and Bucket Ct. **5Bc**
Well Close Sq. **16Dd**
Well Ct. **15Bc**
Well Ct. **25Cb**
Well St. **15Aa**
Well St. **16Ca**
Well St. **16Cd**
Well St. **29Da**
Well Street Ct. **16Cd**
Well Yd. **14Da**
Well Yd. **16Bd**
Wellclose Pl.* **16Dd**
Wellclose Sq.* **16Dd**
Wellington Pl. **6Db**
Wellington Pl. **25Cc**
Wellington Sq. **3Db**
Wellington St. **13Ac**
Wells Mews **12Da**
Wells St. **12Db** **12Ca**
Wells St. **12Dd**
Wells Yd. **13Ab**
Welsh Charity School* **3Dc**
Welsh's Bldgs **5Dc**
Wenlock St. **5Ac**
Wenlock's Barn **5Ba**
Wentworth Row **17Ca**
Wentworth St. **16Ab** **16Bb** **16Cb**
Wesley's Chapel **5Cd**
West
With the exceptions below, names preceded by 'West' will be found under the second element, e.g. Harding St., West
West and Cove's Wharf **14Bc**
West Ham Water Works, Reservoir **8Bc** **8Bd**
West India Dock, Entrance Basin **28Db** **29Ab**
West India Docks **29**
West La. **27Ac** **27Ad**
West Pl. **24Cd**
West Smithfield **14Da**
West Sq. **34Ca**
West St. **3Bb**
West St. **7Cd** **7Cc**
West St. **7Db**
West St. **13Bc**
West St. **14Ca**
West St. **16Aa**
West St. **34Ca** **24Cd**
Westbys Almshouses **5Da**
Western Wharf **23Bd**
Westleys Chapel **5Cd**
Westminster Abbey **23Bc**
Westminster Bridge **23Cc**
Westminster Bridge Rd. **24Ac** **24Ab** **24Bb**
Westminster Hall **23Bc**
Westminster Hospital **22Cd** **22Cc**
Westminster School, Playground for the Westminster Scholars **32Db** **32Da**
Westmoreland Bldgs **15Aa**
Westmoreland Row **35Cd** **35Dc**
Westmoreland Pl. **5Bb** **5Ba**
Westmoreland St. **12Aa**
Weston Ct. **25Cb**
Weston Pl. **3Ca**
Weston St. **3Ba**
Weston St. **4Aa**
Weston St. **25Cb**
Wests Gdns **17Bd**
Weymouth Mews **12Ba**
Weymouth St. **12Aa** **2Ad** **2Bd**
Weymouth St. **34Db** **34Da**
Weymouth Ter. **6Ba**
Whalebone Ct. **15Cb**
Whartons Ct. **14Ba**
Wheatsheaf Alley **15Cd**
Wheatsheaf Brewery **25Aa**
Wheatsheaf Ct. **14Cb**
Wheelers Chapel **16Aa**
Wheelers St. **16Ba** **6Bd**
Whetstones Park **13Db**
Whetstones Yd. **18Ad**
Whiskers Ct. **15Bc**
Whitcomb Ct. **13Ad**
Whitcomb St. **13Ad** **23Aa**
White Bear Alley **16Ac**
White Bear Ct. **14Cb**
White Bear Gdns **6Ab** **6Bb**
White Bear Inn **15Bb**
White Bear Yd. **25Bc**
White Ct. **13Ad**
White Cross Alley **15Ca**
White Cross St. **15Ba** **5Bd** **5Bc** **5Ac**
White Cross St. **25Ab**
White Friars New Wharf **14Bc**
White Friers Dock **14Bc**
White Hall Ct. **26Ba**
White Hart **31Bb**
White Hart **14Db**
White Hart **34Ac**
White Hart Ct. **13Bd**
White Hart Ct. **14Da**
White Hart Ct. **15Cc**
White Hart Ct. **15Db**
White Hart Inn **4Dd**
White Hart Inn **25Bb**
White Hart Pl. **30Aa**
White Hart Pl. **34Bc** **34Bb**
White Hart Row **3Ca**
White Hart Row **24Db**
White Hart Row **34Bc**
White Hart St. **34Da**
White Hart Yd. **13Dc**
White Hart Yd. **16Bc**
White Hind Alley **24Da**
White Horse **14Bb**
White Horse **29Aa**
White Horse Alley **14Ca** **4Cd**
White Horse Ct. **5Bd**
White Horse Ct. **6Bd**
White Horse Ct. **25Ca**
White Horse Inn **15Ab**
White Horse Inn **15Ac**
White Horse La. **16Dc**
White Horse La. **18Ab** **18Aa**
White Horse St. **18Ad** **18Ac**
White Horse St. **22Ba**
White Horse Yd. **13Dc**
White Lion **24Da**
White Lion **33Cc**
White Lion Ct. **4Ca**
White Lion Ct. **6Aa**
White Lion Ct. **14Da**
White Lion Ct. **15Cb**
White Lion Ct. **15Cc**
White Lion St. **4Ba**
White Lion St. **6Ad**
White Lion St. **16Cd**
White Lion St. **31Cb**
White Lion St., Great* **13Bc**
White Lion St., Little* **13Bc**
White Lion Wharf **14Cd** **14Cc**
White Lion Yd. **5Ad** **5Bd**
White Lion Yd. **12Db**
White Lion Yd. **33Cc**
White Lyon St., Great **13Bc**
White Lyon St., Little **13Bc**
White Rose Alley **15Ba**
White Rose Ct. **15Bb**
White Stiles **31Bb** **31Bc**
White St. **6Dc**
White St. **15Ba** **15Ca**
White St. **16Aa** **16Ba**
White St. **16Ab**
White St. **25Bc**
White Yd. **5Ad** **5Ac**
Whitechapel **16Bc** **16Bb** **16Cb** **16Db** **16Da** **17Aa**
Whitechapel Burial Ground **16Da**
Whitechapel Churchyard **16Cb**
Whitechapel Workhouse **16Da**
Whitehall **23Bb** **23Ba**
Whitehall Pl. **23Ba**
Whitehall Timber Yd. **23Bb**
Whitelands **31Bb**
Whites **22Ca**
Whites Alley **14Ab** **14Bb**
Whites Alley **15Bb** **15Cb**
Whites Bldgs **16Cd**
Whites Ct. **15Ba**
Whites Grounds **6Dc**
Whites Grounds **25Dc**
Whites Rents **23Bd**
Whites Rents **28Ca**
Whites Yd. **14Ca**

Whites Yd. **16Cd**
Whites Yd. **17Da**
Whitethorn Ct. **27Ba**
Whitfield St. **5Dc**
Whitfields Chapel **2Dd**
Whiting Yd. **25Db**
Whitsters Ground **23Ad**
Whttington's Almshouses **15Bd**
Widegate St. **16Aa**
Widnalls Pl. **4Bd**
Wiggins Quay **15Dd**
Wigmore St. **12Ab** **12Bb**
Wild Ct. **13Cb** **13Db**
Wild St., Great **13Cb** **13Db**
Wild St., Little **13Db**
Wilderness La. **14Cc**
Wilderness Row **4Dd**
Wilderness Row **5Da**
Wilderness Row **31Db**
Wilderness St. **25Cd**
Wilkes St. **6Bd**
William St. **2Bb**
William St. **2Cb**
William St. **6Ac**
William St. **13Cd**
William St. **14Cc**
William St. **16Db**
William St. **16Dc** **17Ac**
William St. **22Cd** **22Cc**
William St. **24Cb**
William St. **25Ac**
William St. **34Ab**
William St. **34Ad**
William St. **35Aa**
William St. **35Ca**
William Warrens, Sir, Sq. **27Bb**
Williams Bldgs **21Ad**
Williams Ct. **24Da**
Williams Mews **2Bd**
Williams Mews **11Bb**
Willmotts Bldgs **25Bc**
Willow Bridge **38Dc** **39Ac**
Willow Ct. **5Dc**
Willow Row **4Dc**
Willow St. **5Dc**
Willow St. **24Da**
Willow Walk **5Cb** **5Db**
Willow Walk **5Dc**
Willow Walk **6Bb**
Willow Walk, The **32Bb** **32Cb**
Willow Walk **36Ab**
Wills's Yd. **28Bd** **28Cd**
Willsted Ct. **3Bb**
Willsted St. **3Bb**
Wilmot Sq. **7Ac**
Wilmot St. **3Cc**
Wilmot St. **7Ac**
Wilmots Grove **7Ab**
Wilson St. **15Ca** **5Cd**
Wilsons Ct. **25Aa**
Wilsons Pl. **18Cc**
Wilton St. **22Ac**
Wimpole Mews **12Aa**
Wimpole Mews, Upper **2Ad**
Wimpole St. **12Ab** **12Aa**
Wimpole St., Upper **2Ad**
Winchester Ct. **15Ab** **15Aa**
Winchester House **31Ad**
Winchester Pl. **4Ba**
Winchester Row **11Aa**
Winchester St. **3Da**
Winchester St. **25Ba**
Winchester St., Great **15Cb**
Winchester St., Little **15Cb**
Winchester Yd. **25Ba**
Winckworth Bldgs **5Cb**
Wind Ct. **9Cc**
Windles Wharf **14Ac**
Windmill Alehouse **38Ac**
Windmill Ct. **5Cd**
Windmill Ct. **14Db**
Windmill Ct. **16Cd**
Windmill La. **38Ac** **38Bc**
Windmill St. **5Cd**
Windmill St. **12Da** **13Aa**
Windmill St., Great **12Dd** **12Dc**
Windmill St., Little **12Dc**
Windsor Ct. **13Dc**
Windsor Ct. **15Aa**
Windsor Pl. **5Bb**
Windsor Ter. **5Bb**
Wine Office Ct. **14Bb**
Winford Ct. **16Bb**
Winsley St. **12Cb**
Withers Ct. **5Bc**
Wittingtons Almshouses **15Bd**
Wobourn Ct.* **13Ba**
Wobourn Mews **3Bc**
Wobourn Pl. **3Bd**
Wobourn St.* **13Ba**
Wolsingham Pl. **24Ad**
Wonder Wat Pl. **21Bc**
Wooburn Ct. **13Ba**
Wooburn St. **13Ba**
Wood and Co.'s Wharf **14Cc**
Wood St. **3Cb**
Wood St. **4Bc**
Wood St. **5Dc** **5Cc**
Wood St. **15Ab** **15Ba**
Wood St. **16Ba**
Wood St. **23Bd**
Wood St. **33Db**
Wood Yd. **25Bb**
Wood Wharf, Lower, West India Docks **29Cb**
Wood Wharf, Upper, West India Docks **29Ab**
Woodbridge St. **4Cc**
Wooden World **5Ad**
Woods Bldgs **6Ac**
Woods Bldgs **17Aa**
Woods Bldgs **35Cc** **35Cb**
Woods Close **6Cc** **6Dc**
Woods Ct. **6Ad**
Woods Ct. **12Cb**
Woods Mews **11Cc** **11Cd**
Woods Pl. **4Bc**
Woods St. **6Dd** **6Dc**
Woods Yd. **6Bd**
Woodstock Ct. **12Ac**
Woodstock Mews **12Aa**
Woodstock St. **1Dd**
Woodstock St. **12Aa**
Woodstock St. **12Ac** **12Ab**
Woolcombes Yd. **27Db**
Woolpack Yd. **25Bd**
Worcester Pl. **15Ad**
Worcester St. **25Ab**
Worcester St. **27Aa**
Workhouse La. **33Db**
Worleys Ct. **16Bd**
Wormwood St. **15Db**
Worship Ct. **5Dd**
Worship Sq. **5Dd**
Worship St. **5Dd**
Wrestlers Ct. **15Db**
Wrights Bldgs **14Ca**
Wrights Bldgs **35Da**
Wrights Rents **16Dd**
Wych St. **13Dc** **14Ac**
Wycomb Pl. **25Bd** **25Cd**
Wynatt St. **4Cb**
Wyndham Pl. **11Ba**

Yeates Ct. **15Da**
Yeates's Ct. **14Ac** **14Ab**
Yeomans Row **21Ad**
Yoakleys Bldgs **17Aa**
York Bldgs **1Cd**
York Bldgs **3Ab**
York Bldgs **3Da**
York Bldgs **33Ba**
York Bldgs **35Ca**
York Buildings Stairs **23Ca**
York Buildings Waterworks **23Ca**
York Ct. **5Cd** **5Dd**
York Hospital **31Db**
York Mews, Great **1Cd**
York Mews, Little **1Cd**
York Mews North **1Cd**
York Mews South **1Cd**
York Pl. **1Cd**
York Pl. **3Da**
York Pl. **4Ca** **4Da**
York Pl. **5Bc**
York Pl. **18Bb** **18Ba**
York Pl. **24Ad**
York Pl. **24Cc** **24Dc** **24Cd** **24Dd**
York Pl. **34Db**
York Pl. **35Ac** **35Ab** **34Db**
York Pl., Little **1Cd**
York Row **6Bb**
York Row **34Cc** **34Cb**
York St. **3Da**
York St. **4Bd**
York St. **6Bd** **6Bc**
York St. **7Dc**
York St. **12Ca**
York St. **13Cc** **13Dc**
York St. **16Db**
York St. **21Bd** **21Bc**
York St. **22Da** **12Dd**

For Key Map see p. 1

York St. **22Dc** **23Ac**
York St. **27Cc**
York St. **28Bd** **38Ba**
York St. **34Da**
York St. **35Ac**
York St. **35Ca**
York St. **35Cb**
York St., Old **6Bd** **6Bc**
York St., Upper **1Cd**
York St., Upper **11Ba**
York Ter. **1Dc**
Youngs Bldgs **5Ac**
Youngs Ct. **15Bb**
Youngs Quay **15Dd**
Yoxalls Wharf **25Da**

Zephon St. **25Cd**
Zoar St. **24Da**

For Key Map see p. 1